Ki taku tamahine,
ki a Hinauri Moetu

The author delivering a submission before the Waitangi Tribunal during the final hearings of Ngati Awa's case at Whakatane, 1 December 1995.

(Onehou Thrupp, Ngati Awa Research)

Landmarks, Bridges and Visions

Aspects of Maori Culture

ESSAYS BY

Sidney Moko Mead
MA, PhD, FRSNZ

Victoria University Press

VICTORIA UNIVERSITY PRESS
Victoria University of Wellington
P O Box 600 Wellington

© Sidney Moko Mead 1997

ISBN 0 86473 317 8

First published 1997

This book is copyright. Apart from
any fair dealing for the purpose of private study,
research, criticism or review, as permitted under the
Copyright Act, no part may be reproduced by any
process without the permission of
the publishers

Published with the assistance of a grant from

Printed by GP Print, Wellington

Contents

Introduction 1

Education

1. Landmarks, Bridges and Visions 11
2. Maori Studies Tomorrow 21
3. Maori Studies in the Universities in the 1990s 39
4. A Time to Reach Out 50
5. New Initiatives for Maori at Tertiary Level Institutions 54

Te Reo Maori

6. Maori Language Week 67
7. Pronounced Respect for Maori Placenames 71
8. Maori Language and Identity 76

The Meeting of Cultures and Problems of Communication

9. Should Maoritanga be Shared? 89
10. The Day New Zealand Cried 94
11. Two Blankets and a Puff of Tobacco 100
12. The Maori People Tomorrow 113

Sovereignty

13. A Pathway to the Future 119
14. The Rebirth of a Dream 130
15. Maori Representation 133
16. Options for Self-Determination 144

Aspects of Culture

17	Dimensions of Meaning in Maori Art	157
18	The Rahui and its Applications	167
19	The Nature of Taonga	179
20	Traditional Maori Leadership	190
21	Tamaiti Whangai	204
22	Haere, Haere, Haere	213
23	Aspects of Raupatu	222
24	Whenua Tautohetohe	232

Being Maori Today

25	The Maori World and You	245
26	The Significance of Being Ngati Awa	250

Glossary   264

Introduction

Toi te kupu, toi te whenua, toi te mana. Knowledge is the word, knowledge is the land, and knowledge gives dignity. This is a collection of words, ideas, opinions, theories, reactions and prescriptions for the future, written over a period of three decades. This period represented a time of great change for the nation and a time of contrasts, from the confrontational policies of Prime Minister Robert Muldoon in the 1970s, to the mood of optimism and new-right philosophies of David Lange's Labour Government in the 1980s, and then the conservative and mainstreaming policies of Jim Bolger's National Government in the 1990s. It was a time of tumultuous change for Maori, when the rules were changed, services drastically changed, the Department of Maori Affairs restructured out of existence, and the budget for Maori programmes sharply reduced. There was a succession of new populist terms: devolution, tino rangatiratanga, accountability, mandates, transparency, level playing-fields, choice, fiscal caps and envelopes, etc.

It was also a time when new opportunities came for Maori, such as kohanga reo, the *Te Maori* exhibition, the 1990 celebration of waka at Waitangi, Maori radio, *Te Karere*, television news in Maori, the Sealords deal, Maori Congress, the Treaty of Waitangi Fisheries Commission, Waitangi Tribunal hearings of the Ngai Tahu, Taranaki and Ngati Awa raupatu cases, and the beginning of settlements, with the Tainui case becoming a benchmark. It was during this time that the carved meeting-house Mataatua, given on permanent loan to the Otago Museum in 1925, was returned to Ngati Awa after fifteen years of negotiation. Undoubtedly, great progress has been made on some fronts and so there was encouragement and hope for Maori. But there were also some disturbing events and policies that changed the face of the Maori world. Overall it was a tricky time for Maori, when it was necessary to stake out a future for ourselves and to begin to define that future in our own terms. The papers in this collection were written during this time.

As the country's first Professor of Maori, I considered that it was my duty to comment on decisions or policies made by others, supposedly on our behalf and for our good. It is an expected function of universities that people who teach and do research there act as the conscience of the nation. They may criticise the government without fear of losing their heads or their jobs. The right to criticise one's government without fear of being imprisoned and executed is a very important freedom and one to be cherished. However, very few academics actually rush into print or appear on television. It is not a popular activity, nor a comfortable one. In my case I thought I should make an effort.

At times I opposed policies of the government of the day and became most unpopular as a result. I was criticised by Ministers of the Crown who insisted that the government was always right. This was especially the case over Bastion Point. There was the odd occasion when the cause I took up was seen as attacking a sacred cow of the nation, and practically the whole nation turned against me. This was the issue of Maori rugby players going to play in South Africa at a time when the rest of the world was boycotting and isolating South Africa. I proposed a way of stopping Maori players from going. I did not succeed: the tour went ahead. But I did begin a furious debate about Maori customary ideas. On such occasions acting as the conscience of the people or as a critic of society is lonely and difficult for one's family. But it is a matter of choosing the cause one decides to take up. I also set out to stop a well-known school in Auckland from being closed down by the church. This was a more popular cause and many people rallied around to assist. The result of the effort is that Queen Victoria School for Girls, at Parnell, is still open.

But there are far too few Maori commentators putting a strong and clear Maori perspective on the events of the nation. Ranginui Walker and Syd Jackson have been the most consistent. Both have been vilified and condemned by sections of the public, and praised by others. Some well-known personalities have been and gone, or changed sides. Some were too afraid to become involved. Inevitably, many Maori commentators become labelled as activists and protesters. In fact, it might be regarded as a mark of some honour to be so labelled.

Some of our people argue that it is a complete waste of time putting a Maori viewpoint before the public. Muldoon polarised the population during his time. The ordinary bloke he courted turned out to be generally right-wing, racist and nasty. Maori writers are not able to change their attitudes. The ideology of the new right has given encouragement to the racist element, and it has become even more difficult to influence the thinking of such people. The newspapers of the country present a lot of letters that are negative and plainly anti-Maori culture, and anti-Maori people. There is an endless parading of prejudices and misinformation. So some of our people believe it is quite hopeless to make an attempt to change deeply entrenched attitudes.

Regardless of all the negativity, I believe we must intervene and represent ourselves in public discussions and debates. It is important in a society such as ours that several Maori viewpoints are presented. A general practice has been to appoint one Maori to every committee, or to have one Maori provide a comment for a news item. That lone Maori voice is taken to represent all the tribes of New Zealand. For some 'ordinary blokes', even that one solitary voice or pen is too much. For others, the gesture of inviting one Maori to participate is evidence of consulting with Maori.

Maori society is complex. It is certainly not a carbon copy of Pakeha society. Nor are our interests exactly the same. While we share many common needs and interests, such as rugby football, netball and beer, there are other aspects of life that we do not share. Maori culture is different. It has a different history, different origins, different relationships and different traditions and customs. And no purpose is served by pretending otherwise.

These papers represent my views of the world. Those views are underpinned by my upbringing as a Maori, by my being Ngati Awa and having relationships with several other tribal groups, by my experiences as a country teacher in many different Maori communities, by my training as an anthropologist, by my special interest in the arts, by my experience in teaching in universities both in Canada and in New Zealand, by being an advocate for Maori studies as a developing discipline, and by having a commitment to Maori culture. I am an advocate for my culture and for my country.

Some of the papers provide information on selected aspects of Maori culture. These are included to enlighten and to make up for the lack of knowledge about much of Maori culture. Up until quite recently, it was acceptable at university level just to teach Maori language and to apply anthropology and archaeology to Maori society. Acceptance, however, did not come easily. Sir Apirana Ngata and Sir Peter Buck worked hard to have Maori subjects taught at what were then almost exclusively Pakeha universities. Maori studies as a university discipline did not exist in their time. That came later.

Up until the 1970s, courses on Maori customary practices were not included in the curriculum. The event which changed this was the Springbok tour of 1979, and the furore aroused by my suggestion that a customary idea, the rahui, by which a place is ritually placed out of bounds, should be applied to South Africa to prevent Maori players from going there. My suggestion began a debate on whether it was appropriate to employ a custom from the distant and cannibal past of the Maori to a modern international event such as a rugby football tour. The very idea seemed preposterous. But many people wanted to know what the rahui was all about. Out of that debate came the first university course on the customary concepts of the Maori, and it was introduced at Victoria University in 1980. Since then many other tertiary institutions offer similar courses. The paper I wrote to explain the rahui is included in this collection.

Also included in this book is a selection of papers drawing attention to the parlous state of the Maori language. The language is now widely taught at all levels of education, but that came about as a result of a very effective campaign by a group of students from the University of Auckland who called themselves Nga Tamatoa. Their efforts have become an essential part of the history of the struggle to save the Maori language. Maori radio was launched as a way of saving the language. *Te Karere*, a television news service in Maori, was a welcome initiative. Kohanga reo, the language nests for pre-school children, was introduced. In all, many different initiatives were launched during these decades of great change.

I played a small part in this struggle. In the 1950s I was a country schoolteacher in a Maori school called Waimarama, in Hawke's Bay. I decided way back then that te reo Maori ought to be taught in the school because the community was losing the language. The school committee agreed and we began to teach Maori at primary-school level. Officials of the Department of

Mrs Eva Rickard, an outstanding personality who has been involved in politics and in various protests over a number of years. Here she is at Moutoa giving support to the people of Whanganui.
(The Evening Post, Wellington)

Education heard about what I was doing and threatened to send an inspector to chastise me for teaching a prohibited subject. The man came, but when he discovered the whole community supported the idea we chatted instead. Thus, it was not so long ago that the notion of teaching te reo Maori in a school supported by the government was seen to be subversive—not by Maori, but by Pakeha officials. I wrote a language book for primary school use, called *We Speak Maori*, and published it in 1959, through Reed. So I was a little bit ahead of the big movement to save the language.

Progress for Maori initiatives has come generally from the struggles of individuals, or of groups such as Nga Tamatoa, based in Auckland, and the Te Reo Maori Society, based in Wellington. The nature of our society makes a struggle necessary. Maori society is a minority in its own land, a people controlled by another. The struggle is linked inextricably to this Land of the Long White Cloud. Toi te whenua, knowledge is based in the land. Identity is anchored to it. To be landless is to lose your soul.

As a minority, Maori are forced to achieve our political ambitions through the majority Pakeha culture, which controls Parliament and indeed the whole country. The majority culture exercises a power of veto. Its majority vote decides what is done for Maori and what is not. Government members often have to weigh up the consequences of being too supportive of Maori initiatives. And there are vociferous and well-organised elements within the majority population that actively advocate the elimination of any special measures to assist Maori in some way. The Waitangi Tribunal, for instance, is being targeted by such groups. There has to be a struggle to resist the efforts of groups of people who want us assimilated, homogenised and properly packaged. For them, we are the enemy within.

There is another reason why we must engage in a struggle with the dominant society. Once we have achieved a gain, such as having the notion of kohanga reo accepted, funded and put into practice, other ethnic groups can follow. Likewise, once Maori studies was firmly established in the university system, it was possible to introduce Samoan studies or Pacific studies or Cook Island studies. Opening up the parliamentary system to more Maori members also opened the doors for Pacific Islanders and Chinese members. In this sense, the Maori struggle is always difficult, as we have to introduce innovations by changing attitudes. Obstacles have to be overcome and we open doors for others besides ourselves.

Discussions on tino rangatiratanga or self-determination have been happening over the last five years, and have intensified in the Maori world over the last two. Special hui were called at Hirangi by Sir Hepi Te Heuheu to talk about this and issues such as the fiscal envelope concept proposed by the government. Successive governments, however, have not been happy to be seen to be encouraging such discussions. The notion of self-determination or tino rangatiratanga is considered a threat to the sovereignty of the nation, and so nothing happens. Several papers in this collection discuss the issue of sovereignty.

Toi te kupu, toi te whenua, toi te mana. The second phrase of this proverb focuses on land. As already mentioned, Maori identity is linked to this land. Tangata whenua, people of the land, expresses the link. The particular character of Maori has much to do with this part of the Pacific, and with this part of Polynesia. While we share many common features with other Polynesians, Maori have a distinctiveness, a uniqueness, that marks us as an identifiable culture that is tied to Aotearoa.

Aotearoa, marae, tangihanga, wharenui, dawn ceremonies, the obligatory welcome on a marae, protocol, speeches and haka are recognisable elements of Maori culture. The majority culture is rarely involved in the day-to-day activities of Maori. And that is fine so long as not seeing does not translate into believing that we do not exist.

There is a lot of literature about land, our land; and there has been a bewildering legacy of legislation to alienate the land from the people of the land. Today we spend a lot of energy in efforts to get some of the land back. There have been occupations such as the long Bastion Point case, and shorter ones such as the Moutoa Gardens occupation of 1995. There are claims to the Waitangi Tribunal—the Ngai Tahu case, the Taranaki case and the Ngati Awa case—all wanting land given back, or assets allocated in lieu of land lost.

But knowledge of land (toi te whenua) and of traditional land tenure still needs to be untangled from early Maori Land Court definitions and practices. For example, was the ahi-ka (burning fire) principle as important in determining ownership of land as the court judges ruled? Was not that principle overridden by the ringa kaha (strong arm) principle? Was it not true that what mattered was who wielded political influence in the region, and who had the military might to enforce control? Obviously, a fresh look at Maori land tenure is required. I have included a paper that makes a small contribution to the debate on Maori land.

Maintaining the integrity of Maori culture is one of the great themes of the struggle in Aotearoa. It has been the focus of protests about the language, which is held to be the core of the culture. Once the language disappears, much of the culture vanishes with it. A great fear among many thinking Maori is that we might have given away too much of our culture in the quest to become integrated into Pakeha culture. Did we take on the mantle of being Westernised willingly? Did we knowingly abandon our culture so that we could dress up like the best of the Western world? Did we have to give up our culture as the price for becoming Christians, or for adopting Western technology, or for learning the English language? Was it necessary to give up so much? And then the crunch question: who persuaded us that we should sacrifice our culture? How was it done? Were our ancestors and our parents so gullible? Was it

Confrontation with the police at Moutoa Gardens which was occupied by a Whanganui group.
(The Evening Post, Wellington)

because they had no choice in the matter? Probably. The power of Parliament was behind the assimilation policy 100 years ago, and it is still pushing the same policy today. Nonetheless, there are questions which continue to worry some of us. Were we too willing to go along with whatever government-paid officials advised us to do? Are we so colonised in our thinking that we can no longer think for ourselves? Or are we now awakening from a long sleep on a soft assimilated bed? These are all fascinating questions. I touch on some of them in these papers.

An interesting question is this: why do we engage in a continual struggle with our government and its various agencies? Why do we believe in the Treaty of Waitangi? In fact, why do we want to be Maori and maintain our distinctiveness, when society at large is providing so many escape routes? It is possible, as many of our people already know, to leave the Maori world, not to contribute at all to its maintenance, to pretend to be something other than a Maori, and to get lost in the general populations of the big cities. But many who knowingly escape also come home. If they do not, it is when they die that their identity as Maori is reconfirmed by their being brought back to the ancestral marae for the tangihanga ceremony.

There are many answers to the questions posed above. One of them is in the proverb I began with: Toi te kupu, toi te whenua, toi te mana. There is great dignity in being a Maori. There is satisfaction in knowing that we are people of the land, tangata whenua. There is honour in being part of the peoples of

Polynesia and knowing that we have relatives spread across the great Pacific Ocean. We have a place in the world, and it is here in Aotearoa: the centre of the universe for us. But with it all comes a responsibility: to ensure that our culture survives. We have to struggle to improve the lot of our people. Who else should do this but we ourselves? We also want to ensure that the heritage passed on to the younger generations is in good condition, that there is something worthwhile to hand down. In many respects, we have no choice really. If you are born a Maori, then you accept the consequences of that biological fact, and the culture that comes with it. Yes, you are a Maori. And so am I.

S. M. Mead
November 1996

Education

1. Landmarks, Bridges and Visions

The title of this paper has become a more general title for the whole collection of essays. It was prepared for a conference of language teachers, organised by the New Zealand Association of Language Teachers and held in Nelson in the early 1980s. I was not able to deliver the paper in person. There were urgent issues to discuss, as Maori language teachers who had taken up jobs in secondary schools after undergoing a compressed training programme were experiencing difficulties. There were no processes in place to assist them. Demands upon their time were considerable, and several were turning away from teaching Maori. It was another initiative that was failing for lack of funding and lack of forward planning.

In addition, the public of New Zealand was still having difficulties in coming to terms with the needs and rights of Maori. For example, there was still considerable opposition to putting the teachers of Maori language on a par with English. The public has no difficulty in forcing everyone to learn English, nor with the idea of insisting on English as the medium of instruction for everyone. There was the belief that one could not be educated in a language like Maori. It took years for the majority educators of the country to take off their ethnic-centred goggles and see other realities.

Today, many of the ideas put forward at the conference are no longer such large issues. Efforts are being made to offer more choices to Maori students and to offer learning opportunities in their own culture. But as for the bridge, it remains a challenge for future generations.

Visions for Maori have always been made difficult by the fact of being a minority culture and always having to consider the views of the dominant culture. Through various mechanisms, the dominant partner in the Treaty of Waitangi can always veto what Maori want. They can delay, ignore or actively discourage any vision statement they do not like. Or they can demand, as was done with the act to make Maori an official language of the country, to 'tone' it down, change it and make it more Pakeha-friendly. However, not withstanding these conditioning factors, we must state our aspirations, our future hopes, our vision for the future.

My intention in this paper is to review briefly and selectively some of the landmarks in the history of Maori education, with a view towards catching glimpses of the visions some leaders had of pathways to success and salvation for the Maori. Then I will focus on the problems of the present decade and see whether our past experience has something to tell us. These images of the past can sometimes haunt us and they can sometimes uplift us. Whatever you think of them, they always help provide a better perspective and understanding of the problems we face.

Maori is the native language of New Zealand. According to section 51 of the Maori Affairs Amendment Act 1974, it is the 'ancestral tongue' of that portion of the population of New Zealand that is of Maori descent (Benton 1979, p.4). It is, as some would say, the language of the tangata whenua, thus making a statement about the important place of Maori in our country. It is a vulnerable, threatened and surrounded language that has no legal status in its homeland (Benton 1979). This is a landmark that we have reached today.[1] Already it is possible to think of the eclipse and demise of the 'ancestral tongue' of the Maori and to think of it being taught as a dead language such as Latin.

In the introduction to the report of the Canadian Royal Commission on Bilingualism and Biculturalism in 1967 (Bk. 1, p.XXIX), the commissioners said:

> It is language which makes possible social organisation. Thus a common language is the expression of a community of interests among a group of people. It is not surprising, then, that any community which is governed through the medium of a language other than its own has usually felt itself to some extent disenfranchised, and that this feeling has always been a potential focus for the political agitation.

This statement about language in another country has some meaning for us. That the plight of the language has been a focus of political agitation is a point that I need not labour with this audience.

When Captain James Cook visited Aotearoa in 1769, Maori and its various dialects reigned supreme. But Captain Cook opened a Pandora's box and pretty soon we were signing the Treaty of Waitangi which our experts tell us is also not legal. Missionaries set up schools and traders brought marvellous things from Europe and America.

In those early days, schooling, which the missionaries introduced, was seen as a great thing. The Maori people wanted schools and so, very much on their own initiative, they began setting up schools and learning to read and write through the medium of their own language. This great demand for schooling was explained as a desire of the Maori people to 'read for themselves, in their own tongue, the wonderful words of God' (Barrington & Beaglehole 1974, p.26). By the year of the treaty there were schools in almost every village and enthusiasm was high.

It is important to reflect on what was happening in 1840. Maori adults wanted to learn how to read, write and spell. They instructed themselves in Maori and organised their own schools with but minimal help from the missionaries. The main task of the missionaries was to act as facilitators and train a few advisers, who then trained other keen Maori as community teachers. Maori was the bridge to the white man's knowledge, and a most important one, because through the language the Maori people were able to control the traffic across the bridge.

The idea of using education to produce an anglicised elite within the Maori community was very much in vogue at the time (Barrington & Beaglehole 1974, p.35). The state of being a native was seen by educators as a great impediment, though fortunately it was possible to 'eradicate' it by bringing the people into contact with the benefits of British civilisation and by converting them to Christianity. Very boldly stated in the Native Trust Ordinance was the aim of assimilating 'as speedily as possible the habits and usages of the native to those of the European population' (Barrington & Beaglehole 1974, pp.39, 40). The Reverend Richard Taylor, missionary in the Wanganui district, agreed wholeheartedly with this policy because to him a Maori educated in Maori was still a Maori 'ready to return to the blanket' (p.42). This is a useful image to bear in mind—that is, of a Maori wrapped up in his blanket of Maori education. Clearly, the task of education at the time was to remove the blanket.

By 1847 instruction in English had been introduced in the Education Ordinance of that year. This, too, was a landmark decision whose ultimate objective was similar to the proposed Indian model of producing people who were 'Indian in blood and colour, but English in tastes, in morals, and in intellect' (Barrington & Beaglehole 1974, pp.34, 35). The Native Schools Act of 1858 consolidated the general policies of the period and ensured better funding for Maori education.

A result of the policies instituted after the Treaty of Waitangi was that the school became a bridge between Maori and Pakeha. The technology, wisdom and literature of the West were made available at the school through the medium of English. Those who were well trained could communicate reasonably well in Pakeha circles; those who weren't confined their communications within the Maori world itself and wore the blanket that Richard Taylor equated with being uneducated.

The idea of a bridge was clearly in the mind of Donald McLean, the Native Minister, when introducing the Native Schools Amendment Act 1871. English would be maintained as the language of instruction, he assured the populace, because the education of the Maori race in the English language was the factor most likely to bridge the gap between the two races. And you don't need to be reminded that he whose language is the medium of instruction controls the bridge.

It is worth dwelling briefly on the fact that the government of the day was able to persuade Maori communities to
1. give land upon which to build a school
2. pay some of the costs of educating their children
3. allow their children to be taught by Pakeha teachers in English, and
4. agree to the setting-aside of their own language, and their customs, so that they could become more like Pakeha.

It is truly remarkable that successive governments in New Zealand could and did persuade the Maori to assist with the destruction of their own culture and their own language. Ethnocide is a modern term for this phenomenon.

If we now look at the 1900s, it will be easy to understand that the big battle on the hands of policy-makers was to reintroduce Maori language and culture, aspects which were part and parcel of schooling when the teachers were predominantly Maori. By 1930, when a big revolution in Maori education occurred, the position was that anything Maori had been banished from the classroom. Education was equated with matauranga Pakeha. Maori knowledge was not accepted as education in the Pakeha sense and was ignored. The task of anglicising the Maori was given over to Pakeha teachers entirely, thus tightening the control over the bridge. A Maori teacher was a rare being in those days.

What did the 1930 revolution bring? First, Maori art and crafts were allowed legally into the schools. At the time, it was seen as a huge concession by the government and the Department of Education. Second, Maori culture as understood by the policy-makers was permitted into the curriculum of Maori schools. Finally, a more practical sort of schooling, such as homecraft, woodwork and agriculture, was re-introduced, thus effecting a balance, it was claimed, between academic subjects and practical subjects. W. Parsonage (1954), an inspector of Maori schools, reported that homecraft cottages were built at Whakarewarewa, Manutahi, Tikitiki, Te Araroa, Te Kaha, Ruatoki and Rangitahi. Examined in the cold light of present knowledge, the whole effort was misguided and aimed no further than preparing girls for domestic work.

There was great excitement in the 1930s and the 1940s following the change in policy. But the change came at a time of recession and war. Adequate funding was therefore not likely. Moreover, the teachers who were to put the new policies into effect knew very little of Maori culture, let alone the arts. So the revolution fizzed and failed. As a result, the battles which we thought had been won had to be re-fought and re-negotiated, and funds found for their implementation.

Great efforts were made in the 1950s to generate enthusiasm and drum up public support for Maori education. The campaign launched by E. B. Corbett, Minister of Maori Affairs, on 14 July 1955 began the Maori Education Foundation, which we now take for granted. The Hunn report (1960) came out and, amidst all the excitement, Maori schools were abolished one by one and handed over to education boards. This was the other face of assimilation, later to be called mainstreaming. Maori schools could not be allowed to become too Maori and so the government assimilated them into the Pakeha system to be under Pakeha control.

The vision put forward was that of equality between Maori and Pakeha, of both going to the same school and receiving the same education. It was like Brian Talboys' image of Maori and Pakeha men heaving, grunting and sweating it out together in a rugby scrum. That helped to produce a uniform model of cultural understanding in all those who participated in this meeting-place of dubious value, the rugby scrum.

A fair question to ask is: what have the policy-makers and administrators of education achieved? What have they done to us and to our people? When we look back we see that there was a time when the education of the people was, in large part, carried out by the Maori people themselves. They knew what they wanted and set to work to learn what they felt they had to learn. In a remarkably short time, Maori teachers had taught perhaps just over half the adult population to read and write in Maori (Barrington & Beaglehole 1974, p.28).

They had succeeded, too, in creating a huge demand for books and in encouraging a healthy respect for the Bible and the prayer-book. It happened that the knowledge they sought for their salvation was religious knowledge, which in their view held the key to the availability of Western technology. Who can be sure now? All we know is that the book became a highly valued taonga in the early days.

After that burst of success, the education system was tidied up and control removed from the community. A foreign language became the medium of instruction and Pakeha teachers had to administer education. A predictable result is the feeling of disenfranchisement mentioned in the report of the Royal Commission on Bilingualism and Biculturalism (1967). Today there seems to be a widespread feeling among Maori children of missing out on something and having something else imposed upon them. Rejection of the education system appears to be more common and more audible now.

Moreover, all of the bridges that have ever been put between Maori and Pakeha have been fragile affairs. When the economy is good the bridge holds, but as soon as times are bad people jump off it and do not want to cross from one culture to the other. For example, spectacular increases were made during the 1970s in the numbers of both secondary and primary school students learning Maori and in the number of schools offering Maori. The figures would persuade our own people that they had nothing to fear about the culture and language. Both had become widely accepted in Pakeha society in the 1970s and the gains made must surely last. The old people could die secure in the knowledge that Pakeha society was a lot more caring and supportive of things Maori than they had ever imagined. The optimistic bridge of the 1970s would surely endure.

After all, look at the gains. Maori is accepted in most of our universities. Honours programmes are offered at Auckland, Waikato and Victoria. It is now possible to do a PhD in Maori studies. There are more students sitting School Certificate and UE Maori. The schools have hundreds of students taking Maori as an option. Adults are learning Maori in a variety of institutions. Wherever one looks, there are Maori language classes, some taught by the rakau method. And, as this conference ought to confirm, there are now many Maori in the teaching profession so that we have a better chance of doing traffic duty on the bridge. The overwhelming impression one gets from the 1970s is that at long last we had done something significant to get Maori firmly planted in the curriculum.

Sid Mead, Bishop Manuhuia Bennett and Harawira Gardiner, who all went overseas for part of their higher education. Photo taken at Waitangi, 1990.

(Mead collection)

But here we are, today, in the 1980s. What do we see? Should I spell it all out for you, or do we take all the negative facts as read? What progress have we really made? Are race relations any better now than before? Are we as honest with one another as we should be? Is the teaching of Maori really secure in your school and are you holding your own, gaining or losing ground in terms of students? Is the job any easier? Are you happy in your position of teacher of Maori? Do you have a real role in looking after the bridge, or would you be happy to see it washed away! Are you supported by your colleagues at school, or are you an island in a vast ocean? Do you find that you do not have to worry about the status of Maori in the school curriculum, that people do regard it as the equal of English, French or Russian? Are the battles that were fought in earlier decades really over?

The revolution of the 1930s was dampened considerably by an economic recession. We are now in another period of recession. So will the gains of the 1970s now be lost? There are obviously many questions which one can ask, and it is probably good to ask them, even if we do not know the answers.

But obviously there are some responses which we can make at this meeting. For example, I believe that many policy-makers (and this includes the teachers) still believe in the Richard Taylor dictum that a Maori educated in Maori and wrapped up in his blanket is not educated. Instead of us being thankful that Richard Taylor was wrong, and understanding why he was wrong, a good number of people still want to see as small a component of Maoritanga in the curriculum as is possible to get away with. To them, subjects with a Maori emphasis still do not constitute education—only English can open the doors of edification and, as it turned out, unemployment.

So the first recommendation we might make is this: that as a matter of principle Maori options in schools be increased. Through the last fifty years we have put our faith in one option, Maori language. Isn't it time to introduce subjects such as the myths and traditions of Aotearoa, customs of the Maori, tribal organisations in New Zealand, the technology of the Maori, and so on. And shouldn't these options be included as School Certificate and UE subjects.

Following the same principle through, we might consider offering two language subjects: spoken Maori, where the emphasis is entirely on speaking the language; and written Maori and grammar, in which the emphasis is more academic.

The increase in options will bring several benefits. For the student, and especially the Maori student, this helps achieve a cultural balance in the curriculum and so remove at least some of that feeling of disenfranchisement. The student should get a fairer go at public exams because now the exams would have been indigenised. For the teacher, the obvious benefit is in immediately increasing one's value to the school. In addition, one would be able to specialise in one's area of competence, Maori studies, much more than before. Lastly, and importantly, the increase in options ensures that more students walk the bridge between cultures and that fewer escape than at present. Increasing the opportunities for contact with Maoritanga in the school system would seem to me to be a good thing.

Compulsion or Choice?

Another matter which we should look at seriously is whether the Maori component of the curriculum should be optional in every case and at all levels of education. Is there a place for the compulsory teaching of Maori to all Maori students, or to all New Zealand students regardless of race?

Compulsion is a hot political issue for the Maori language, although it isn't for English—it is all right to force all citizens to learn English. However, this issue is worth examining with a view to ensuring that the rights of access of Maori students to their Maori heritage are not jeopardised by the tardiness and unwillingness of many Europeans to use the Maori language bridge. Nor should

Maori children be prejudiced because Pakeha parents do not want their children to learn Maori.

Matauranga Maori

Another recommendation we might discuss at this meeting is the call to all teachers to respect matauranga Maori and to unlearn ideas which they have inherited, such as that education begins with the English language. Represented here is a sufficient number of languages other than English to highlight the point that English is not the only key to education. It is as possible to be educated in the Maori language as it is to be in French, Japanese, Samoan, German and Tokelauan. This is so obvious that we should not have even to say it. Teachers of Maori might need to re-educate themselves so that they are able to teach the expanded Maori curriculum. This means insisting that they all have degrees in Maori studies or have some other comparable qualification. The task before us does not become easier, so the need to upgrade the professional qualifications of all teachers of Maori has to be considered. I would also suggest that more attention be given to becoming sophisticated in the techniques of teaching Maori language and culture.

The reason I would stress for upgrading qualifications and skills is that yours is a particularly difficult job, which always includes focusing a great deal of attention upon the bridge. Sometimes, whatever you do to encourage two-way traffic on the bridge, few people want to hear you, let alone see you. At other times, people really do appreciate whatever you do about the bridge and so they will encourage you in your work. Always challenging you are the negative attitudes which teachers, parents and students bring to you. You need to be emotionally strong, culturally secure, professionally competent, saintlike in patience, and a good backstop for the Maori children in your school. That is the profile of a person of rare qualities.

Some Proposals for Discussion

1. A child can be educated in languages other than English. This is a fundamental truth that is self-evident.
2. Matauranga Maori is knowledge clothed in Maori terms and categories. It is an integral part of the heritage of every Maori child, and of every other child whose parents believe in the bicultural nature of New Zealand society.
3. It is consistent with the spirit of biculturalism that education should embrace and reflect both Pakeha and Maori forms of knowledge.
4. As a general principle, opportunities for learning about Maori forms of knowledge should be increased in the school system, and such increase should be in the direction of providing a wider selection of subjects so that

Maori stands a fairer chance of being selected by a more representative group of students than at present.
5. Examples of additional subjects might be:
   a. the myths and traditions of New Zealand
   b. spoken Maori
   c. written Maori (including grammar)
   d. social and economic organisations of the Maori
   e. the history of Maori–Pakeha associations
   f. New Zealand society
   g. Maori art
   h. the Treaty of Waitangi
6. Increasing the opportunities for students to experience biculturalism in the schools means that the teachers of Maori must acquire the qualifications appropriate to the new demands which would be made of them.

Visions

Different groups have their own views of the future. There are many visions—some are imaginative, some are inspiring and idealistic. However, there are some visions that we would reject out of hand. The 'one people' concept of a fully assimilated Maori population lost in the whole is an example. That is the sort of vision a dominant group wants to impose on everyone else.

Another vision is represented by the concept of a multicultural society, the notion of a cultural mosaic which was popular in Canada in the 1970s. While it is an appealing image, Maori groups distrust the political agenda embedded in the idea. For one result of it is to treat Maori society, the tangata whenua, as just another ethnic group, no different from any other. The country was founded on the Treaty of Waitangi in 1840. Maori are a Treaty of Waitangi people who have a special constitutional position in the country. The cultural mosaic image does not recognise our special position in Aotearoa, and therefore the multicultural vision is rejected.

In my vision of the future, Maori culture is alive and well. It remains a vital part of the nation and is, in fact, a nation within a nation. Maori people are in charge of their culture and of their future. They have achieved a greater degree of self-determination and self-government, are economically self-sufficient to a degree never seen before. The Maori population has retained its unique features, and is highly visible and able to speak for itself. It has not allowed itself to be assimilated or intimidated into accepting the mainstreaming ideology of successive governments.

In cultural terms, the language has recovered and is widely used on radio and television. The arts are strong and vibrant and the self-esteem of the people never better. Maori communities run their own justice systems, organise and manage their own education, from kohanga reo to wananga, and run their own social and welfare programmes. By this stage the government of the land has little choice but to hand over the funding to allow these self-help initiatives to succeed, because Pakeha attempts have continued to fail. Moreover, Maori are tired of other people running their affairs.

While Maori have achieved a large measure of tino rangatiratanga in managing their own affairs, they have also linked into international communication networks, they trade all over the world, are frequent fliers, are up with technological developments and are making alliances with indigenous peoples or trading partners.

Most iwi have become economically strong and are able to use their combined influence to affect national policies. Political parties cannot operate without a strong Maori membership. Maori make their voice heard through the Maori Congress, which has reformed and redeemed itself to become a powerful political voice for Maori. If the Maori Congress disapproves of a government measure, it will not be passed in Parliament.

Conclusion

It is our duty at a gathering such as this to support one another and to give our rourou of understanding and of aroha. You should be strengthened and encouraged by a meeting such as this one to tackle the job with new vigour and confidence. The difficulties you will undoubtedly face must not deter you as a professional group from giving your best, not only to the development of matauranga Maori in the school system but also to the quality of the service you provide. That familiar piece of advice which we give to the rising generations we need to say to one another: kia kaha, kia maia, kia manawanui, kia whanui te titiro. Pikitia nga pikitanga kia eke ai ki nga taumata o te maramatanga.

References

Barrington, J. M. & T. H. Beaglehole, 1974. *Maori Schools in a Changing Society: An Historical Review*. Wellington, New Zealand Council for Educational Research.
Benton, Richard, 1981. *The Fight of the Amokura Oceanic Languages and Formal Education in the South Pacific*. Wellington, New Zealand Council for Educational Research.
Hunn, J. K., 1960. *Report on Department of Maori Affairs*. Wellington, Government Printer.
Parsonage, W., 1954. 'Practical Education for Maoris', *Te Ao Hou*, 2 (4), pp.42–3.
Royal Commission on Bilingualism and Biculturalism, 1967. *The Official Languages*, Bk. 1, General Introduction. Ottawa, Queen's Printer and Controller of Stationery.

Footnote

1. The Maori language was made an official language of New Zealand on 20 July 1987, thus introducing a new landmark.

2. Maori Studies Tomorrow
Te Wananga i te Matauranga Maori

This paper was prepared for a winter lecture which I was invited to deliver at the University of Auckland in 1983. It gave me an opportunity to look at Maori studies as a university subject.

At this time I advanced the idea of a national whare wananga or university as an option. Subsequently, I changed my mind and decided that regional or tribal institutions were preferable. Now there are three Maori tertiary institutions in place: Te Wananga o Raukawa, Te Wananga o Aotearoa and Te Whare Wananga o Awanuiarangi.

At the time I presented this paper, diplomas or degrees in Maori studies had not been introduced into the universities. In 1996 they are commonplace.

Matauranga Maori (Maori philosophy and knowledge) was also relatively new as a topic of study in tertiary institutions. It should be noted that Eruera Stirling and Anne Salmond discussed and recorded this notion in 1980 in Eruera: The Teachings of a Maori Elder. *The idea is discussed often in the 1990s at wananga, and there is now a master's degree in Matauranga Maori at Te Wananga o Raukawa. Change is occurring all around us and sometimes we hardly notice that there is progress.*

When university teachers of Maori met in 1978 to discuss the subject of Maori studies, my colleague Professor Bruce Biggs thought that it was important to talk about 'what we are actually doing at this university or that' (Biggs 1978, p.5). From this statement it is reasonable to infer that teachers of Maori have some idea of what Maori studies is. At every university in which the subject is taught as a major in a bachelor's degree, there is a programme of courses which can be divided into two categories. The first is language, and Professor Biggs considered this aspect of Maori studies to be 'basic and major' (1978, p.5). His view is supported by the fact that it is mainly language courses that are taught in secondary schools across the country. The second category is culture, or the cultural aspect. According to our colleagues in other disciplines, we Maori do not have a 'civilisation', and so it is that courses in Maori culture and not 'civilisation', as in the Indo-European languages, are taught at New Zealand universities. Thus, as practised in our universities, Maori studies consists of two types of courses: those which focus on the language (te reo), and those which deal broadly with culture, including such topics as prehistory, traditions, tribal histories, art, oratory and customary concepts (nga tikanga, nga matauranga Maori i tua atu o te reo).

It is plain from these introductory remarks that my intention is to discuss the very questions which most of us want to avoid: namely, questions about what we select for inclusion in Maori studies courses, who should teach it, and why. That the enterprise is full of pitfalls and snares is probably to be expected, but one should not surrender without an attempt.

At the outset I shall try to lay out a broad framework for the discussion that follows. In doing so I borrow extensively from Bullivant (1981), who published in *Canadian Ethnic Studies* an article entitled 'Multiculturalism—Pluralist Orthodoxy or Ethnic Hegemony'. According to him, university teachers, along with teaching associations and the professorial board, are 'knowledge managers'. These managers of knowledge are 'the formal agents appointed by the group to ensure that its culture is transmitted' (Bullivant 1981, p.3). They devise a curriculum which Bullivant defines as 'a selection from the socio-cultural group's stock of valued traditional and current public knowledge, conceptions, and experiences, usually purposefully organised in programmatic sequence' (1981, p.3).

The selection involves 'a rational process based on value judgements (i) about the type, quantity and purposes of the knowledge and conceptions; (ii) about the present and anticipated future demographic, social, economic and cultural features of the society and the relationships of the individuals that comprise it'. This seems like a straightforward task, but it isn't. First, the judgements are influenced 'by the prevailing ideologies and counter ideologies about education and society' that are held by the agents or the knowledge managers. They are apt to select features of the knowledge and conceptions of the group which are compatible with their respective ideologies. The definition of ideology accepted by Bullivant is that provided in *A Dictionary of the Social Sciences* (Gould 1964): 'a pattern of beliefs both factual and normative which purport to explain complex social phenomena with a view to directing and simplifying socio-political choices facing individuals and groups' (Bullivant 1981, p.4).

The knowledge managers are in turn influenced by a variety of other groups, such as 'political bodies, interest and pressure groups and other power-holding managers of curriculum decision making'. An example is the 'hidden' decision made by Dr C. E. Beeby (personal communication), on the advice of Sir Apirana Ngata, not to introduce the teaching of Maori language into Maori schools in the 1930s. Few people knew that a decisive discussion between two important knowledge managers had occurred and that they had agreed on a course of action which proved to be ill advised and plainly wrong.

Had this discussion been open to all knowledge managers, it is more than likely that 'counter ideologies' which challenged the status quo would have been heard. As visualised by Bullivant, counter-ideologies are proposed by persons who challenge 'the basis for allocating knowledge/power, who envisage emerging trends in the society that might conceivably generate a new socio-historical context, or who try to bring about an ideal-type, future society based on philosophical speculations'.

In many countries, ideologies and counter-ideologies are talked about in shorthand form. For example, in New Zealand we are hearing increasingly about bicultural education. These labels were rarely mentioned when I began teaching; rather, the emphasis was on assimilation and integration, and we tried hard in the wake of the Hunn report (1960) to propose that integration meant something other than fitting Maori society into the mould of the dominant Pakeha society and that it was more acceptable than the other ideology.

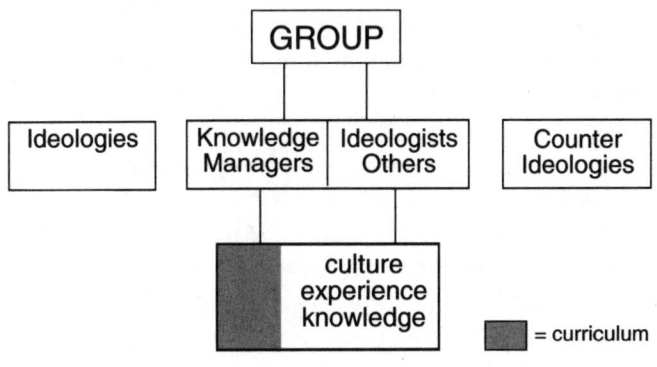

Figure 2.1
Summary of the Bullivant framework.

In Figure 2.1, the shaded area in the diagram represents the curriculum of Maori studies as taught in our universities. The model suggests that the material selected for inclusion has resulted from extensive discussions among many groups of people, including representatives from the ethnic group, whose knowledge, experience, and conceptions are to be transmitted to later generations. One might be forgiven for thinking that there had been a lot of talking since

1. Maori was included as a University Entrance subject as far back as 1929 (Royal 1975, p.35)
2. the teaching of Maori as a university subject did not begin at Auckland until 1952, and
3. graduate programmes did not begin until 1978 at Victoria and Waikato; Auckland followed in 1979 and Canterbury begins in 1984.

I suspect, however, that there were not really many open discussions held about this emerging subject. The trouble was that Maori studies as a subject was seen to be neither separable from anthropology nor worthy of a place in its own right. It was out of sight and out of mind.

Furthermore, from the 1920s onwards, two of our influential Maori thinkers, Sir Apirana Ngata and Te Rangi Hiroa, were both thoroughly preoccupied with anthropology (Sorrenson 1982, p.17). In fact, rather than push for the establishment of Maori (or Maoritanga or Maori studies) at university level, they were both concerned with attempts to introduce anthropology. If Te Rangi Hiroa had had his way, Raymond Firth would have had a lectureship in anthropology in 1931, and if Sir Apirana Ngata could have done it, anthropology would have been introduced probably in the 1930s and Te Rangi Hiroa would have been the subject's first director (Sorrenson 1981, p.17). But nothing came of these early discussions, most of which occurred in the zone Bullivant describes as the 'hidden curriculum of curriculum decision making'. As far as most of the thinkers of the pre-war era were concerned, Maori did not exist as a subject. It was an adhering child of anthropology and, if not attached to anthropology, then it would be given to some other Western university subject, such as German.[1]

In the 1950s many Pakeha scholars had great difficulty in accepting Maori as a proper university subject. Professor Biggs would be very familiar with such ethnocentric knowledge managers, because he had to overcome their prejudices in the years when Maori was introduced into Auckland University. But if one analysed their attitudes it would very likely be found that they believed in the ideology of total assimilation, and probably also believed, as fact, the evolutionary three-step ladder which put Pakeha culture at the top and that of the Maori some distance down. Since universities were concerned with Western subjects such as classical studies (for Greece and Rome are acceptable), history, geography, Latin, and geology, there was no room for this non-Western, non-European and non-Pakeha subject called Maori. Lacking the honourable suffixes of academia, as in Maorigraphy or Maoriology, the subject stayed out in the quadrangle until Professor Biggs added the word 'studies'.

The rise of Maori studies as a subject in its own right is a fascinating historical research topic, and somebody should do work on it. Many difficulties have hindered its progress. Professor Biggs would have touched on some of the barriers which had to be cleared away in order that Maori studies could emerge from the coffin which earlier knowledge managers, and some still living, prepared for it. Thus it is necessary to add further elements to the Bullivant model in order to better reflect the reality in New Zealand.

The tangata whenua ethnic group does not exist as an entity or clearly identifiable enclave within New Zealand society. Rather, it is a fractured Humpty-Dumpty that is scattered all over New Zealand, and all the king's men and all the king's horses cannot put the pieces together again very easily. As a dispersed group of 385,000 people, it is surrounded and feels hemmed in and oppressed by the larger Pakeha population of about 2,500,000. Even though in 1840 we signed the Treaty of Waitangi and became partners with Britain, Maori people cannot seek help from the Queen, or from the British Parliament, but must turn to the local Pakeha people who are the cause of nearly all our problems. This, too, is part of the reality Maori society has to face.

The deliberate fracturing of Maori society made it easier to domesticate the pieces and integrate them into the various parts of Pakeha society. In terms of curricula, this means that every subject area or discipline within, say, a university has its slice of the Maori cake. Thus anthropology often has Maori within it, history has a strong interest in Maori land issues and Maori leaders, education in the pedagogy of the Maori minority, medicine in Maori health, and so on.

Many knowledge managers would argue that this is proper because it does reflect a reality on the ground. From this vantage point, Maori people are scattered and widely dispersed among the institutions of the land. Some argue that these institutions should become aware of the 'bicultural imperative'[2] and reflect it both in the personnel who work there and in the manner in which the institution operates. In fact, these very issues are at present under discussion in the State Services Commission, and the ideological positions of those who believe in integration, multiculturalism or biculturalism are voiced.

This kind of thinking is, in my view, ethnocentric. It is an argument of the sort that, since the word Pakeha was spelt in Busby's 1835 Declaration of Independence with a lower case 'p', and since a host of Pakeha editors to this day spell it with a small 'p' on the good authority of a now-retired Pakeha professor of English, the word should continue to be spelt with a lower case 'p'. The ideology behind the thinking is not acceptable because it is clouded by racism. Many Pakehas reject the label which the Maori people put upon them because they want to be called by the more pretentious term 'European'. They claim that the term 'bloody Pakeha', is different from 'bloody Maori', and sounds worse! Most of us would surely argue that the intention of the speaker is the same and that the status of the victim is also similar in each case.

It can be shown that the 'pepper potting', 'domesticate in small portions', 'spread them out' thinking is similarly ethnocentric and self-serving. Maori people are being asked to accept the social reality, the categories and vision of truth of the dominant society. They are also expected to accept that imposed reality as scientific truth.

Given the sorts of ideology which have dominated New Zealand life for so long, it is easy to see why developments in Maori studies have been so disappointingly slow. As it has become gradually more acceptable as a subject, several landmark events have occurred—and all of them recently!

1952   Maori studies first taught as a university subject at Auckland.
1967   Maori studies introduced as part of anthropology at Victoria University by Joan Metge and Koro Dewes.
1974   Big increase in number of secondary schools teaching Maori, from twenty-five in 1960 to 117, involving 10,482 students (Royal 1975, p.36).
1974   Fifteen lecturers in Maori language and Maori studies had been appointed to teachers colleges (Royal 1975, p.37).
1975   Victoria University advertised a chair in Maori.
1978   MA programmes in Maori introduced at Victoria and Waikato.
1979   MA programme introduced at Auckland.
1982   Te Wananga o Raukawa established, with emphasis on iwi and hapu studies on the one hand and administrative studies on the other, and culminating in the award by the wananga of a Bachelor of Maori and Administration (BMA) degree.
1983   Maori studies included in subjects discussed at fifteenth Pacific Science Congress held in Dunedin in February.

The name of the subject still presents some problems for some of the knowledge managers. Teachers at the secondary level tend to separate the two aspects of Maori studies. Thus they speak of Maori language, which they teach for the School Certificate and University Entrance examinations. Maori culture includes all of the non-language activities which they teach and is apt to be dominated by song and dance. More recently, Eruera Stirling and Anne Salmond (1980, p.249) have focused our attention upon matauranga Maori, as a term to include a body of knowledge which contrasts with Pakeha or Western knowledge.

Matauranga Maori can be seen as constituting the knowledge base which Maori people must have if they are to be comfortable with their Maoritanga and competent in their dealings with other Maori people. It represents the heritage of the Maori, the knowledge which the elders are said to pass on to their mokopuna, the wahi ngaro, which our youth long for, and the tikitiki mo to mahunga (the topknot for your head), which Sir Apirana Ngata talked about. This concept of matauranga Maori helps bring back together into a united whole the shattered pieces of Humpty-Dumpty that I spoke of earlier. Moreover, it helps us to understand the nature of our subject and hence provide some guidance as to what our responsibilities are to the Maori people.

I assume that, by being responsive to the survival needs of the Maori society, we will make a contribution to the nation as a whole and thus to the wider community. Matauranga Maori is like a stand of native trees that must be saved from the sawmills of the timber merchants, or like the kokako, a rare native bird that enhances the landscape and enriches the life of the nation. Like a native forest full of tall trees or a beautiful native bird, matauranga Maori is to be regarded as an important part of the national heritage.

It is a reality that, after some 140 years of a very grim struggle by Maori society to survive as a group, we face cultural defeat. We managed to survive biologically, and now there are 385,000 persons of Maori descent in New Zealand to prove it, and several hundred more in Australia. We have learnt how to survive as biological, sort of culturally neutral, inoffensive, silent beings. By and large we keep our complaints to ourselves and we tend to express our frustration with Pakeha society by often violent actions against ourselves and especially against our women. We reflect the behaviour and the contradictions of an oppressed people somewhat like the peasants of Brazil, as described by Paulo Freire in his 1970 book, *Pedagogy of the Oppressed*.

We have been less successful at cultural survival. To begin with, as Professor Biggs (1981, p.ix) and Dr Richard Benton (1978, pp.11-12) pointed out, the Maori language is in rapid decline. Massive migration from rural to urban communities where no facilities were provided to support the continued use of the language was a major factor. Another was that the school system was slow to accommodate the cultural needs of Maori children. The widespread adoption of television and radio played their part also in assimilating the urban Maori into city life. The result is that we now face the prospect of the death of our language, and this threat to the traditional vehicle of matauranga Maori threatens much of the culture. Many art forms that are based on the use of language, such as waiata, karanga, whakapapa and whaikorero, are 'endangered species'.

Our conceptions of the universe, our ideas about the nature of man, the myths and legends that have become part of New Zealand literature were given to us through our language. But what is most important, as has been proved over and over again in recent times, is the fact that for Maori people matauranga Maori, the experiences of our people, the conceptions mentioned by Bullivant, are part and parcel of our reality. They comprise an important component of the material which gives us a grip on life, which enables us to be human, and which gives us dignity in this land.

The struggle of the Maori people to survive biologically and culturally has been a long, lonely and often bitter one. In the hundred years just passed there has not been too much evidence of genuine Pakeha aroha and understanding. In my view, the university cannot be an institution that stands back and records every poignant moment of the death of Maoritanga, like geologists watching the eruption of a dying mountain, and catching everything on video and various other recording machines. I know that our colleagues are capable of doing a good job of observing and recording. Nor should we be an institution that accepts the demise of Maori culture fatalistically and regards it as an inevitable consequence of Pakeha dominance, that academics can do nothing about, except to prepare the bed and put the dying pillow in place. Personally, I reject that position and I cannot commend it to anyone in Maori studies and in anthropology.

The counter-ideology affirms that there is only one honourable and dignified pathway that we can follow. There is no real option but for the knowledge managers of our universities and departments of Maori studies to become involved in the struggle of the Maori people to survive culturally. We must work with the people in the sense described by Paulo Freire (1970, p.52). He said: 'Critical and liberating dialogue, which presupposes action, must be carried on with the oppressed at whatever stage of their struggles for liberation.' Liberation is the opposite of cultural death. Liberation from the present reality of a culture under threat and bound tightly under the machinery of Pakeha government and its institutions helps all who participate become more human. To become more human is a worthwhile reward because we can live more easily with ourselves.

Alarmists are bound to say that it is dangerous to become so involved. However, most of us who are trained in anthropology cannot really say that with conviction. Nevertheless, some colleagues are bound to worry about the nature of our involvement and it is right that we should clarify our contribution. A useful background paper to this issue is by Raymond Firth (1981), who deals with the problems of engagement or detachment of social anthropologists in social affairs. The tradition of anthropologists becoming advocates for the indigenous people they study goes back to Malinowski, who was clear about our duties. What we should do is 'present facts, develop concepts, destroy fictions and empty phrases and so reveal relevant, active forces' (Firth 1981, p.195). For knowledge managers who are Maori I see no conceptual problems: all of us are bound to participate in plans to free our people's minds, make them more aware of our reality, and as well to help develop and maintain the institutions of Maoritanga. Most of us play a part already in the affairs of our tribal groups, especially when we are reasonably close to the heartlands. Those who are removed some distance from the tribal headquarters find other ways to contribute. For most of us, the problem is how much time to give to one's iwi. There are limits which need to be recognised and new rules, perhaps, which need to be negotiated. Otherwise, the students we teach may not get a fair deal. Only a few of us are in the happy position of working simultaneously for the university and for the tribe. I can imagine no greater pleasure in life than being able to fuse my role as university teacher and researcher with a similar role in my own tribal region. I sometimes feel that if my students were all members of my tribe we could achieve great results and take greater pleasure in the tasks of teaching and learning.

These issues aside, I do feel that the university has much to offer in ways that are part of its traditional role. Most students coming to us now want to learn Maori in order to speak it. As Professor Biggs (1981, p.x) put it: 'More and more Maori will use the language as an identity card, shown for a moment to establish one's Maoritanga, then returned to an inner pocket.' While it is true that some who identify as Maori do that, I happen to view the need to learn to communicate in Maori quite seriously, and I believe we have an obligation to train speakers of Maori as quickly and as economically as possible.

The challenge to the universities is to discover new and more effective ways of teaching Maori and to make these new ways available to every group that requests it. We should find out how best to teach children to be native speakers of Maori and explore new structures for dealing with the new demands of our students. We ought to be able to find ways of transforming the pain of language learning into a joy, because this has a bearing on the survival of Maori. We need to explore new techniques of teaching that perhaps make greater use of the marae, so as to reduce as dramatically as we can the time taken to teach a student to become a reasonably competent speaker of Maori. Can we do it in the three years that it takes a student to obtain a bachelor's degree? Should we design a new degree? Or should we set up a new kind of university that best meets our cultural needs?[3]

With regard to culture courses, we need to discover what the new, educated and bicultural person needs to know in order to make a contribution to marae-based activities. This person is likely to replace knowledgeable elders who have died out, either from natural causes or from being assimilated and thereby suffering a cultural death. We need, therefore, to produce students who have a good grasp of these portions of matauranga Maori which we offer at our universities.

The questions we need to ask ourselves have to do with what we should be selecting for the curriculum, what part of matauranga Maori our people need. Should we decide that we really do need a course called whakapapa (and not kinship), then we have to find out how to teach whakapapa as effectively as possible. There is no doubt in my mind that few people have been able to master whakapapa to the point of being able to use this creatively in Maori ceremonial life. There is also little doubt that whakapapa experts are given great respect in Maori communities because of the knowledge (matauranga) they exhibit during moments of great social importance to the people. Maori people look upon whakapapa as being a very intellectual and difficult art, and that is why I think we should try to offer courses on this topic.

Recent events arising out of the Waitangi Tribunal's report to the government on the seafood resources of Taranaki suggest very strongly that we should be teaching courses on Maori land and sea tenure. And, indeed, Victoria University is introducing such a course in 1984. Another obvious gap is a course on Maori organisations such as the Waitangi Tribunal, Maori land incorporations, trust boards and so on, for the resourceful and knowledgeable graduate should know about them. Where else should students find such a course but in Maori studies?

Not forgetting Bullivant's inclusion of experience as part of the material for the curriculum, we should bring into the programmes of Maori studies courses such as cultural survival, the history of Maori survival, Maori–Pakeha relations, the Treaty of Waitangi, unsung and forgotten heroes of Maoritanga, and the effects of Pakeha government on Maori culture. As people who have felt the effects of oppression and who are vitally concerned with what Pakehatanga is up to almost every day of the year, we ought to have something to say to our students about our experiences—the bitter, the poignant, the tragic, the triumphant and the happy.

Beyond explorations of new courses and developing an appropriate pedagogy for Maori studies, I believe we should assist through our writings and publications, such as *Paanui*,[4] in engaging the Maori people in the critical and liberating dialogue which is necessary for us to understand our social reality. Paulo Freire (1970) offers a theory about how we, as a people, might free ourselves intellectually from the bonds of being a minority group within our own country. I notice that the Canadians have not been afraid to deal with self-determination and 'the right to exist as distinct peoples and to prosper in their own cultures and traditions' (Jackson, McCaskill & Hall 1982, p.1). In fact, the *Canadian Journal of Native Studies* published a special issue on 'Learning for Self-Determination: Community-Based Options for Native Training and Research' in which most of the articles were written by activists rather than scholars. The editors of the issue noted that 'It seems as if the use of Native Studies as a means of reflecting on political and social action taken by the native movement has declined in recent years' (Jackson, McCaskill & Hall 1982, p.2). They hoped that the special issue would 'encourage others to reflect on the activities of the native movement and to feed this analysis back into the movement in a spirit of solidarity, mutual support and dialogue' (ibid).

I do not think Maori studies people as a group consider seriously that we might have an obligation to support with our skills various projects which the Maori people are required to do in dealing with the institutions of the Pakeha. Rather, we have been content to let a few of us, such as Rangi Walker[5] and Pat Hohepa,[6] operate in the disapproved arena of politics. Some of us made brief forays into politics and then retreated into the relative safety of academia. Yet others of us appear not to be associated or identified with the people whom we, as knowledge managers, are supposed to represent. I sometimes wonder why.

It should be pointed out very strongly to knowledge managers everywhere that we are going through a very difficult period in the life of our nation. It is a time when one has to scream in order to attract attention and fight hard for a share in the resources of our institutions. Maori people are facing many crises. Never before has the Maori community needed its educated and skilled people more desperately. But there are too few educated Maori men and women, too few with MAs and too few with PhDs. The consequences are many. But the one which concerns Maori studies immediately is that a strong community pressure is being exerted on our staff for help. Many of us are involved in various tribal initiatives or community projects, thus reducing the time that we can give to writing papers and books. The few who serve are overworked. Moreover, some able Maori students are responding to the call of the communities and are 'going home' to live and work. A few are becoming like monks in that they are renouncing affluence and city life for the opportunity to serve their own people and teach their children to become native speakers of Maori. One of my students has three children who are native speakers and it is now very difficult to persuade him to come back to university.

I come now to the question of who should become knowledge managers of Maori studies. A few years ago a student of mine complained that he came to university to seek and find his heritage. He regarded his Maoritanga as very sacred and precious. When he found that some of the transmitters of the heritage were Pakeha, he protested. He found that he could not accept his heritage from a Pakeha teacher: it seemed quite wrong to him. This had nothing to do with the quality or expertise of the teacher. Rather, it was a matter of ethics as far as he was concerned. The appropriation of the heritage of the Maori by the knowledge managers of all the other disciplines is what worried him. He resented it and, in telling me about his personal difficulty, he alerted me to a problem I was not aware of until then.

All of us are now aware of the sensitivities of the modern Maori. These resentments and sensitivities are, in my view, a direct consequence of feeling and being oppressed. How can a victim of oppression take from the hand of the oppressor the very substance of his identity? That was the problem of my students and it is a general issue that we must face. In our New Zealand context the university has favoured the Pakeha student. Even in a subject such as Maori the organisation of courses, the writing of essays, the lecturing in English have all conspired to favour Pakeha students. No wonder that some Maori students, who may be no less bright, resent the institution, the department and those who teach Maori studies as a university subject.

It is interesting to me to find that a few Pakeha students also want to be taught by a Maori. They want an 'authentic' source: a person who has experience in the difficulties of being Maori. Some of them are worried about the integrity of Maori culture and are no less concerned about whose hand it is that feeds matauranga Maori to them. Many members of our Maori public accuse us of 'selling out' to the Pakeha and of giving to them jobs which Maori teachers should have. They point to the scarcity of Maori teachers on any university campus and to the fact that in many cases the only Maori lecturers on the university staff are those in Maori studies. These are not matters we can ignore, for it is a fact that there are too few Maori teachers at our universities.

Our greatest difficulty is that the universities were slow to respond to the need to train people for the various Maori studies jobs throughout the land, and particularly short-sighted in not training people in matauranga Maori and in Maori language so that qualified people would have been available. So we have to be staffed the way we are at present and we must live through our present difficulties. We must have access to the branches of knowledge that we require and at this present time there are a surplus of Pakeha academics and a desperate shortage in all disciplines of Maori PhDs. The shortage is so critical that it is possible that, in the immediate years ahead, Pakeha professors will be appointed to take charge of Maori studies departments. I would regard that as a backward step; some would call it a backlash step! The important question remains: where are our successors?

In the paper I referred to earlier, Firth (1981, p.198) described anthropology as 'the uncomfortable science', following the line of thinking which resulted in economics being called 'the dismal science'. Firth pointed out that anthropologists tend, through their research, to identify human problems which policy-makers find awkward. Moreover, they tend to offer no practical solutions to problems but, more typically, reveal other elements to the issue than had been known at the time. As a daughter science of anthropology, Maori studies qualifies very definitely to be described as 'the uncomfortable science'. A lot of people, including many Maori outside the university, are somewhat suspicious of it, and knowledge managers in other subjects do not regard it as a science and question its right to exist as an independent discipline in a university. Teachers within Maori studies also feel insecure. Pakeha scholars feel threatened by the changes occurring in Maori society today and within the subject itself. On the other hand, Maori scholars feel threatened by the university and are often intimidated by it. Our students come to us often afraid of their own heritage. So for these and many other reasons we are going through an uncomfortable period in our development.

Among knowledge managers at all levels of education are people who still question the mana of Maori studies. They see the subject as being too narrow, too limited, not part of an international network and not academic. While such accusations tend to reflect the attitudes of the accusers more than anything else, there are nevertheless some problems to discuss. But in dealing with this matter I find it useful to follow the model of Tane, who turned himself upside down in order to bring maramatanga (light and understanding) into the world.

Ideally, Maori studies is Polynesian studies, because Polynesia is the region against which we can understand our situation. The Maori case is but one example of events in Polynesia, of which we are an integral part.

If we want a broader perspective for our understanding, we must traverse the world. Thus, in a geographical sense, it is not Maori studies that builds limiting fences around itself, but rather the other disciplines such as history, political science, sociology, geography and anthropology.

In terms of colleagues in other parts of the world, there is a network to which we belong because we are not the only country that has developed ethnic studies. Others are Australia, Canada, the United States, Denmark and Norway. That the network is not properly developed is a function of ethnic studies being a relatively new development worldwide.

In the world of ideas, I recognise no boundaries for Maori studies. In fact, it is easy for me to visualise anthropology, sociology, history, geography, linguistics, art history and economics as working for Maori studies. They have very valuable contributions to make towards our subject. Anthropology is part of the legacy of Maori studies and we claim it without apology. The world of ideas has always been open to us and we must travel that world and learn from it.

It is obvious that I see Maori studies as being organised more like a school than a department. I can visualise the anthropology department in Auckland becoming the first School of Maori Studies. Education and geography might well be included in the school. In this sort of arrangement, it is possible to put Humpty-Dumpty together again, and it also becomes possible to repossess our heritage, hold on to it, and exercise a measure of control over it.

I should be quite happy to see Maori studies move towards a Maori university which could exist side by side with, say, the Auckland campus. This sort of arrangement has been adopted in at least one campus in Canada. In such a university I would see Maori topics being taught entirely in Maori. A marae would be a central physical feature of the campus. Its students would be able to share the same basic facilities as the other students, and have access to subjects that we could not otherwise offer. The university would be funded by the state, and offer degrees in its own name, say as the University of Aotearoa. People to fill the teaching posts—who are bicultural and bilingual—would need to be trained for such a university.

An idea such as this offers a challenge to Maori academics to come forward and be trained. It also presents an opportunity for far more Maori knowledge managers to be employed by the university system in New Zealand than is the case now. At the moment, all of our universities are bastions of Pakehatanga and are dominated by Pakeha teachers, technicians, administrators, typists, carpenters and gardeners.

Ngati Raukawa, Ngati Toa and Te Ati Awa have made a move towards establishing their own university and they are now into their second year. They chose to move outside the structures of the present university system, finding little sympathy in those quarters for their enterprise. We could well find other tribal universities being established in the next few years. I am very keen on setting up a whare wananga at Whakatane but I know that there are enormous difficulties ahead. The largest difficulties have to do with funding.

To bring this discussion to a conclusion, I now focus upon some tasks that must be addressed in the years ahead. A start has already been made on some of them.

1. Te Wahi Ngaro (The Lost Portion of the Heritage)

There is an urgent need for research which focuses upon discovery, rediscovery and reconstructions of the heritage. The people want this information and are hungry for it. Our national aim should be to record the heritage for every iwi and whanau in the country. This is an immense task, which needs to be shared out among Maori studies departments and undertaken purposefully in the full knowledge of what we are trying to achieve.

Such research illustrates a sensitivity to the needs of the Maori people and emphasises the point that the university can meet the need without compromising its scholarly and research aims.

2. Te Reo Tuku Iho (The Language Heritage)

Some necessary resource materials have already been produced by both the universities and the New Zealand Council for Educational Research. But a tremendous effort needs to be made to produce good teaching programmes which are aimed at achieving communicative ability in the language as a first priority. Other aspects such as reading, writing and translating come next.

I believe we need to direct some of our effort into putting the new technology of computers and word processors into the hands of our students. If by using this sophisticated technology Maori can be learnt more systematically and faster, we must encourage it.

But there is a less spectacular revolution that we are quite unprepared for: the availability of tape-decks in motorcars. Hundreds of our young people have such equipment. We ought to make available to them programmes of language instruction suitable to their needs and necessary for going to a hui—instructions on how to behave at a tangi, waiata that they can learn as they travel, and so on. However, we might need to find ways of making such resources available. One way of dealing with it is to encourage the establishment of a company which specialises in selling resources of this sort. Such a company would become a commercial arm of all Maori studies departments everywhere and, if set up properly, could be controlled by us and made to work for the people. It would handle sophisticated word-processor programmes and distribute materials which we cannot handle easily ourselves.

3. Nga Tupuna Rongo Nui (Famous Ancestors)

I have already mentioned the need to bring out into te ao marama outstanding men and women of the Maori world. These are the heroes and heroines of our people, who must be seen as Maori leaders who crossed the stage of life and made important contributions to our life, our struggle to survive, and our efforts to contain and domesticate Pakehatanga. More recently, there are people who are already making a name in the struggle to reassert our right to a place of prominence in our country.

I refer to leaders such as Te Ua Haumene,[7] the first Maori leader ever to be exhibited like a monkey and publicly humiliated and ridiculed—and this with state funding and full government approval. Titokowaru,[8] an outstanding military tactician in the Pakeha sense, is another unsung hero who needs to be brought forward so his achievements can be viewed again.

The important essential is to free our heroes and heroines from the smothering blanket of government propaganda and of news media smear campaigns. Recently I was told that some descendants and relatives of Te Kooti did not want to talk about their ancestor because he was a 'rebel' and they are ashamed of him. This is the sort of nonsense that must be overcome.

4. Te Tangata Whakaiti (The Humble Person)

It is most important that, in all we do at university, we keep certain values before us. Students must not think that they know everything and, worse, know more than any other Maori. Matauranga Maori learnt at university must be accepted with humility as a very good foundation upon which to build. Maori graduates should be made to spend at least a month among members of their tribe in order to learn that ahead of them lies the task of winning the confidence of their people. Pakeha graduates should spend a month doing community service among Maori people. Most importantly, however, they must realise that they face a more difficult task of gaining acceptability in the Maori world than do Maori students. That is a fact of life, although life is often full of surprises and contradictions! All of our students also must learn (and probably the hard way) that humility is an important taonga to possess not only soon after graduation but always.

University education often alienates, and just as often teaches values which encourage some of our people to become arrogant knowledge managers. Matauranga, according to our late kaumatua Eruera Stirling, 'is a blessing on your mind, it makes everything clear and guides you to do things in the right way . . . and not a word will be thrown at you by the people' (Stirling & Salmond 1980, p.247).

One of Te Kooti's prophetic sayings reminds the Maori people that it is all right to receive Pakeha education and learn to read and write, but he and the Ringatu church had matauranga too. Though he did not amplify his statement, it is clear that Te Kooti recognised the danger of Pakeha education and what it can do to our people if it is not tempered by a humility towards our own matauranga and towards our people. University education must work with us and for us and not against us.

5. Te Waihanga i Nga Whare Hou (Building New Houses)

I have already talked about building new structures such as a School of Maori studies or a tribal university or Te Whare Wananga o Aotearoa. We must address ourselves to the task of finding the most appropriate structures for teaching our subject. Maori studies is more than a university subject area. It is closely linked with the identity of Maori and Pakeha alike, though more for the former than for the latter. Its knowledge managers must reach beyond the present confines of the university and bring in the buildings that we all know we must have—for example, a marae. There are already some twenty teaching institutions throughout the land that have a marae and I understand that the Education Department is already at the point of accepting a marae as a legitimate teaching structure in our secondary schools. It is up to us to ensure that a marae becomes an integral part of departments of Maori studies at university level.

There are, however, other structures such as a Diploma in Maoritanga which we at Victoria University are trying to establish. This will be a one-year undergraduate diploma which might be very attractive to students who want to study Maori only and nothing else. Such a diploma might be the most effective way of meeting the identity and heritage needs of many of the students who come to us.

New degrees and courses need to be introduced. I would see these as being selected on the principle of community need and offered because the knowledge gained is very important.

6. Te Toi Matauranga Maori (The Knowledge of Maori Knowledge)

Finally, it is our duty to study the nature of our subject. I see matauranga Maori as being Maori studies, one being a translation of the other. But what we teach at university is but a selection from the whole. The part that is selected is usually the portion which is seen to be most valued and most central to Maori society as it exists today. One of the tasks before us is to focus upon the meaning of the word 'toi' and so become involved in studying the nature of knowledge, or in grander terms the epistemology of matauranga Maori. My selection of 'Te Toi Matauranga Maori' as the Maori title of my paper was deliberate because I hope that in Maori studies tomorrow we give our subject the academic mana that it should have. It is up to the knowledge managers to accomplish that goal.

Conclusion

It is impossible in a paper of this nature to cover everything and to say everything. The remarkable thing about our subject is that it is still relatively new, so a whakatauki of my tribe can be applied to it: 'He manu hou ahau he pi ka rere' (I am a new bird, a fledgling that has just learnt to fly). The next part of the whakatauki spoke of allowing one to drink deeply of the water from a certain river before one's life was taken away. It is important, I believe, that our subject does have time to develop and that we have time to see and appreciate its good works. I would not want to see it die for lack of imagination, dedication and funding.

Let me end by saying that Maori studies has proved so far to be a 'blessing on the mind' of the nation. There are exciting developments ahead and I believe there is no time to lose. We must do everything we can to encourage the manu hou to fly, enjoy the freedom of the skies, and adorn the breast of Ranginui who stands above us.

References

Belich, James, 1979. 'Titokowaru's War and Its Place in New Zealand History'. MA thesis, Victoria University of Wellington.

Biggs, Bruce, 1978. *Te Whakaako i te Reo Maaori i te Whare Wananga o Akarana*. Talk given at Inter-University Maori studies Conference, Victoria University, August 17–19.

Biggs, Bruce, 1981. *The Complete English–Maori Dictionary*. Auckland, Auckland University Press/Oxford University Press.

Bullivant, Brian M., 1981. 'Multiculturalism—Pluralist Orthodoxy or Ethnic Hegemony', *Canadian Ethnic Studies*, XIII (2), pp.1–22.

Clark, Paul, 1975. *'Hauhau': The Pai Marire Search for Maori Identity*. Auckland, Auckland University Press.

Firth, Raymond, 1981. 'Engagement and Detachment: Reflections on Applying Social Anthropology to Social Affairs', *Human Organisation*, 40 (3), pp.193–201.

Freire, Paulo, 1970. *Pedagogy of the Oppressed*. New York, Harper and Herdes.

Jackson, Ted, Don McCaskill and Budd L. Hall, 1982. 'Introduction to Learning for Self-Determination: Community-Based Options for Native Training and Research', *Canadian Journal of Native Studies*, II (1), pp.1–9.

Royal, Turoa, 1975. 'Culture Change and Educational Administration in New Zealand'. MEd Admin thesis, University of New England, Australia.

Sorrenson, M. P. K., 1982. 'Polynesian Corpuscles and Pacific Anthropology: The Home-made Anthropology of Sir Apirana Ngata and Sir Peter Buck', *Journal of the Polynesian Society*, 91 (1), pp.7–27.

Stirling, Eruera and Anne Salmond, 1980. *Eruera: The Teachings of a Maori Elder*. Wellington, Oxford University Press.

Vice-President's Report, 1977. 'Proposals for Increased Response through Teaching, Scholarship and Service to the Expectations of the Native Peoples of Alberta'. Calgary, University of Calgary.

Footnotes

1. At Canterbury University, Maori was introduced under the mantle of the Department of German.
2. This term is attributable to Ken Piddington and is meant to indicate that settling the problems of inter-relationships between the two main groups in New Zealand, Maori and Pakeha, has a priority over all else. Multiculturalism as an ideology is rejected by many Maori thinkers because it removes the special and legitimate claims of the Maori people, as tangata whenua, and relegates them to being the same as all the immigrant minorities now living in New Zealand.
3. The attitude of our universities can be compared with that of the University of Calgary, in Canada, whose vice-president commissioned a report entitled 'Proposals for Increased Response through Teaching, Scholarship and Service to the Expectations of the Native Peoples of Alberta' (December 1977).
4. *Paanui* or *Panui* is a publication of Maori studies departments begun in 1978, and issued by each department which is identified in the title adopted—for example, *Panui a Waikato* (publication of Maori Department at University of Waikato), *Paanui a Aakarana* (publication of Maori studies section at University of Auckland), *Panui a Wikitoria* (publication of Department of Maori Studies at Victoria University), *Paanui-a-Waitaha* (publication of Maori sections at Universities of Canterbury and Otago). The Maori studies section of Massey University has not yet issued a *Panui*.
5. Dr Rangi Walker, of continuing education at Auckland University, writes a regular feature on Maori–Pakeha relations in the *New Zealand Listener* and has been subjected to abuse by Ministers of the Crown, by Prime Minister Muldoon, and by many members of the public who resent a view of reality that is counter to their own.
6. Dr Patrick Hohepa, who is engaged in activities of the New Zealand Maori Council and of Mana Motuhake (a Maori self-determination political party), is seen to be a very political person and therefore bad. There is also resentment of all educated Maori men and women who become advocates for their people. Many Pakeha New Zealanders feel that it is wrong to use Western (Pakeha) knowledge in pursuit of Maori social and political issues. This is an attitude that we must try to change.
7. Paul Clark (1975) has helped considerably in allowing us to get a better appreciation of Te Ua.
8. See thesis by James Belich (1979), who has revealed the military genius of Titokowaru.

3. Maori Studies in the Universities
Te Kaupapa Maori i Nga Whare Wananga

This paper was a keynote address delivered at Te Herenga Waka Marae, Victoria University of Wellington, in 1990. The occasion was a conference of Maori university teachers and staff who belonged to a recently formed organisation called Te Matawhanui. The subject of Maori studies was explored further and I stressed the wisdom of relating the curriculum to the needs of the clients, the Maori people. What was taught at universities should relate to the cultural, social, economic and political needs of the people. It needed a social intent, as universities are required by Act of Parliament to act as the conscience of the people and accept that scholarship be brought to bear on current issues so that views contrary to government policy can be stated without fear of being jailed and persecuted. There are few Maori academics who are willing to become the conscience of the Maori population by writing to newspapers and countering the many biased and anti-Maori statements that frequently appear in the newspapers of the country. As a group, Maori academics do not and are not asked to comment on world events. We seem to be confined to our own world, possibly through default.

There was another important task for Maori academics: to help make the world more coherent for the Maori public by providing theories, analyses, commentaries and ideas to help give some order to a rapidly changing world. In other words, Maori academics should become the intellectual leaders of their people, or at least try to be. These were some of the issues for the conference.

Tēnā koutou te whānau o Te Matawhānui kui huihui mai nei ki Te Herenga Waka marae i tēnei ahiahi. Ka nui te mihi ki a koutou i roto i tēnei tau hou, i roto hoki i ngā mahi o te rā o Te Tiriti o Waitangi. Kua tangihia te hunga kua wehe atu ki te pō. Nō reira waiho rātou kia moe i te moenga roa. Ko koutou ēnei ngā kanohi o ō koutou mātua, ō koutou tīpuna. Ka mihi atu ki a koutou, tēnā koutou, tēnā koutou.

This is 1990, the 150th birthday of the Treaty of Waitangi. In February I was at Waitangi as a participant and an observer in the activities leading up to and including the commemoration of the treaty on the sixth day. Queen Elizabeth II and the Duke of Edinburgh have been and gone from Waitangi. Whakahuihui Vercoe, the Bishop of Aotearoa, made his forthright, honest and appealing sermon on Waitangi ground, and the critics have attacked him on the seventh and eighth days of February.

At Waitangi there was a huge tent city where cultural groups and canoe crews, together with supporters, camped. I observed the huge tent the Tainui people brought and put up for their 1000-plus contingent and I saw their refrigerated truck and the piles of food they brought to feed themselves. This is self-reliance on a scale some of us can hardly contemplate. But this is not something new; our people used to travel like this a century ago. They housed themselves and prepared their own hangi.

I saw the tent where the crew of Mataatua waka stayed. There were some 500 people of Mataatua who went to support Te Toi o Mataatua, the canoe constructed at Poroporo, Whakatane and brought to Waitangi to join in the celebrations. The twenty-two canoes on the beach and some anchored in the bay presented an awesome sight. Over a century ago an observer would have seen a sight something like this. There were canoes of many sizes, some magnificent in their grandiosity of scale, some modest but beautifully constructed and carved. Ngati Kahungunu's huge waka, Tamatea-Ariki-Nui, had a crew of 140 earnest

The waka being launched at Waitangi on Waitangi Day 1990, easily one of the most memorable celebrations of the treaty held so far. *(Derek Fox)*

young men and could carry a tira of eighty passengers—truly a jumbo waka. This canoe had a slight mishap and for a while it looked as though the mana of Ngati Kahungunu was fractured, but only for a while. Ngati Whatua's presence in the water was represented by a very large, 150-man waka and it, too, was very impressive. Some of the canoes were constructed with fibreglass, some were made of totara and others again were of laminated timber. There were more canoes at Waitangi than I have ever seen in my lifetime and looking at the men handle them stirs the wairua Maori in me. I marvel at this wondrous spectacle.

It was also remarkable to see hundreds of young men stripped to the waist performing their various duties of launching their canoes, lifting them out of the water, or applying the paddle and chanting as they laboured, or getting down to the serious business of a haka. Nearly every canoe crew was sheltered by a large contingent of their kuia and koroua as well as many supporters of the iwi. And when I walked the beach and looked into the faces of the men and women associated with the canoes, I saw complete dedication and commitment. One detected pride in their eyes, and joy to be part of a cultural revival. Our people at the flax roots successfully snatched up a whole complex of skills and knowledge from the past, re-educated themselves, and at Waitangi elicited a reaction of ihi, wehi and wana even from the most sceptical of our people. By Waitangi Day there was admiration for these dedicated rangatahi and their waka.

The nation has just witnessed a very successful Commonwealth Games at Auckland city. The opening ceremony was an event of great significance for us, because for a change the Maori dimension was not an afterthought, like the Japanese addition to the Auckland harbour bridge, nor a token gesture, as has often been the case. Instead, the Maori welcome was an essential and fundamental part of the ceremony. It was given its proper place and emphasis in the proceedings.

During the games we saw on television a reflection of the new Commonwealth. We saw new interpretations of 'Englishman' and 'Englishwoman' which would have delighted any Maori. We saw that talent is widely distributed and is not concentrated among the white performers. This should be a timely reminder to our people that what we saw the Kenyans doing, the Jamaicans and the Nigerians, we can do also, given the right structures, appropriate promotion and funding, the right mind-set and control in our hands. Perhaps we should consider entering the Commonwealth Games as Aotearoa and present ourselves more effectively to the international community. If we appeal to iwi competitiveness, an Aotearoa Games for Maori sports men and women could become successful within a short time.

Exciting developments are occurring all around us. Maoritanga is alive and becoming stronger and more interesting. Te Maori and the year of the waka have caught the imagination of our people and motivated the rangatahi to seek knowledge on an unprecedented scale. The canoes have encouraged large groups of young Maori men to rededicate themselves to their iwi. They have had to learn the skills of the paddle, of navigation, of dealing with waves, winds and rain, of reading the sky and the clouds, of karakia, paddling chants and haka. The remarkable thing about all of this is that, when called upon by their iwi, the young men submitted themselves willingly and enthusiastically to a strict regime of physical training and learning. In addition, the people at home took over the tasks of training and education, and with few exceptions they have done all of this without us. One of my staff was grateful to be called upon to be a paddler! Is that the lot for us university teachers?

Then, as far as the Commonwealth Games are concerned, what is our contribution? Sir Hugh Kawharu played an important ceremonial role at the opening, but he was clearly speaking as a Ngati Whatua leader and was not representing us. Dr Peter Sharples of Ngati Kahungunu is a graduate of Auckland University, and we might shelter under his wings for that reason. I did not see any of my students limbering up at the starting lines. There may have been some students from other Maori studies departments but I rather doubt it. In the overall tally of medals, the white countries of the Commonwealth scored far more than the non-white countries such as India (fifth), Bangladesh (seventeenth), and Papua New Guinea (twenty-first). Australia, England, Canada and New Zealand occupied the first places, in the order given.

Another event was the Aotearoa Maori Festival of 1990 at Waitangi. This, too, was an exciting occasion which drew hundreds of enthusiastic spectators, mostly of our own people. One had to be present to enjoy the atmosphere and to participate in the joy of being Maori and to be lifted in spirit by our performing arts. The festival also connects with iwitanga, so that supporters travel by the busload to be on hand to stimulate the performers to greater efforts. Two university groups took part, Te Whare Wananga o Waikato and Te Kapa Haka o te Whare Wananga o Otakou, and for us of Wikitoria several of our students were in the Pukeahu team and that group trained at this marae. Professor Timoti Karetu is a member of the runanga of the Aotearoa Maori Festival of Arts. Here we seem to have had some involvement over a long period of time, thanks to the efforts of Maori studies at Waikato University.

In the *New Zealand Herald* of 3 February 1990 an announcement was made by the general manager of the Iwi Transition Agency (Te Tira Ahu Iwi) that a major research project aimed at 'auditing' the iwi of the land was to be launched this year. Spread over two years, the research was to involve both iwi researchers and Maori departments of the universities. This is the first time to my knowledge that Maori studies departments have been invited to assist with what is basically iwi research. The invitation was based on the assumption that Maori studies staff:

1. have research skills
2. are willing to be involved in iwi research

3. want to make a contribution towards building up the information and knowledge base of the iwi, and
4. are willing to play a leading role in supervising, co-ordinating and writing up the results of research.

This is a new development for Maori studies staff and indeed for all university teachers of Maori descent. An opportunity has now come to test our years of education, our training and skills against the needs of our people. It is accountability time. Have we used our resources and skills to assist the iwi not only at home but all round us in the cities? Can we admit that there is an obligation upon us to respond to the iwi, to show that higher education is worthwhile and can make a contribution to the task of building up the knowledge base of iwi?

These new developments come at a time when we need to look seriously at two aspects of our work in universities. The first is the task of building up the credibility and status of Maori university teachers. We tend to have low status in the world of universities and among our colleagues here in New Zealand. While we might feel equal to other university teachers, they do not necessarily see us as their equals.

Maori studies itself suffers from the way it is perceived by our colleagues in other disciplines. Maori studies is given a low status by a majority of the students today who mirror all the old prejudices against it. For example, the opinion of a large number of Pakeha and some Maori students is that Maori studies is a side road that leads nowhere, it is no use anywhere else in the world but here, and it will not help get a student a job. We know that the facts are quite different. In fact, Maori studies is a useful career path that leads on to many interesting jobs which are increasing every year rather than diminishing. There is a demand for graduates who have competence in the language and who know Maori culture and tikanga.

Maori studies belongs to the international group of studies variously called native studies, black studies, indigenous studies or aboriginal studies, all of which have sprung up in Fourth World countries. The emergence of these studies reflects the need of various indigenous groups to make the university systems work for them and to use the resources, skills and status of the institution to give a better understanding of and respect for the cultures of the native peoples. Perhaps the subject needs to be internationalised in order to give more status to Maori studies—that is, we should have meetings with our international colleagues and exchange ideas with them through shared journals.

A more serious problem which confronts us is the attitudes of our own teachers, and sometimes of our students, to Maori studies. Let me deal first with the attitudes of staff. Why has *Te Panui* failed? Why is the Maori University Teachers Association (MUTA), formed last year at Dunedin, a non-event? Why is Maori studies held in low esteem?

While it is true that the fundamental issue is the attitude of our colleagues and students in the Pakeha world, some of the fault lies in ourselves. A professional attitude is necessary, and this should be reflected not only in the manner we present ourselves to the world at large but also, in particular, to the students we teach. Students need to know that we are competent, committed, professional and demanding people who in our very attitudes reflect what we want Maori studies to be. If Maori studies is to be a professional, high-profile academic discipline, we should act as though it is. My thesis is that, if we work hard to raise the status of Maori studies as a university discipline, we would in fact help to make it more useful to iwi development, more responsive to iwi needs, more positive and raising of self-esteem for Maori people working within it. Professionalism would help raise the status of our subject.

Another problem is the freedom of Maori students to choose Maori studies. Do they in fact really choose, or are they already streamed in the secondary school to the point that later choices are limited? Is taking Maori studies really a matter of choice for Maori students? Are Maori students caught in a cultural bind at the tertiary level by not being adequately prepared culturally at the primary and secondary levels? Is this situation changing with the development of kohanga reo and kura kaupapa Maori?

A point I want to emphasise is that the iwi at home and in the cities demand that the best of our rangatahi should be the future leaders and managers of our people, and that they should give of their best to the maintenance and development of our culture. These leaders must be competent in the language and culture of Maoritanga. Our duty is to give them the best education and training possible for the tasks ahead. It is not in the interests of Maoritanga that our most promising young people are alienated from their culture.

I also want to draw your attention to the scarcity of Maori graduates who pursue Maori studies to PhD level. Where are the mokopuna and why are they are not enrolling? These questions need exploring and we need some answers. The apparent failure to attract more graduate students to Maori studies and our failure to enthuse and inspire students to do a PhD in Maori studies indicate that not all is well at our universities.

Student reaction to our courses and our degrees falls short of the enthusiasm and dedication among the rangatahi that was inspired by Te Maori and now by the waka taua. Could it be that the courses we teach are outdated, irrelevant and not related to any real community need? Is the structure of the department not appropriate? Are we approaching our task the wrong way? Are we too timid to teach the sort of courses our students really want? Are we out of tune with our iwi and with our own Maori world? Is it that, in trying to be multi-tribal, national, international and academic in a Pakeha sense, we have missed some vital lessons from our Maori heritage?

Perhaps the 'iwi audit' which the Iwi Transition Agency wants is needed just as urgently by us. Perhaps most of what we do at university comes more out of the Pakeha world than out of our own world and its needs, its dreams and its quest for a better world for our mokopuna.

Since the increase over the last few years of Pakeha anxiety about our demands for resources, Maori studies appears to have lost the active support of other disciplines in our universities. There are some exceptions, such as Anne Salmond of anthropology at Auckland. But it seems to me that anthropologists and archaeologists around the country are not actively supporting us to the same degree as they did before. There is little or no help from sociology, political science and others. The closing of the door of support appears to have coincided with the allocation of more resources to Maori studies, by way of marae complexes and increased grants. Maybe this has nothing to do with the cooling towards Maori studies, but the silence of our colleagues is noticeable. It seems that Maori studies has to fight some of its greatest battles in the universities alone, and this might be a new reality for us to consider. I would hope, however, that what is really happening is our colleagues are waiting for us to ask them to support us.

Bishop Whakahuihui Vercoe, Bishop Brown Turei, Morehu Te Maro, Lewis Moeau at a powhiri for the centennial of Hinetapora meeting-house at Mangahanea, Ruatoria, 26 October 1995.
(S. M. Mead)

As we assert our identity as Maori people with increasing confidence, as we press for proper expression of the notion of 'tino rangatiratanga' everywhere, including the universities, as we establish schools such as kurakaupapa Maori which demand that all teaching is done in Maori, as we strive to alter some of the structures within universities and as we move towards iwi development and self-determination, it could well be the case that we will find ourselves standing more and more alone. We should be prepared for that to happen.

The day after Waitangi Day 1990 the *New Zealand Herald* gave front-page billing to the rousing speech of Bishop Whakahuihui Vercoe. The Rev. Maori

Marsden of Te Taitokerau was quoted in the *Auckland Star* (7 February 1990) as saying: 'Bishop Vercoe was straight up the middle. He gave us the reality of this so-called partnership. Maori have become marginalised.' He was so honest about how we feel about the treaty, and about our dissatisfaction with the performance of the government in really honouring the treaty, that some of our conservative Maori leaders and many Pakeha elders were upset by it. They were upset by the truth and by the unusual and unexpected phenomenon of a Maori leader speaking the truth to the Queen. I find it remarkable

1. that we do not expect any 'reasonable' Maori leader to speak truthfully about our situation
2. that we expect our leaders to join in a conspiracy of silence or to lie to the world and to the Queen about what is happening to us, and
3. that some of us do not want to hear us tell them what is happening to us but prefer to hear the view of the dominant group.

The straight-talking stance taken by Bishop Vercoe was applauded by the great majority of people at Waitangi that day. He was cheered for his honesty and for his courage to break with a Waitangi Day orthodoxy of taking an official Pakeha view of great progress towards unity and goodwill. I believe the bishop articulated a need felt by thousands of people to tell the truth. This means avoiding the views of the politicians and of all those who are opposed to the treaty and who are in fact traitors to the sacred compact signed in 1840.

I would like to think that the new spirit of honest thinking and straight-talking which the Bishop introduced at Waitangi should be taken up by us in our workplaces. The days of being afraid to speak the truth should be set aside. After all, universities are places which stand for integrity and truth.

Conclusions

The few days I spent at Waitangi, and events before and after Waitangi Day, helped me to focus upon a few ideas that might help us get our house in order.

The most powerful force among our people is their identification with their tribal groups. I call this iwi force or mana iwi. While it might lie dormant for decades, the force can be activated given the right challenge, for example, by Te Maori or Nga Waka Taua. In each case the people were moved to become involved in aspects of their heritage (art in one case, war canoes in the other) and they were encouraged to organise themselves according to their iwi groups. Each event moved tribal groups to relearn matauranga that had been neglected for a century, and they did so willingly and enthusiastically. Mana iwi is becoming progressively stronger and, if we as university teachers want to be part of it, we must re-examine what we do, how we do it and why. The rising force of mana iwi provides some guidance to us about how we operate in the future. Accountability to the iwi is a new aspect of our work that I believe will be helpful. Our public, our target clients, consist of iwi groups which are identifiable and named. Up to now we have managed to do our work without reference to them and without formal structures of communication and accountability. Those days are over and we now need to prepare to deal with mana iwi.

If we approach mana iwi with sensitivity and good sense, the result could well be more students coming to university than we have had before, better training, more enthusiasm for our teaching programmes, more graduates, and more students pursuing higher degrees.

The dramatic increase in the number of kura kaupapa Maori indicates that with mana iwi comes another aspect that could have a powerful influence upon both the shape of tertiary education and the standards of teaching. This new movement in Maori education is the drive to teach in Maori, to explain in Maori, and to give order, commands and instructions in Maori. It was standard practice among all the crews of the waka taua at Waitangi to give all commands in Maori. We should not be surprised if our students begin to demand that they are instructed in Maori so that the language is the tool of instruction, the vehicle by which the wairua of Maoritanga is captured, and not the end-point of teaching. When this happens, the teaching of language has to be vastly improved so that students can move quickly into 'total immersion' classes or what might be called kaupapa Maori courses.

These changes signal a greater degree of co-operation with iwi and a more imaginative way of dealing with the issues of cultural maintenance and development. The invitation to conduct research *with* iwi and *for* them is also a healthy sign and indicates a coming together of university education and iwi. The details of the partnership are still to be negotiated over the next few years, but I see this as an exciting time.

I turn now to measures of a tu tangata nature that are aimed at strengthening ourselves professionally.

At this conference we must take steps to alter the perception our colleagues have of us. I suggest we strengthen MUTA or Te Matawhanui by demanding a real commitment to it by our members and some dedication from our leaders. The tasks before us are important not just to us but to future students and ultimately to the iwi. If we demand commitment from our students, we must make similar demands of ourselves in regard to the subject we teach and the students we serve. The excuse that we are all too busy is not acceptable.

I suggest, too, that the inter-university Maori studies journal called *Te Panui* be upgraded to an academic journal for Maori university teachers, that we change its name, and that we appoint the sort of editor who will lift the standards to a high level. The present *Panui* lacks a rigorous standard, it lacks academic status, we all hold it in low esteem and consequently we allow it to languish. We pin our faith upon the well-established Pakeha journals and we neglect to build up the mana of our own. We have to establish its mana ourselves—no one else can do it for us.

Other measures need to be taken to lift the status of Maori studies. The task needs to be faced with some imagination, otherwise we will be forced to wait for racism in New Zealand to decline. I prefer taking some active steps to improve the situation rather than the other option of giving up or of ignoring the problem. I leave it to you to suggest how we might improve the status not only of Maori studies as a university discipline, but also of Maori university teachers generally.

Bishop Whakahuihui with his Waitangi sermon has taken a giant step forward in speaking out openly about what is happening to us. Our organisation needs to do that, too. We should be speaking out for our people. And when one of our leaders is attacked by the Prime Minister and others for speaking out we must defend that person. I recommend that we declare support for Bishop Whakahuihui Vercoe and that we do this as effectively and as strongly as we can, that we defend his right to speak openly about how we feel we are being treated and that we begin to attack people who are traitors to the Treaty of Waitangi. For too long Maori university teachers have had no voice, no influence over events, no organisation and no kaha.

Following the example of Bishop Whakahuihui Vercoe, we should be speaking out and commenting on issues that are of local, national or international importance. Should we not say something about the great desire of our people to form a congress? Should we respond to the crisis in Western Samoa by encouraging and leading fundraising efforts on all university campuses? Should we support the quest of the Palestinians to form a nation in which they can enjoy tino rangatiratanga? And what about the rebel English cricket tour in South Africa and the fact that the tangata whenua of the land are being treated brutally by the South African police? Or is it your wish that we limit our vision and not live up to the wairua of our name, Te Matawhanui? These are issues we need to discuss.

As an organisation we must be represented on committees that are important to the future of tertiary education such as the National Education Qualifications Authority, which has a Maori representative from the polytechnics (Marina Hughes) but none from our organisation. We need members who are willing to serve and who are moved by the necessity to protect the interests of all iwi and to make the future brighter for our students. In this sense our representative is speaking for a much larger population than MUTA itself.

The future is always hard to predict, and the particular skills that we have do not necessarily prepare us to be good social engineers. But I believe we have an obligation to help make the future more coherent and exciting by providing theories, methods and ideas to give some order to what is otherwise hard to visualise or articulate. There is no doubt in mind that we need to be a part of the great changes occurring at the present time.

Let me close with the words which are familiar to all of you: kia kaha, kia manawanui, kia pono ki te kaupapa. Ko te Matawhānui te ingoa o to tātou rōpū, no reira me whānui ta tātou titiro i nga kaupapa kei mua i a tātou. Tēnā koutou katoa.

4. A Time to Reach Out

In 1992 I was asked to give the keynote address at the graduation ceremony of Victoria University of Wellington on 28 April. This ceremony was held at Te Herenga Waka marae for Maori students wanting to receive their diplomas and degrees on the marae rather than in the larger Town Hall ceremony.

During my tenure as Professor of Maori at Victoria University, I developed a marae complex and was able to have built a beautiful carved meeting-house called Te Herenga Waka. My colleagues Ruka Broughton and Wiremu Parker assisted me in the project, but neither of them was able to witness the opening ceremony for the marae which was held on 6 December 1986.

I also helped to pioneer the idea of a special graduation ceremony for Maori students. Some members of the University Council were against the idea, which they saw as being 'separatist'. But we went ahead anyway and began to develop a ceremony at Victoria University in the early 1980s. Since then a marae graduation ceremony is accepted around the country as quite normal. Many Maori students prefer to be honoured in a marae ceremony.

My graduation address was, in effect, my farewell address to the marae I helped establish, to the Maori Studies Department I developed, to the university where I had worked since 1977. It was a message to the students of my time who were now passing through 'the system', as it were, and about to face the challenges of life.

Graduation is a time to feel good, a time to be happy, a time to celebrate, because an important goal has been reached, personal struggles have been vindicated, sacrifices justified and one's self-esteem has received a boost. Success alters your view towards the world and its many challenges. In fact, success can make you feel so good about yourself that your mind is free to float upwards towards Rangi-e-tu-nei. You can soar like a bird across the world and there are no limits to what a free mind can do.

This should be a time when you can share your success with your whanau, your hapu and your iwi and be honoured in a way which affirms your being Maori and enhances your view of yourselves as Maori. I congratulate the university for opening the doors of cultural understanding a little further to give Maori students the cultural right to be capped at Te Herenga Waka marae if they so choose. Those who criticise what is happening today are trapped in a world of ignorance and racism and cannot understand that the process of education is enhanced by working with the culture of Maori students. In fact, the legacy of ignoring this principle is the under-achievement of Maori students throughout the education system of the country.

I want to congratulate all of you who are receiving your degrees here today. It is perhaps difficult for you to realise that it has taken several years of negotiating to have this happen, so that you should enjoy the moment.

The Americans use the word 'commencement' to characterise their graduation ceremonies. It is a gentle reminder that the qualification you are receiving is not the end of the education process but rather the beginning. Your journey into matauranga or knowledge has begun and the pathway ahead is long. Our ancestors were well aware of the nature of matauranga, its value to society, its dangers if misused, and its power for good. Knowledge is respected in the Maori world and in this sense we are no different from other societies. University education is concerned with the pursuit of knowledge and not really with getting jobs, although it undoubtedly helps. Matauranga is about developing the creative powers of the mind. It is about expanding horizons and reaching beyond the limitations of circumstance and adversity. It is about learning to analyse critically and logically. It is about searching and collecting data and organising information in a coherent way. Most importantly, it is about reading and writing and so becoming literate.

Our ancestors saw the process of education as focusing light upon an area of study, hence the word 'maramatanga' or light. The more light one could focus on a subject, the greater the understanding of that subject. Maramatanga means being educated or having understanding. This is entirely consistent with what a university education is supposed to do. It focuses light on areas of darkness, on ignorance, prejudice, racism, on mumbo-jumbo humbug, on falsities, on harmful government policies, and it should be the conscience of the nation in these matters.

There are two concepts our ancestors applied to the pursuit of knowledge. One is 'te hohonutanga o te matauranga', which means going deeply into learning and not being satisfied with surface knowledge. Knowledge is like the ocean, most of which we cannot see and understand. The learner therefore has to dive in and explore the areas of darkness, that is the unknown parts of the ocean, and by exploring come to understand.

The second term is 'te whanuitanga o te matauranga', and this refers to the unreachable horizons of knowledge, to its breadth as opposed to its depth. This means that a student needs to swim the ocean of knowledge, and how far you are able to go determines the degree of maramatanga you will achieve. In terms of our own culture, the journey you have begun today is to seek more light, more understanding and that most elusive of all educational goals, wisdom.

There was a time when the Maori world considered a pass in School Certificate or University Entrance a great achievement. Armed with those qualifications, the young people went home to make their contribution to their communities. Then over the last thirty years we raised our sights to a bachelor's degree and, while we have produced many graduates, few of them actually went home. So today Maori communities are badly under-resourced and are suffering from under-population, from the loss of the rangatahi, and very definitely from a scarcity of well-educated and able young people to do the work of the iwi. It has become increasingly important to our survival that you equip yourselves far better than ever before for the urgent work that needs to be done. A bachelor's degree is not sufficient, and so we must encourage you to expand your educational horizons and now focus on high degrees such as a master's or better still a PhD.

Another good reason for pursuing higher qualifications is that we are entering an interesting phase of becoming involved in the education of our people. We are taking charge of matauranga and of the process of educating and schooling. The kohanga reo and kura kaupapa Maori provide evidence of this trend. We have also entered the area of tertiary education and are establishing whare wananga in different parts of the country. The Wananga o Raukawa is the pioneer in this new trend, and I understand that it will become the first whare wananga in the country to be registered under the new legislation and that is expected to happen this year. I congratulate my colleague Professor Whatarangi Winiata and all who assisted him in establishing their university. Theirs is a wonderful achievement and it is something to be proud of. I cannot, however, resist the temptation to add that I hope that Te Whare Wananga o Awanuiarangi at Whakatane is the next one to be registered. The important point I want to make, though, is that these developments demand more people with expertise and better-qualified graduates to fill the teaching positions that are now being created. Moreover, the fruits of your hard work need to be taken back to our communities. The repatriation of matauranga to the wa kainga is urgent and we need a new breed of missionaries to carry out this task. In order to establish the whare wananga properly we need the best, not only because we want to succeed to our own satisfaction but for another important reason which I now turn to.

Many years ago Professor Winiata and I and our families met in Canada. We went there to prove a point: that we could hold our own in the international community of scholars. This is a crucial test for scholars and for whare wananga, and we owe it to ourselves to tap into the knowledge base of the world and become a part of the big world out there. This is te whanuitanga o te matauranga I spoke of earlier—that is, the reaching out to the boundaries of knowledge—which is very exciting. The iwi at home are already doing that in various ways, and have become international travellers. We are the new octopus, te wheke a muturangi, that reached out to the margins of the horizon. Now our people are exploring the countries of the world and they are travelling for business, for the arts, for entertainment and for pleasure. Universities must keep up and be aware of where the Maori world is heading. The concept of the global wheke or octopus is one we need to pursue, and we have to be the octopus.

I now need to bring several threads together. You are graduating at a very challenging moment in our development as the indigenous people of this land. We have arrived at a time when Maori university graduates with high qualifications are in desperate need. The measures taken previously by universities and by successive governments to increase the number of Maori graduates are shown up to be hopelessly inadequate and typically far too slow. Where are the Maori masters and the Maori PhDs? They are still far too rare a breed.

But while it is possible to lay the blame for this state of affairs in various quarters there are several steps which we can take ourselves. Obviously, one way is to open more whare wananga and take an active role in producing, first, a better-educated public and, second, more graduates with PhDs. But the pace is far too slow and the response of government far too conservative. Another is for the Maori Studies Department here and at other metropolitan universities to become more active and better organised to meet the challenges of our time. Another is for the Maori Education Foundation to target funds specifically at encouraging Maori students to go on and complete degrees at the master's and PhD levels. Some bold and imaginative steps are necessary if there is to be any real change. Then one can ask you, the graduating classes of today, to become a part of this new drive for high qualifications. Give it some thought and reach out to the world and soar like an eagle as you explore the limitless sky or the depths of the oceans of knowledge that exist in the world. The quest for matauranga is indeed an exciting challenge, and you have begun the adventure. Go forth into the world and explore.

Tena koutou katoa.

5. New Initiatives for Maori at Tertiary Level Institutions

This paper was presented at a tertiary education conference held at the Plaza International Hotel in Wellington in April 1995. Since 1990 there had been further developments in tertiary education. The establishment of wananga had been included in the Education Amendment Act of 1990 and by 1995 at least two had been established, one at Otaki and the other at Te Awamutu. A third, Te Whare Wananga o Awanuiarangi, was in the process of becoming registered.

I was personally involved in establishing Awanuiarangi and had first-hand experience of the difficulties. This article is about wananga and what we expect of them.

Introduction

Education is an important activity which the state funds and organises in order to meet certain objectives which are seen to be in the best future interests of the government of the day. At present the entire education system in New Zealand is undergoing drastic change. This includes the tertiary education sector. The thrust of change is driven by marketplace interests or by new right ideology. There is an emphasis upon increasing efficiency, upon creating national standards, upon increasing the share of student costs, and upon greater transparency in expectations and outcomes that students have to meet.

As these general trends are occupying the minds of communities and families everywhere in the country, Maori are attempting to set up structures that better meet the requirements of their people.

The unfavourable and negative statistics of Maori are generally well known. That the national system of education has failed to adequately address the needs of Maori at all levels of schooling is also well known and accepted by most Maori. It is partly in recognition of the relatively poor performance of Maori at school that some new initiatives have been accepted. Well-known examples are kohanga reo and kura kaupapa Maori.

Some statistics give an indication of what is happening in the Maori world.
1. The number of children enrolling in some form of early childhood education between 1991 and 1993 increased by 31 per cent. Of the 28,503 Maori children, about half were in kohanga reo ('Nga Haeata' 1994, p.13).
2. By 30 June 1994 there were twenty-nine kura kaupapa Maori schools established or approved ('Nga Haeata' 1994, p.11).
3. A pilot kura tuarua (a secondary school with kura kaupapa Maori philosophy) was being tested in 1994 at the Hoani Waititi Marae in Auckland ('Nga Haeata' 1994, p.11).
4. Total immersion units within mainstream secondary schools were being developed ('Nga Haeata' 1994, p.11).

It is important to point out that Maori have demonstrated a keen interest in education, not just recently but from the beginning of first contact with Western culture. Recent developments in kohanga reo and kura kaupapa Maori provide evidence that, once opportunities are provided for Maori to deliver education programmes to their own people, they are grasped with great enthusiasm.

Hirini Mead, June Mead, Kate Walker visit the kohanga reo at Waititi Marae, 1989.
(Mead collection)

Kura kaupapa Maori at Maungawhau, 1989. The class is doing arithmetic with abacus.
(Mead collection)

Students at Te Whare Wananga o Awanuiarangi at Whakatane, 1995

(S. M. Mead)

Progress in Maori participation in the education of their own people is usually hampered by government procrastination, lack of vision by officials, and most of all by lack of good faith. Pakeha ideologies often get in the way. For example, there is an accusation of separatism because Maori want to do things for themselves. But it is all right for Pakeha to do things for Pakeha. That is not seen as evidence of separatism. There is also the ideology of assimilation, which conspires to impose mainstreaming upon the Maori people. This is supported by the Pakeha-driven movement of 'one people, one nation', which the One New Zealand promoted in the country. These sorts of ideologies become gate-keeping mechanisms to prevent Maori from developing their own structures and their own delivery systems.

It does appear to be true that the views and interests of the dominant ruling culture are not the same as those of the minority indigenous culture, whose people see themselves as victims. The government that reflects the views of that dominant culture in effect becomes the problem, as it tends to resist pressures from Maori to do things for themselves. This applies to Maori efforts in the areas of crime, social welfare and education.

Education can be a liberating force, but only when it is passed into the hands of the people who want to be liberated. To some extent this happened in kohanga reo and kura kaupapa Maori.

The Role of Te Reo Maori

Teaching in te reo Maori has become an important issue, both as a means of improving the performance of pupils in the curriculum subjects of the school and in helping to save the language. In other words, there has been a shift away from studying the language as an end in itself to actually using it as a medium of instruction. Kohanga reo, kura kaupapa and immersion classes have created an urgent need for qualified teachers who are competent in te reo Maori—that is, they can speak it as well as talk about it and teach in it. There is a shortage of such skilled people.

Trends in Mainstream Institutions

I turn now to the tertiary sector. Two main trends are emerging in Maori education at this level. The first might be described as indigenising the mainstream institutions, as universities, colleges of education and polytechnics strive to improve their service to Maori. There has been a dramatic increase in the number of Maori studies departments in all of these institutions. It is now necessary to have a Maori department which stands alongside other departments.

It was not so long ago that such institutions either did not have a Maori studies department or, if there was one, it was placed under the authority of some other Pakeha-controlled unit, such as anthropology, sociology or German. We have made some progress over the last twenty years.

Another sign of the indigenising trend is the use of Maori names for tertiary institutions. Te Whare Wananga o Te Upoko-o-te-Ika is Victoria University. Te Whare Wananga o Waikato is the University of Waikato. There is, however, an irony in this practice. While a mainstream university can appropriate a Maori name, a Maori whare wananga is prevented by law from using the word 'university'. So we cannot have a 'tribal university', and I understand we are prevented also from using the terms 'vice-chancellor' and 'chancellor'.

More Maori staff are employed in mainstream tertiary institutions than twenty years ago. In the 1970s Maori staff were very uncommon. It would have been rare to find one in a department of education, but not any more. Education has leapt ahead of Maori studies in attracting Maori students at the graduate level.

The indigenising of tertiary institutions is well advanced. One of the reasons for this is that enrolments of Maori students have increased over the last few years. The following table indicates the increase in the number of Maori students attending these institutions.

	1991	**1992**	**1993**
University	5742	6566	7924
Polytechnic	5371	10 591	9434
College of Education	798	1043	1106
TOTAL	**11 911**	**18 200**	**18 464**

('Nga Haeata' 1994)

Table 5.1
Maori enrolments at tertiary levels.

The Establishment of Wananga

The second trend at the tertiary level is a continuation of what is happening at lower levels. It might be described as a self-determination model, as a move towards greater Maori control and participation in the processes of education.

The structures being established are wananga, as provided for in the 1990 Education Amendment Act.

Only two wananga have been fully established under this act. These are Te Wananga o Raukawa at Otaki, and Te Wananga o Aotearoa at Te Awamutu. Another, Te Whare Wananga o Awanuiarangi at Whakatane, is in the process of being officially registered. Several others have begun and are waiting to register.

Already there are several types of wananga. One follows the intent of the act seriously and teaches degrees up to master's level. Raukawa and Awanuiarangi are of this type. These are more like universities but cannot be identified as such.

The next type offers polytechnic courses and Training Opportunities Programme (TOP) courses that are funded by the Education Training and Support Agency (ETSA). Their programmes and courses are accredited also by the New Zealand Qualification Authority (NZQA), as is the case with Raukawa and Awanuiarangi. Te Wananga o Aotearoa follows this second type of wananga. It is the largest of the wananga and has outposts at Rotorua, Hamilton and Auckland.

A third type of wananga is established at Manuariki, near Te Kuiti, as part of a large church complex. Unlike the other two, this type is not funded by the state but might be described as an independent, church-based wananga that does not have to comply with the regulations of an act of Parliament, nor is subject to NZQA monitoring. In this sense it might be seen as being more independent and more able to meet the needs of Maori. However, Manuariki has yet to prove its case.

Characteristics of Wananga

In a broad sense there are two avenues of access to tertiary education for Maori: mainstream institutions and wananga. But wananga is a relatively new option for Maori, being a post-1990 phenomenon. The idea, however, was pioneered by Te Wananga o Raukawa some ten years earlier. In addition, the name whare wananga or wananga has a traditional base and a cultural history behind its own body of literature. See, for example, *The Lore of the Whare Wananga* (Smith 1913) and 'Whare Wananga Development in 1993–1994' (Winiata and Winiata 1994).

The 1990 act itself speaks of Maori tradition (ahuatanga Maori) and Maori custom (tikanga Maori), and thus there is an expectation that cultural issues such as te reo, matauranga Maori and tikanga Maori are given a high priority in wananga. Maori students therefore look to this new institution to provide a more culturally sensitive and welcoming environment in which to learn.

These institutions tend to be iwi-based. Thus Te Wananga o Raukawa is an initiative of three tribal groups: Ngati Raukawa, Ngati Toa and Te Ati Awa. Te Wananga o Aotearoa is a Ngati Maniapoto initiative, while Awanuiarangi is clearly associated with Ngati Awa. The close link to iwi contrasts with the larger metropolitan institutions which serve a region and a largely urban population.

Because of the tribal links, wananga tend to be more attuned to iwi needs, and so it is no surprise that te reo is a major concern and wairua Maori is evident in the way the institutions operate. Also evident is a large percentage of Maori students—95 per cent or more. The Maori presence is very strong, and overwhelming for some non-Maori. This, in itself, makes the institution more Maori-friendly. The contrast is with the metropolitan universities, where the percentage of Pakeha students is overwhelmingly large and where Maori will always be a minority.

Definition of a Whare Wananga

A whare wananga of traditional times is a different institution from the whare wananga or wananga of modern times.

The Education Amendment Act 1990, Section 162 (4), defines a wananga as an institution that 'is characterised by teaching and research that maintains, advances, and disseminates knowledge and develops intellectual independence, and assists the application of knowledge regarding ahuatanga Maori (Maori tradition) according to tikanga Maori (Maori custom)'. The modern wananga or whare wananga is required to carry out a number of functions. These include:

1. teaching
2. research
3. maintaining knowledge
4. advancing knowledge
5. disseminating knowledge

60   *Landmarks, Bridges and Visions*

6. applying knowledge to ahuatanga Maori according to tikanga Maori
7. developing intellectual independence.

There are some additional functions mentioned in the act as characterising universities and 'other tertiary institutions'. Wananga are included in the latter group. These characteristics are:

1. they are primarily concerned with more advanced learning, the principal aim being to develop intellectual independence
2. their research and teaching are closely interdependent and most of their teaching is done by people who are active in advancing knowledge
3. they meet international standards of research and teaching
4. they are a repository of knowledge and expertise, and
5. they accept a role as critic and conscience of society.

These are sensible and responsible aims which present a challenge to the managers and lecturers of wananga.

The Funding of Wananga

Funding of wananga is by the EFTS system. One EFTS is the equivalent of a full-time student and is the unit used in funding all tertiary institutions. Money is allocated to various categories of EFTS. Category A is relatively low, and other training programmes such as dentistry and medicine attract larger amounts.

WANANGA	1994 EFTS	1995 EFTS	% INCREASE
Aotearoa	200	337	68
Awanuiarangi	125	133	6.4
Raukawa	81	137	65

('Nga Haeata' 1994)

Table 5.2
EFTS allocations for wananga in 1994 and 1995.

The sharp discrepancy in the percentage increase for Awanuiarangi was due to a number of factors. The main one was that, because Awanuiarangi was not registered as a wananga under the act, its allocations did not come out of a wananga allocation of EFTS. Instead, as it is funded through a system of conduits, the EFTS were taken from the pools for polytechnics and colleges of education. The conduits for Awanuiarangi are Waiariki Polytechnic at Rotorua and the Auckland College of Education. The reason given by the Ministry of Education for the low increase in EFTS for Awanuiarangi was that there were no spares available in the pools for colleges of education and for polytechnics.

Putting this matter aside, it is clear that there was a big increase in the allocations for the other two institutions and this high rate is achievable in the immediate future.

Student Enrolments at Wananga

Wananga enrolments are growing, as these figures show.

WANANGA	1995 EFTS	1995 TARGET	1995 ACTUAL
Aotearoa	337	400	380
Awanuiarangi	133	200	168
Raukawa	137	200	145

('Nga Haeata' 1994)

Table 5.3
Enrolments in wananga in 1995.

The association of wananga called Te Tauihu o Nga Wananga is an umbrella body for the three wananga. Its projections for wananga growth are shown below.

YEAR	AOTEAROA	RAUKAWA	AWANUIARANGI
1995	400	200	200
1996	600	300	300
1997	900	450	450
1998	1350	675	675
1999	1350	800	800
2000	1350	1000	1000

('Nga Haeata' 1994)

Table 5.4
Projections for growth in wananga enrolments, 1995–2000.

The goals may not be targeted as realistically as is possible but each institution will attempt to reach its target. There are several factors to consider, however:

1. meeting the needs of Maori students and gaining their support
2. maintaining good national standards
3. the effects of government policies in increasing the amount students must pay for their education
4. Ministry of Education willingness to provide EFTS funding at rates which will allow high growth
5. finding other ways of funding wananga, such as an alternative to EFTS or a combination of several methods.

Indigenising the Curriculum

One trend that is working itself out in the wananga is the indigenising of teaching programmes. There are two forms of this at wananga. The first is the definition of a subject area called matauranga Maori, which is being developed at Raukawa. Matauranga Maori can be described briefly as Maori philosophy and Maori knowledge in its broadest terms. Wananga are working towards restoring Maori knowledge and reintroducing it into the curriculum of modern whare wananga.

Another trend is the concentration on adapting teaching programmes to the local culture, so that the wananga works within Maori culture and on its behalf rather than against it, as was the case previously. Education at a wananga is not to be an alienating experience but rather is to enhance Maori culture and build up the self-esteem of students as Maori persons located in a social universe of whanau, hapu, iwi, waka and the state. We do not over-emphasise the individual and what the institution might do for the individual. Rather, the focus is upon what the wananga can do for the hapu, iwi and nation, and how the individual might serve the people.

International Links

Already wananga are developing global links in order to participate in the indigenous peoples' movement, and be in touch with what is happening in other parts of the world. Awanuiarangi participated in the 1993 International Conference on the Protection of Intellectual and Cultural Property of Indigenous Peoples. Out of this important conference came the Mataatua Declaration on intellectual and cultural property, which has become a part of the literature of the United Nations. People from around the world visited Whakatane and saw Te Whare Wananga o Awanuiarangi. Staff and students participated in the week-long conference.

Last year a group of Hawaiian students with their elders visited Awanuiarangi, and this year some of their students will be coming to Whakatane for the second half of the year to take courses at our institution.

We are negotiating with a community college in Hawaii and an Indian college, Standing Rock College in North Dakota, to establish a three-way link with indigenous peoples' initiatives in tertiary education. These moves are designed to globalise our outlook and to encourage our students to reach across the world for knowledge.

National Links

At the same time, we are mindful of our position at home and the need to establish a recognised place in the education system of our land. While we are linked to the other wananga, we are also developing an association with the University of Auckland, which will assist us in some aspects of our work. Graduate studies is one area where the assistance of the University of Auckland is appreciated.

There are seven MA students enrolled at Awanuiarangi and working towards a Master in Indigenous Studies or a Master in Maori Studies. With this number of graduate students, we are already competing with established departments of Maori studies around the country.

Conclusion

The development of wananga is an exciting initiative that is covered by legislation and funding by government. There are some 600 students attending courses at wananga this year. Many of them may not have attended any other tertiary institution. Many of them choose to attend a wananga run by Maori. Graduate courses are being taught at Raukawa and Awanuiarangi.

In a very short time, wananga are already making an impact on Maori participation in tertiary education. The Secretary for Education, Dr Maris O'Rourke, said in 1994:

> It is of concern to the Ministry that despite increased participation and increased levels of achievement by Maori in the mainstream, the gap between Maori and non-Maori does not appear to be closing. ('Nga Haeata' 1994, p.6)

Wananga are able to help change the statistics and may help close the gap. Efforts made in mainstream institutions are not sufficient on their own, and Maori will always be a step behind others. With the wananga as a tool of change, Maori are able and willing to become involved in the education of our people so that it is more democratic in its delivery to the people—that is, education is more of a liberating and positive force than it has been in the past.

> Ka pu te ruha, ka hao te rangatahi.
> The old net is cast aside and a new net goes fishing.

References

Ministry of Education, 1994. 'Maori Education', *Education Trends Report*, 6 (1). Wellington, Ministry of Education.

Ministry of Education, 1994. 'Nga Haeata Maatauranga', *Ministry of Education Annual Report 1994/94 and Strategic Direction for Maori Education 1994/95*. Wellington, Ministry of Education.

Smith, S. Percy, 1913. *The Lore of the Whare Wananga*. New Plymouth, Thomas Avery.

Winiata, Calm Pakake and Whatarangi Winiata, 1994. 'Whare Wananga Development in 1993–1994'. Paper prepared for Education Review Office.

Te Reo Maori

6. Maori Language Week

The thrust to save the Maori language, have it recognised officially and taught in schools, came from two sources: from Nga Tamatoa, based at the University of Auckland, and from Te Reo Maori Society, based at Victoria University. Both groups were committed and dedicated and worked hard to highlight the plight of the language. Holding an annual Maori-language week was one step along the way.

This article, written for News VUW *2 (14), 1977, pays tribute to the work of Te Reo Maori Society and its members and chronicles some of its achievements. The language issue gave both groups a good cause, as all members had suffered from the consequences of the English-only policy of the Education Department. Several generations of Maori were disenfranchised by the schools and in a sense culturally retarded by them.*

Nga Tamatoa and Te Reo Maori Society all attacked the institutions of learning and had to deal with elders who had, in modern language, been 'colonised' in their minds. The arguments were powerful and the moral ground was unassailable.

Based at Victoria University, Te Reo Maori is characterised by an unusually high degree of dedication to the cause of promoting the Maori language and of ensuring its survival. It is one of the few voluntary organisations which focus most of their attention, year after year, upon promoting in New Zealand the use of the Maori language and the oral literature which goes with it.

While there are many voluntary organisations which exhort the people to hold on to their language, there are few which actually try to do something positive about it. It is this willingness to work without pay for what they believe in that sets Te Reo Maori Society apart from other organisations. In dedication it ranks with Nga Tamatoa, and the two together form a powerful pair.

The message of Maori Language Week is this: Maori is a language spoken only in New Zealand, and as such it is the rightful heritage of all New

Zealanders. What happens to this language in the future is a matter of concern not only to the Maori people but also to the Pakeha.

We should combine our resources to ensure that the language remains a living and breathing language, that it is allowed to grow by teaching more people to speak it, that it is allowed to enrich the cultural life of this country, that it is given due respect as the language of New Zealand's largest ethnic minority, that, like English, it be used as a bridge of understanding between Maori and Pakeha, and that we are all proud of it and manifest this pride by at least trying to say Maori words correctly and insisting that everyone tries.

In 1972 Te Reo Maori launched National Maori Language Day, on 14 September. This was one day in the year when the people of this land were asked to think about the Maori language. That year the society undertook as its main task the presentation of a national petition to Parliament, asking for Maori to be introduced into all schools.

While the petition caused a storm of protest over what may have seemed like a linguistic imposition upon the monolingual speakers of English, the fact of the matter is that today the Maori language is being taught in an increasing number of schools throughout the country. And it is being done calmly and, in many instances, with a great deal of enthusiasm. No one is being forced to learn Maori. Instead, opportunities are being presented for the students who wish to learn Maori to do so.

In 1973 Te Reo Maori approached the Minister of Education, Phil Amos, and asked that in certain cases the Maori language be used as the medium of instruction in primary schools. These cases included schools where perhaps a majority of the children were native speakers of Maori. As a matter of interest, this same request was made twenty years earlier, at a time when there was a larger number of Maori-speaking children. The request was denied.

Ironically, when there are hardly any schools left in the country where Maori is the first language of the children, the Education Department has agreed to implement bilingual schooling. This year Ruatoki became the first experimental school where both languages are to be used systematically in the teaching programmes.

In 1974 Maori Language Day was increased to a week, and as the main focus of its activities Te Reo Maori turned its attention to radio and television. The students asked that 10 per cent of radio and television time be devoted to programmes with a Maori content. They asked for a Maori-language radio station and for a Maori production unit in television. Their attempts that year failed to bring any positive results.

The group also approached the Ministers of Maori Affairs and Education to discuss bilingual schooling, the training of teachers of Maori and other matters pertaining to the Maori Affairs Amendment Bill.

As their 1975 project, Te Reo Maori pressed for the establishment of a

National Maori Cultural and Language Board and, for good measure, a Maori Language Institute. But 1975 was not a good year, for neither proposal was accepted by anyone. Perhaps, too, Te Reo Maori was reaching too high for comfort.

The society returned to an unfinished issue in 1976, and this time sought wider approval of its radio and television policy. This year it continued the task of gaining more support from other Maori groups in preparation for a more concerted attack on radio and television.

But even before Te Reo Maori was ready to make a move, Radio New Zealand announced its new expanded Maori programmes and the formation of a Maori programming unit to be located in Auckland. The expected battle with radio evaporated, thus leaving the way clear for a concentrated attack on the problem of introducing programmes with Maori content on television.

The present year has been a heartening one for Te Reo Maori. It has received more support than ever before for National Maori Language Week. The Maori Affairs Department announced its support publicly. But the most important support has come from the Education Department, whose considerable resources and manpower can now be directed towards making the week a success.

At the moment, no one body has a greater influence on the promotion and teaching of the Maori language and of publishing literature in the Maori language than the Education Department. By comparison, the efforts of all other bodies, including the universities, become rather small.

Quite apart from its yearly projects, Te Reo Maori has tried to persuade people, singly or in groups, to carry out some project during Maori Language Week. Over the years, its own members have engaged in a variety of activities to publicise the week, often to an extent which has put their university subjects in jeopardy.

The society receives calls from all over the Wellington district, asking its members to visit, put on a performance or help with some local project. The society cannot, in all conscience, refuse such calls for help because National Maori Language Week is an institution which it began. Until such time as another organisation, with perhaps greater resources at its disposal, takes over the organisation of Maori Language Week, Te Reo Maori Society is obligated to see it through each year.

It has always been a problem for the student group to co-ordinate on a national basis the activities of Maori Language Week. The biggest problem has been in persuading chiefs outside the Wellington district that the week is a national one which ought to be celebrated at the same time throughout the nation.

Each year, some group decides to hold its celebrations at a different time. This year is no exception. Auckland, Hamilton and Christchurch chiefs decided on their own to begin the week on 14 September. They 'beat the gun', as it were, and officially opened the week on television, thus upstaging the chiefs of Wellington and ignoring Te Reo Maori Society who began the whole thing.

This sort of difficulty highlights the importance of persuading the members of the society to allow the Education Department to take control of the week and to use its mana and resources to co-ordinate the week's activities on a national basis. That Te Reo Maori has managed to develop Maori Language Week to its present level of importance and acceptance is an achievement of which its members can be proud. The 'child' nurtured by Te Reo Maori has matured and is now ready to leave its home at Victoria University and face the larger world beyond.

At this point, one can say to Te Reo Maori members: 'Tukuna ta tatou mokai kia haere. Kua pakeke i naianei' (Let our child go. It has now grown up). And so it came to pass.

7. Pronounced Respect for Maori Placenames

This article was published in the New Zealand Listener, *29 July 1978, and was prompted by a comment published by Professor of English Ian Gordon in a regular* Listener *column. He argued that speakers of English should be allowed to mispronounce Maori words and anglicise them. There was a proper English rendition of Maori placenames such as Otaki and Paraparaumu and we should accept the anglicised versions as normal and proper.*

It was my duty as Professor of Maori to respond to his article and defend te reo Maori. A straightforward request addressed the Pakeha population: they should respect our placenames and personal names and pronounce them properly.

Eighteen years later there is still a problem—not as bad as before, certainly, but there are still prominent citizens and some media persons who have an attitude. While they will make every effort to say foreign names correctly, they mangle Maori placenames and personal names with impunity. It offends Maori sensibilities.

On the other hand, an increasing number of English speakers have mastered the sound system of Maori and are able to say Maori names correctly. Newsreaders, public speakers, government ministers, officials, weather reporters, radio people all face the challenge. Pronounced respect is being accorded to the language by a growing number of people. That is a positive outcome.

It is now all right to say 'Kia ora', on the phone, on radio, television and on our airlines. Is that progress? Yes, but there are more 'little battles' to face.

The issue of how Maori names should be pronounced refuses to die in peace and apparently is not allowed to do so. Two writers have recently rekindled the argument and reopened the coffin. Not only are we invited to view the corpse again but, more importantly, we are asked to resurrect the body of

Parrerperam and replace it with a different corpse—Paraparaumu.

In his regular Language column in the *Listener*, Professor Ian Gordon fanned the face of the corpse and blew as hard as he could into its mouth. As I recall, the title he used for his column was 'Sheep Talk', which seemed to establish a tone for the article and the arguments it contained, but in fact camouflaged a very serious attack.

The burden of Ian Gordon's thesis is this: the speakers of English ought to be allowed to pronounce Maori words in the manner that most of them are now because it is in the nature of any language to borrow and incorporate words from other languages. He gives examples of borrowings into Maori: words such as hipi (sheep), hoiho (horse) and teepu (table). He also argues that placenames such as Paraparaumu and Otaki have been incorporated into the sound system of the English language and that each has a 'proper' English pronunciation.

For a number of reasons, this thesis will find some very responsive and relieved followers. First, it provides a linguistic argument to legitimise present practice. Second, it soothes the conscience, because Ian Gordon has apparently provided a cloak of respectability to pronunciations which are condemned as almost obscene by many New Zealanders—both Pakeha and Maori.

More recently, another writer has taken up the cause. Writing in the correspondence columns of the *Evening Post* (29 April 1978), S. C. Brown wants to go a step further and actually change the spellings of Maori names which have become a part of the vocabulary of English. In other words, he wants evidence of incorporation into the sound system of English. Following Mr Brown, then, Hori would become Hoary, Paraparaumu would be Parrerparreroommoo or Parrerperram and Otaki, Oh-tack!

Brown limits his proposal to placenames, and he sees it as a gift of God for 'radio and TV frontmen'. They would be spared the agony of saying Maori placenames the Maori way, while Brown and his sympathisers would be spared from hearing such names ('crack potteries', he calls them) pronounced properly.

While Ian Gordon and S. C. Brown are poles apart in their manner of argument, they do want virtually the same thing; in this sense, they belong to the one club. Of the two, Ian Gordon is the more dangerous. His colleague S. C. Brown can be quite easily dismissed as being too emotive, too dogmatic, too ready to ingratiate himself to the radio and TV announcers, and not a little 'crackpotted' himself!

On the other hand, Ian Gordon appears to be a level-headed and knowledgeable professor who uses reasoned and reasonable argument to inform his equally reasonable readers. As a consequence, more people are inclined to believe him. But should he be given any more credence than S. C. Brown? I don't think so.

The whole question of how Maori words (including the names of people) should be pronounced has little or nothing to do with linguistic arguments.

Rather, the issues are moral, political, sociological and psychological. At the centre of the argument is the nature of the relationships between Maori and Pakeha. Are we to treat each other with mutual respect, or should we ignore each other and pretend that the other fellow does not even exist?

If we accept that the only reasonable policy is to work and live together and respect each other, then as evidence of that respect we must show proper deference towards our respective languages. This means that, on the one hand, the Maori people should say English placenames and personal names correctly and if called upon to speak English should do so as correctly as possible. On the other hand, there is an equal obligation upon speakers of English to say Maori placenames and personal names correctly and if called upon to speak Maori should do so as correctly as possible.

Take the matter of personal names. By and large, English names are said correctly by the Maori so that the bearers of those names are not hurt, do not feel put down or made to look ridiculous in public. Most Pakeha monolingual speakers of English (and some Maori monolingual speakers of English as well) mispronounce the Maori names of students, friends and colleagues. A large number fail to make the slightest effort to say these names correctly.

This failure is evidence of a certain attitude towards another culture. It is not lost on the Maori that people of other countries and other ethnic backgrounds, such as the Dutch, the Swiss, the Americans, the French and people from South-east Asia, tend to have little difficulty in pronouncing Maori placenames correctly. It is also noticed that some visitors who are in New Zealand for only a short time make a determined effort to master the pronunciation of Maori placenames and are soon saying them correctly. The Telethon of 1977 provided some remarkable examples of overseas visitors pronouncing Maori placenames with a fair degree of accuracy. The question is: why cannot the home-grown Kiwi do the same? Or, to put the question differently: why do they refuse to make an effort? Most of the answers to these questions are quite disturbing and are not complimentary to a large number of Pakeha New Zealanders.

If these questions were properly researched, it would probably be found that, besides attitudes differing according to a socio-economic scale, they also differ according to the ethnic backgrounds of the people interviewed and the nature of their social history. It is generally believed among Maori people that the Scots, Irish and Welsh people, among those who came from Great Britain, exhibit a more sympathetic and open attitude towards the Maori and their language than do the English. Furthermore, New Zealanders whose roots are in Europe proper are believed to have a more positive attitude towards the Maori. In a group which is believed to be more likely to be anti-Maori language in their attitudes are those of English background and those coming from Australia and Africa.

None of this common knowledge should be accepted at face value until the facts have been properly researched. However, a good deal of it is based on 'grass roots' experience and is indicative of the sociological dimensions of the problem. It would be very instructive, therefore, to probe the backgrounds of both Ian Gordon and S. C. Brown in order to discover why they think the way they do.

Another dimension of the issue of pronunciation is how we identify as New Zealanders, and with what. The Maori people have always been quite certain of their identity: they are the people of this land and have been New Zealanders since the signing of the Treaty of Waitangi. The symbols of their identity are the land (mountains, forests, plains, rivers, lakes and oceans), the people (including the great figures of bygone days), the language, literature and the arts, and finally the style of life. Important within this group of symbols are the named features of the environment, names such as Tongariro, Waikaremoana, Waikato, Kahuranaki, Te Moana o Raukawa and Hikurangi. These names should evoke images of the significant parts of the land and positive feelings towards them. Each is like the title of a fascinating story. Names such as these mean a great deal to the people most closely associated with them. They often appear in the love songs and laments of the Maori and it is certainly not unusual to find a Maori weep over a place with which he or she identifies.

Such placenames are part and parcel of the Maori heritage. Today they comprise a legacy to the nation—a gift to all New Zealanders. But what is to happen to this legacy? To rush in and anglicise the lot, which is what Ian Gordon and S. C. Brown advise, is thoughtless and short-sighted politics. It is the sort of thing conquerors do to the culture and language of the people they subjugate. Do the Pakeha New Zelanders still think of themselves as the conquerors and do they still feel that they have a right to ride roughshod over Maori culture? We are supposed to be partners in a modern New Zealand society and it is about time we all began behaving accordingly.

The Maori people make a simple request: that all New Zealanders preserve and respect the names associated with our landscape and with our common heritage; that all help to maintain the stories which are an integral part of each name and that all say them correctly. This is by no means an unreasonable request, because Pakeha New Zealanders also claim to identify with these same names. Indeed, there are many who honestly do just that.

Citizens who identify with our country find that, increasingly, what they identify with are the same things as the Maori people value. However, many Pakeha New Zealanders (and I suspect they are mainly the old ones) appear to resent and resist this inevitability. They want nothing whatever to do with the Maori and probably regard everything Maori as 'crack pottery' and beneath their perceived status.

Part of the Pakeha problem (and I believe we do have one) is that as a people they have no antiquity and no real concept of a past history in New Zealand. With few exceptions, they are not interested in maintaining a continuity with our history as a nation. Sadly, they do not even recognise a responsibility to act as guardians of the nation's cultural heritage and to ensure that there is something of value to hand on to future generations. They are mostly sheep and butter, beer and betting, and here and now people. But this is surely a passing phase in our social history. An increasing number of Pakeha people are concerned about our cultural heritage and are doing something about it. What we need to guard against is that, 100 years from now, the New Zealanders (or will it be the Australians?) living then will curse our generation for its stupidity and short-sightedness in being too quick to bury the Maori and its culture and language.

The strategy used by Ian Gordon in his effort to win every phase of the linguistic battle between Maori and English is well tried in New Zealand. It has worked very well for the Pakeha and has consistently beaten the Maori on many fronts. Usually, what happens is this: some property of the Maori is wanted by the Pakeha but he has no moral right to it. He then seeks an authority to take the property anyway—by calling on some act or other, by using the courts as in the Bastion Point issue, or by rationalising the action in a manner which is seen to be respectable at the time.

Ian Gordon must know that Maori as a living and spoken language is a threatened language, that it is struggling to survive. This part of our national heritage is dying before our eyes. And people like him don't seem to care. Rather, they want to give us a kick on the way down.

It is true that efforts are at present being made to save it, or at least to prolong its life for as long as possible. The battle to conquer the Maori language has already been won by the speakers of English. This being so, I am absolutely appalled that Ian Gordon has not the good sense to leave well alone. Rather than salve his conscience by helping to keep the language alive, he has elected to participate in the mopping-up operations to hasten its death. There is apparently no moral component to his sort of scholarship and no sense of responsibility.

8. Maori Language and Identity

The previous articles on Maori language were reactions to events. This time a more serious attempt was made to review the state of the language. That the language was losing ground as a living language and no longer actively spoken in homes was noted by many commentators. And, as the older generations of native speakers die, and some notable exponents of it, such as Dr Pei Te Hurinui Jones, Dr Henare Tuwhangai, Pumi Taituha, Ruka Broughton, Sir James Henare, Dame Whina Cooper, John Rangihau, Haami Mitchell, Sir Monita Delamere and many others pass on, one may be forgiven for becoming fatalistic. The urgency of the matter becomes very evident in different tribal localities: for example, in the Mataatua region, within a very short time the two high-profile orators in the accompanying photo, Pokai Waiari of Te Teko, Ngati Awa, and Te Makarini Temara of Tuhoe, both fluent exponents of Maori, died. Both are survived by their wives, who are also fluent speakers of Maori. In addition, other high-profile speakers were lost: Sir Monita Delamere of Whakatohea and Te Whanau-a-Apanui, and Turi Tekani of Ngai Te Rangi, Tauranga, and Hohua Tutengaehe, also of Ngai Te Rangi. All belonged to Mataatua. Thus in a ten-year period there was a huge loss of native speakers. This has happened in other areas as well.

I argue in this paper that the struggle to maintain the language of a group must be taken up by the members of the threatened group. We cannot buy into the fatalistic belief that our job is 'to smooth the dying pillow' of the language. This is called 'the Featherston-Newman-Walsh attitude', which is characteristically adopted by non-Maori commentators. On the other hand, Maori, whether speakers of te reo Maori or not, have to become active advocates for their language. Steps have to be taken, such as establishing a kohanga reo or a kura kaupapa Maori or a wananga, to help in the struggle for the survival of the language. In the end, the best strategy for maintaining the language is to use it everywhere and to persuade thousands of Maori speakers to speak it and write it.

At the same time, hundreds of Maori youth and elders are actively learning the language so that they are able to use it. These signs are hopeful. We cannot give up without a determined fight to revive, maintain and develop te reo Maori.

The thinking of New Zealanders about the future of the Maori people and their culture has been marked by a strange fatalism about the inevitability of the passing of everything—from the people themselves to parts of the culture such as language. We can go back to 1856 to the learned Dr Issac Featherston, whose prophecy of doom probably carried with it the earnest wish of many white colonists at that time. 'The Maoris are dying out,' he said, 'and nothing can save them. Our plain duty, as good compassionate colonists, is to smooth down their dying pillow. Then history will have nothing to reproach us with' (Sutherland 1940, p.28).

Mrs Kitty Temara, Pokai Waiari and Te Makarini Temara, mature speakers of te reo Maori. Pokai Waiari and Te Makarini Temara were both notable speakers and important leaders, one of Ngati Awa and the other of Tuhoe. *(S. M. Mead)*

This is an important statement because it was earnestly believed then to be the correct conclusion to draw, not only from the evidence of what had happened in New Zealand and elsewhere, but also from the assumptions in the minds of the educated colonists about the superiority of Western man and his assumed right to govern the world. That the learned men of the time considered themselves to be fair-minded Christians in their dealing with the Maori over land and other important resources is hinted at in Featherston's words. His idea of 'compassionate colonists' was developed later into an elaborate mask of delusion about the wise and gentle Pakeha who presented the world with a model of how to lead a once-barbaric horde of cannibals towards equality with the white man. Sadly, history has a way of providing a perspective on events which help to distinguish the good scholars from the people who are blinded by their own prejudices.

Just over 100 years ago, in 1881, another doctor, this time Dr A. K. Newman, uttered the same words of doom about the Maori, but added his own particular flavour to the announcement. He said that taking 'all things into consideration the disappearance of the race is scarcely a subject for much regret. They are dying out in a quick easy way and are being supplanted by a superior race' (Sutherland 1940, p.28). His words came twenty-five years after those of Dr Featherston. About the same interval of time had elapsed when, in 1907, that other famous person, Archdeacon Walsh, considered the fate of the Maori, surveyed the causes of our demise and concluded that 'The Maori has lost heart and abandoned hope.' He added, 'The race is sick unto death and is already potentially dead' (Sutherland 1940, p.28).

These three commentators, whose statements spanned half a century, all agreed that the Maori was sure to die. The compassionate Featherston gave us the poignant image of preparing the bed and patting down the pillow on which the last Maori was to expire. It would have been an ideal episode for colour television. Because of his sensitivity to history, Featherston would certainly have opted for proper 'cover' to show that the bed had been properly prepared. Newman added the image of the master race, whose very presence killed off the local natives almost painlessly, he thought. Walsh voiced the important idea of the Maori being 'potentially dead'. A combination of these attitudes towards anything Maori prevails to this day.

By the 1980s, we as a nation are no longer concerned with the death of the Maori. Rather, we accept, somewhat reluctantly, that people identifying themselves as Maori will inhabit the earth a bit longer. The concern now shifts to the question of whether these individuals are genetically Maori or half-breeds conquered at last by the superior genes of the Pakeha. Matters of definition of what constitutes a Maori occupy the minds of our politicians and many Pakeha voters at election time. It is at this time that more than usual attention is given to the future of the Maori language, and it is this topic which symbolises better even than the land problem the great changes which are occurring in New Zealand today. On the part of the Pakeha majority the attitudes expressed at an earlier age about the future of the Maori population are now directed towards the Maori language. For many of them the task is first to prepare the bed—the New Zealand way is either not to do anything positive that might allow the victim to live longer, or to act as slowly as possible to achieve the same result. Very prevalent among people who write to the editors of the local newspapers are the attitudes relating to the superiority of English: that Maori has no right to compete with it, that Maori is not a proper language, that Maori is not a language of the workplace, nor of commerce and hence should not be taught, and so on.

The great majority of people subscribe to the attitude that the language 'is already potentially dead' and that therefore trying to save it is a waste of time. Some unseen authority greater than all the Pakeha scholars and government officials of New Zealand put together has ruled that the language must die or has already died; what we must do is bury it decently so as not to offend the sensitive Pakeha, and then get on with the real job of speaking English!

The position of the scholars in the 1960s is, perhaps, best represented by Biggs (1967, p.84), who concluded that there would be a '*slow* but inevitable further retreat of Maori before the overwhelming pressure of English'. Although Dr Bruce Biggs is a lot more cautious than earlier commentators, he is nonetheless a fatalist. And for him, too, the language is 'sick unto death and is already potentially dead'.

But, in accusing Biggs of being a fatalist, I must admit that during the decade in which he wrote his paper I held much the same view myself. Where I might demur, however, is at the accusation of being a 'pillow smoother'. Various activities, such as writing short stories in Maori (Mead 1960), producing a small textbook for teaching Maori in primary schools (Mead 1959) and preparing material for teaching the language at university level (Biggs, Hohepa & Mead 1967), provide sufficient evidence of a more active interest than one might expect from a 'pillow smoother'. Nonetheless, it is possible to do all of these very practical tasks and still believe that the language is 'potentially dead'. Activity can become an end in itself.

One might argue that those who are engaged in teaching the language represent a group of people who are guilty about preparing the 'dying bed', and so instead busy themselves in the hope of delaying the demise of the language for as long as possible. At the same time the conscience is assuaged. We continue to delude ourselves and Maori continues to lose ground as a living language.

I believe that nearly every educator in New Zealand is aware that the language is dying. Members of the group who speak and understand Maori have seen the evidence acted out before them. Every year, as the old people in the sixty years and above age-group die, we know that they are not being replaced by new native speakers of the language. Already in many marae around the country there are no local competent speakers to man the orators' benches and no women to perform the ceremonial calls.

What laymen know by experience to be the case, Dr Richard Benton and his New Zealand Council for Educational Research team has confirmed by research. He has, however, done more than confirm the trend indicated a decade earlier by Biggs (1968) and more than assure the descendants of Featherston that the language is surely dying. Benton has provided us with a global picture of the problem and with facts and figures to think with. In a 1979 paper (Benton 1979, p.6), for instance, he informs us that in 'more than half of the localities surveyed including all the smaller townships, Maori speakers are a tiny minority—less than one in ten of the Maori population in this age group (under 25 years old)'. He correctly points out that this particular group represents about two-thirds of the total Maori population.

Group photograph of people of the Waiariki district (Te Arawa and Mataatua) taken in front of the Tuhourangi house at Whakarewarewa in 1986. In the ten years since, fifteen mature speakers have died. Roughly thirty-two out of every 100 mature speakers will die in any ten-year period. This is a tremendous loss to the culture. *(Mead collection)*

Generalising his findings from selected regions of the North Island to the Maori population at large, Benton (1979, p.23) calculates that there are about 70,000 speakers of Maori and 115,000 able to understand the language. An optimist would immediately add these figures together and report that 185,000 of the 300,000 Maori in New Zealand know Maori, while a pessimist would point out that already three-quarters of the population can neither speak nor understand their own language. That is surely convincing evidence of decline.

What has become clear recently is that ethnic distance seems to affect the conclusions and recommendations of various academics and government officials in New Zealand. A Pakeha with no affinal or other relationship to the Maori minority, and who is thus separated from them by a great distance, can calmly adopt the Featherston–Newman–Walsh attitude. The passing of the language would elicit probably no more than a shrug of the shoulders from such a person. On the other hand, a Pakeha who has some affinal link, either with a Maori family or indirectly through another ethnic minority, is less likely to feel comfortable about playing the role of a 'pillow smoother' and might become an active supporter of minority causes.

While reactions of this sort are not foreign to some modern Maori, who have already given up hope of ever saving the language, the attitudes of all of these people can be contrasted with those of two groups of contemporary and mostly youngish Maori. The first group represents those who are Maori by upbringing and to whom a large amount of Maoritanga was transmitted by someone by some means during their formative years. A few of these people are involved in movements to save the language, but generally they are not able to appreciate fully the nature of the problem because they were not culturally deprived. Members of this group tend to enjoy the fruits of being Maori.

The second group of the same age represents the alienated Maori, to whom little or nothing was transmitted by parents who were often themselves victims of earlier policies of cultural suppression and denigration. This is the group from which has already emerged some of the most outspoken champions of the Maori language: Nga Tamatoa (the Brave Sons), a protest movement which began in Auckland, and Te Reo Maori (the Maori Language) from Wellington. For this group the language, and indeed Maori culture generally, have been transformed by default into inestimable treasures that are now worth fighting for.

Biggs (1968, p.84) predicted correctly that the study of Maori would increase, for it seemed to him 'in the nature of things that we value our treasures most as they pass from us'. He may have guessed shrewdly that the day of the Maori studies scholar and teacher was coming, and is indeed here now. But he may not have anticipated that a rising percentage of Maori youth is placing a value on Maoritanga that far exceeds anything we have yet seen. In the years to come that value may rise further, like the price of gold, and bring with it even more determined, and perhaps seemingly more extremist, efforts at saving and redeveloping the Maori language.

For members of the Maori minority the language issue is crucial. We are not able to afford the luxury of keeping some distance away from the events which seem to be overtaking our culture and our language. Nor can we hide behind the distant objectivity of what has been described by some social scientists (Willis 1978) as the 'bloodless humanism' of the academics. For, as I have suggested above, in the context of the colonial experience of the New Zealand variety, the learned men are not to be entirely trusted. They are prone to act out the role of 'pillow smoothers' because it happens to be someone else's culture and not their own that is at risk. We have to be wary of their 'cerebralised compassion'.

Nonetheless, as active participant members of Maori society, we have to take note of the findings of researchers such as Biggs and Benton and try to use their research results to our advantage. We need to be aware of the forces acting against the retention of the language, such as social and biological assimilation, accelerating urbanisation, rural depopulation, and the effects of television and radio, mentioned by the researchers (Biggs 1968, Benton 1979). We must be aware that the playcentre movement in the 1960s may have become a weapon that was used against us, the victim being the Maori language.

Though we cannot deny that the language is at risk, it would be immoral and heartless for our people to follow the 'couldn't care less' attitude of the bloodless humanists of New Zealand. It seems to me that we cannot become accomplices in linguistic or cultural genocide that is directed consciously or otherwise by the majority group at Maori. Rather, the only appropriate moral position is to fight for the retention and development of the language, not only for itself but also for the culture as a whole. But more than the language is at stake. Rather, the credibility of Maori academics, politicians, government officials, school teachers and others requires reconfirmation, for the situation that holds today is quite different from any before. It is a time of renegotiation, of demonstrating a commitment to the culture, of testing one's credentials and worth.

This concern for cultural credibility is an 'in-group' affair, which in a sense reflects both the triumph of the Western type of education imposed upon the Maori, and its ultimate defeat. It is a triumph for democracy in the sense that we can think as free men and rise intellectually above the conditions which constrain us today. The education system provided us with the means to think about freedom. Conversely, it represents the defeat of that system. If we are wise, we will not again accept a passive role in the education of our people. Nor should we allow ourselves again to be put in the position of being unknowing and naive partners in the alienation of our children from our culture.

Our language has gone through a history which in a sense symbolises what has happened to us as a people. First, the language reigned supreme as the only language spoken in New Zealand. Then, from 1769 onwards, other languages were brought into contact with Maori and ultimately one major overseas language took hold. Western education was first introduced through the medium of the Maori language, and evidently very successfully, in mission schools from as early as 1816 (Barrington & Beaglehole 1974, p.10). That was a time when Maori interests had a great influence on what was done, how, when and by whom. There followed various political moves which brought in a bilingual phase to the schooling of Maori children. This period was short-lived, however, and was replaced by the linguistic position we face today, in which English dominates the country and Maori is metaphorically engaged in a struggle for survival.

The above is a brief and crude summary of a sequence of very complicated events which are described in more detail by others—for example, by Dr Bruce Biggs (1968) and Barrington & Beaglehole (1974), and by Mrs Hana Jackson (1972) in the submissions on behalf of the Nga Tamatoa Council. Of great importance today is the fact that increasing pressure is being applied by

Maori, including Nga Tamatoa, to return to a bilingual phase in education. Already there is an active bilingual programme at Ruatoki in the Bay of Plenty. Programmes are beginning to be implemented in two schools in the Hastings area: Fernhill public school and St Joseph's School, a Roman Catholic school. Another had begun at Waverly, near Wanganui, at a small Catholic school called St Michael's.

There are several other schools waiting for inclusion in the bilingual programmes of the Department of Education. These include Hiruharama on the East Coast, Te Teko in the Bay of Plenty, and Otaki, just north of Wellington. There are probably others. Such is the desperate position of the language in many areas where it was formerly strong that there is bound to be an escalation in the requests and demands to begin bilingual education programmes in which the ordinary school curriculum is taught in both English and Maori, ideally apportioning equal time to each. In these schools the aim is clearly to produce bilingual children who are capable of using both languages.

Bilingual education is the new hope before us today. It presents the best chance so far available to us for the survival and development of Maori. That there are difficulties in the way of implementing more broadly a programme of this sort can perhaps be anticipated. And they are coming from predictable sources. Unfortunately, these side skirmishes serve only to delay national efforts at saving the language, and to encourage Maori people to be suspicious and plainly sceptical of the lack of support from teacher organisations.

Another difficulty is the fear of many speakers of English that their children might be forced to learn Maori. They are accustomed to English being the only language of instruction and cannot yet accept that Maori has a place in the education even of Maori, let alone of Pakeha children. I suppose it is no surprise that the laws of the land support the monolingual speakers of English and discriminate against the indigenous language, Maori.

There are certainly some problems to be sorted out with the majority population, and I trust successfully. Meanwhile, the majority group does not have the right, in my opinion, to deny the Maori people the opportunity for their children to learn both languages. Indeed, there are probably hundreds of Pakeha parents who would want the same opportunities for their children.

Another hope for the present decade is that either the language will be made an official language of New Zealand, or that a trustee of the Maori language will be established by statute and charged with the task of maintaining and developing the language into the future as part of the cultural heritage of the nation. In the case of the first alternative, I initiated some action in 1979 to encourage the Minister of Maori Affairs to frame appropriate legislation that would make the language official. In the second, the idea of a trustee has come from Dr Whatarangi Winiata (personal communication 1979) and the Raukawa Trustees, who submitted a proposal to this effect to the minister. This sort of move will encourage immediately the continuing survival of Maori by making it legally feasible for Maori parents to demand bilingual education for their children, and generally by helping to restore to the language some of the prestige and status which has been eroded as a result of some 200 years of contact with one of the most powerful languages in the world today —English.

Modern Maori are exploring many different ways of keeping their language alive. Besides the efforts of the Education Department and its machinery for teaching Maori at both primary and secondary levels, besides the contributions of the university system, the teacher training schools and the technical schools of the country by teaching courses in both language and culture, there are less public and little publicised attempts, such as those sponsored by the Department of Maori Affairs. This department encourages the learning of Maori by people who identify as Maori. Classes are offered and taught as a 'grassroots' response all over the country.

There are today literally hundreds of Maori adults and children learning their language. I see this quest as an unexpected consequence of three-quarters of the population not being able to speak Maori and hence experiencing difficulties in gaining full acceptance into the minority group. A rising nationalism and a movement towards greater political, economic and social control over the affairs of the people have together conspired to make the ability to speak the language a prime asset. This, in part, helps to explain why there is an unprecedented number of Maori persons learning their own language. It is a hopeful sign. But, as our population seeks to learn to be Maori and to understand its own culture, new problems begin to emerge. For example, Maori students are beginning in increasing numbers to reject the Pakeha teacher as the guardian and transmitter of Maori knowledge. For example, Victoria University Maori-language classes are taught by teachers who are ethnically Maori. Several Maori students cannot learn and especially cannot accept teaching in language or in the traditions from persons other than Maori. The moral issue of who should properly teach Maori language and other 'Maori' subjects is a new one that we must face.

For the Maori people the language is not dead; it must not die and cannot be regarded as even potentially dead. For them, Maoritanga, the language, their identity as Maori, the visual symbols of the culture, such as the carved meetinghouses and the marae, all merge together as a symbol of growth. There cannot be any doubt that the teaching of Maori language should be a compulsory part of the education of any Maori. There is really no choice at all for a Maori; only the Pakeha can enjoy that privilege.

The point needs to be reiterated that we, as educators, cannot seduce the Maori into believing that they have a choice of affiliation in this country. The option to become a culture-free amorphous New Zealander is tantamount to cultural sabotage; its ultimate aim is to define us off the face of New Zealand.

There is no point in trying to deny an obvious fact of life: a Maori is a Maori and it is that which makes us New Zealanders. Enrolling on the European political roll to vote for a European political seat is part of the seduction away from a perfectly straightforward identity as a Maori. There are many other such subterfuges which aim at confusing us and sidetracking us from our own concerns.

Ironically, while this is happening the Pakeha section of our population is trying to come to terms with its own identity problem. There is a kind of poetic justice in the fact that the new identity which is currently being formed is closely associated with Maoritanga. In fact, the Pakeha New Zealander needs us—especially our culture and language—so that he can define a place for himself in the context of the international community.

What this indicates to me is that we need a new kind of honesty between us, one that is touched with some humility. We need to discuss and examine the Pakeha attitude that everything Maori is 'potentially dead'. In the long run the nation suffers as we blunder along, with our blinkers continually affecting our vision not only of today but also of tomorrow. We need, too, to consider seriously the Maori attitude that the language must live and that it must become a part of the cultural and educational heritage of every Maori child in New Zealand. If Pakeha parents want their children to share in this heritage, it is all for the good of the nation. But let not those Pakeha parents who do not want their children to learn Maori deny us the right to use the education system to teach our children what they should know.

As an article of faith I believe that, if we are culturally honest and establish our roots where they belong, we would have fewer psychological problems than at present and we would find schooling more rewarding. The task of the Maori people is to forge ahead with the development and rejuvenation of our culture. A possible but at present unlikely consequence is that Pakeha New Zealanders will be able to define a more satisfying identity for themselves than they would if we were moulded in their image. Unfortunately, the majority of Pakeha New Zealanders cannot, and refuse to, come to grips with the Maori component of their identity. Until they do, the struggle to save and develop the Maori language will continue to be unnecessarily difficult.

References

Barrington, J. M. and T. H. Beaglehole, 1974. *Maori Schools in a Changing Society: An Historical Review.* Wellington, New Zealand Council for Educational Research.

Benton, Richard A., 1979. 'Who Speaks Maori in New Zealand?' Paper prepared for 49th ANZAAS Congress. Wellington, Maori Unit of New Zealand Council for Educational Research.

Biggs, B., P. Hohepa and S. M. Mead, 1967. *Selected Readings in Maori.* Wellington, A. H. & A. W. Reed.

Jackson, H., 1972. Submissions on Maori Language Petitions, presented on behalf of Nga Tamatoa Council.
Mead, S. M., 1959. *We Speak Maori* (New edition 1971). Wellington, A. H. & A. W. Reed.
Mead, S. M., 1960. 'Ko te Taahae nei ko Taawhaki', *Te Whare Kura I*. Wellington, Government Printer.
Sutherland, I. L. G., 1940. The Maori People Today: A General Survey. Wellington, New Zealand Institute of International Affairs and New Zealand Council for Educational Research.
Willis, P., 1978. *Profane Culture*. London, Routledge & Kegan Paul.

The Meeting of Cultures & Problems of Communication

9. Should Maoritanga be Shared?

The issue of sharing Maori culture with the population of New Zealand is a sensitive one for members of the Maori minority. There is a bitterness on the Maori side when it is remembered that many governments of New Zealand actively undermined the culture by enacting some anti-Maori legislation, for example many land laws and the suppression of tohungaism. The language was suppressed and cultural development was either underfunded or completely ignored.

While it is true that a renaissance of the culture has occurred in modern times, a lot remains to be done. Society-wide cultural loss continues, especially in the language arts and in spoken Maori. Government has only recently begun to fund Maori development, so there is a lot of ground to make up.

It is hard to share the culture with the descendants of people who tried their best to banish Maori culture from this land. It is also difficult to share one's cultural treasures with others, especially when these treasures are a part of one's identity.

On the Pakeha side, the argument is that the descendants were not the ones responsible for damaging Maori culture. The descendants are more open and supportive. They also see elements of our culture in a different light from their ancestors. They want to participate in Maori culture because they identify with this land. Many of them want to distinguish themselves from our neighbours in Australia.

At the time the following article was written the issue had just emerged as a talking point. Or put another way, it had always been there but no one dared to bring it out in the open.

Published in the New Zealand Listener, 87 (1977), *pp. 24, 56.*

Now that Maori Language Week has been celebrated for this year, it is appropriate to take a serious look at some issues which are of fundamental concern to both Maori and Pakeha. I suggest we consider the notion of Maoritanga. What are we doing with and to Maoritanga? Do we know what we are about? Are Maori and Pakeha pursuing a common goal, or are we following different paths which might later lead to collision or, at the least, to competing conceptions of Maoritanga?

Nearly everybody in New Zealand thinks they know precisely what Maoritanga means. To some, it is action songs and haka and nothing else. To others, it is that terrible practice of sleeping together in a meeting-house and of eating pork bones and puha. Or it is that portion of New Zealand culture we use as bait to entice the tourists. Yet another group of New Zealanders may throw up their hands in despair and say that it is surely those activities which Maori do on their own and don't want to share. So Maoritanga is something which, however important it might be to the Maori people, tends to divide the nation.

A more comprehensive definition of Maoritanga focuses on the Maori way of living, on our attitudes to people and to the environment. Included in this definition is reverence for the past—that we of today are the legacy of yesterday and that what we do now has an influence on the lives of our children who will take over the land when we grow old and die. Thus, our aim in life is to make things better, not worse, for the next generation.

To oversimplify the concept of Maoritanga, or say that there is no such thing, is to evade the issue. And it doesn't help to point out that there is considerable overlap between the lifestyles of Maori and Pakeha. We know this. Yet Maori people continue to identify ourselves as Maori and to feel threatened by the dominant European culture. We also assert that there are differences between Maori and Pakeha.

Maori people tend to do things in a different way. For example, a hui is quite different from a Pakeha meeting, not just in the use of the Maori language. Despite the various networks of activity in which Maori and Pakeha participate, there are still social, political and economic aspects which are dominantly Maori. The striking example is the tangihanga, where complex networks come into full play, during which the Pakeha is an occasional contributor or is treated as a guest. There are many hui—such as the tangi—where the costs are partly shared or borne entirely by the Maori participants. When money is needed, a variety of social and financial networks begin to operate as soon as the event is announced.

Apart from the difference in style, a different range of skills is required at Maori gatherings. Oratory is a field where there is a certain amount of competitiveness in the dramatic performance or in the ability of the orator to turn a neat phrase. The highly skilled orator is admired and loved because he adds quality to the event. Likewise, people who can sing waiata with beauty and artistry add depth to the occasion, thus contributing to the ecstasy which some people experience at a hui.

Generally, Maori speakers draw on their own generously endowed heritage for the poetic inspiration they need. And here is the parting of the ways between

Maori and Pakeha: our cultural heritages are not equivalent and what is ecstasy for one may be agony for the other.

These few remarks about Maoritanga are not meant as a full explanation of the concept; rather, they are to give an idea of some of its dimensions and to indicate some of its difficulties. There are few people in New Zealand who are capable of giving an adequate definition of Maoritanga, so one should treat with caution the 'expert', Maori or Pakeha, who claims to understand it all.

The problem is whether Maoritanga properly belongs to the Maori minority of New Zealand or whether it is the legacy of all who claim to be New Zealanders. On the Maori side, there are some of us who claim that Maoritanga is for Maori only, that the language is for Maori speakers only and that our culture is our business. This belief goes back a long way and the grounds are quite strong. After all, it was the Maori people who refused stubbornly to give up our culture in the face of a concentrated Pakeha effort to erase it. The memory of the Maori is a long one. We recall the time when the Pakeha did not want to have anything to do with Maoritanga. Could it be that some time in the future the Pakeha might again turn against the Maori culture? The missionary fervour of the early settlers remains with us today, for there are still some Pakeha who want the Maori people to become 'one' with them and forget all that nonsense about Maoritanga.

Then there is the question of trust. Can the Pakeha of today be trusted with Maoritanga? Unfortunately, our history is interspersed with cases of misplaced trust, resulting in losses of thousands of acres of land. Can the governments of today be trusted any more than those of the past?

Nevertheless, there are many Maori people who do not regard Maoritanga as being theirs only and are quite prepared to share it. But even this liberal-minded group are in two minds on the issue: sometimes they genuinely welcome the Pakeha into the fold of Maoritanga and applaud their efforts in learning the language, but at the next moment are beset with fears that eventually the Pakeha might take over their culture too.

Is there any basis for this fear? Let us look at the Pakeha side and find out. Since World War II, Pakeha New Zealanders have undergone a transformation in their identity. Before then, the Pakeha was a sort of mixed-up fellow whose body and material possessions were located in New Zealand but whose loyalty and cultural affiliations lay with the 'home country'—his body belonged to New Zealand but his soul belonged to a little island somewhere else. Now all of this has changed. The Pakeha belongs body and soul to New Zealand; at least this is how they want it. They seek a New Zealand identity and are working steadily towards that aim.

But this quest for national identity has some implications for the Maori. Consider this: Maori and Pakeha both claim to be people of the land, that is, to be tangata whenua. According to the Pakeha, the hills and the valleys, the mountains, lakes and rivers, the beaches and their bounty of kai moana, and the forests of this land belong equally to them. The activities of environmental groups all over the country attest to a deep concern for this land. Another point: not long ago the Pakeha did not compete with Maori gatherers of seafood. Today they not only identify with the land and sea but, heaven help us, they also go in search of our food. A lot of Maori would wish they didn't and yet are pleased to see this change in the Pakeha—who are now even eating eels!

If the Pakeha want to construct a distinctive New Zealand identity, where will they find the unique features they desire? Rugby, racing and our beer-drinking reputation are hardly the stuff on which to focus a New Zealand identity; yet they are part of it. Our fame as sheep-farmers can be a disadvantage—for instance, the suggestion that the humble sheep become our national symbol. All of these activities are not sufficiently distinctive if we wish to mark ourselves from Australians, Canadians, South Africans and Rhodesians. Plainly, it is Maori culture and the special relationship between Maori and Pakeha, for so long the envy of the world, which provide the source for a distinctive New Zealand image.

The Pakeha are reaching into Maori culture and pulling out features with which they can identify, taking hold of quite generous portions which they then try to fit into a Pakeha cultural world. Our Pakeha colleagues now argue that Maori art is really New Zealand art and is thus part of the New Zealand image. Maori people may challenge that claim, but it could be agonising to discover that the Pakeha will have to be admitted as part-owner of that heritage.

Consider also the history and lore of the Maori. These, too, have been elevated (or appropriated) to the status of New Zealand literature, thus becoming part of the national heritage. Look also at the Maori language. Teaching programmes in our schools are expanding so that there are now about 140 secondary and 240 primary schools offering Maori as an elective part of the curriculum. We are told by the Education Department that there are about 45,000 primary school children who are exposed to the Maori language. This great push in the teaching of the language came, in part, from Maori initiatives and pressure campaigns to have the language offered to all New Zealanders. Some of us are not too sure where Pakeha enthusiasm will lead us. Yet we know that without their help and resources our language will eventually die.

We, the Maori people, are willing to accept help in maintaining our language, though we reserve the right to play a major role in decisions regarding the teaching of Maori.

We further assert that most of that teaching be done by Maori people. Together we are making efforts to have the language taught more widely and we smile at the results we are achieving. I assume that our common goal is that the Maori language be transformed into a New Zealand language. Are we in agreement with this goal?

Does the case of language provide a model for how we are to treat the rest of Maoritanga? Must the Pakeha wait until we say to them: 'We give you permission to incorporate our art and our literature into your New Zealand identity. You need them in order to catch up to us who have always had a New Zealand identity.' Perhaps some of us want to say 'no' to the Pakeha. And what about the Pakeha view of this problem? They are already taking what they feel they need and the use they make of it sometimes enriches the culture and sometimes demeans it. They feel that they have a right of access to Maori culture because in their minds it is New Zealand culture. Yet, there are many sensitive responsible Pakeha who are not happy with the policy of simply taking without some negotiation.

Negotiation provides the key to our mutual problem. We must examine the case carefully, discuss it fully, think our way through the issues involved in our joint claims to Maori culture, work out ways of enriching the heritage to the benefit of the nation and at the same time avoid clubbing the Maori with the cruellest blow of all—taking what is left of our culture away from us and denying us the right to play the most important part in controlling its destiny.

The whole matter is a very sensitive issue which is likely to affect our relationships in the future. Our reputation for happy race relations in New Zealand has been tarnished internationally. We are no longer admired by the world community and it seems that we almost need to establish a new reputation. We owe it to ourselves to ensure that we handle the issue at home in a sensible and sensitive way.

And the exercise need not be an agonising one only; there could well be some joy in it.

10. The Day New Zealand Cried

Published in the New Zealand Monthly Review, *XIX (July 1978), pp.1–3.*

New Zealanders are not easily shocked. Yet thousands were on Bastion Point Day, 25 May 1978. This was the day when the nation did two things. First, in the name of law and order it mounted a para-military operation against the protesters of Bastion Point and moved them off the land. We were told by the press that this was the largest operation of its kind ever mounted in New Zealand. The police, the army and the air force were all involved in an operation that was frighteningly precise, and awesome in the sheer power that was demonstrated.

But the second thing the nation did was that its citizens, both Maori and Pakeha, cried in front of their television sets. How many cried I do not know. Probably thousands, when you count them up. I have heard of many cases, and even of large numbers of secondary school students. Whether proportionately more Maori cried that day than Pakeha, I do not know. The exact statistics are probably less important than the reasons why so many people cried.

A large number of people did not cry; they reacted in other ways. Some fell silent, others became angry and disgusted, while a few were simply upset at what they saw on television. There were many New Zealanders who did little work that day. I was among them. Measured against the awesome happening at Bastion Point, one's own work faded into insignificance.

No doubt there were some, perhaps a majority of our citizens, who applauded the actions of the police, who delighted in the successful removal of the protesters and who were glad to see Joe Hawke's group of 200 arrested and herded off in trucks to the police station. There may have been several citizens who were proud of their country that day. I don't know their number but I suspect that Pakeha and Maori are included in the count. Why they were proud is a question that they can best answer for themselves.

Among the people who cried were the police. I was told of this by eyewitnesses. If we include policemen among that proportion of the population that was upset and cried, and if we remember that the whole operation was to be seen as upholding law and order, we can ask an interesting question. Why did so many people cry on Bastion Point Day?

There are probably many different reasons and I could not do justice to all of them. The sheer scale of the operation frightened a lot of people. It was an object lesson in the mobilisation of part of the nation's power. Previously, most New Zealanders had no idea or concept of large-scale power until television presented them with an example of it.

More important, however, was that this unexpected scale of power was being used internally against our own citizens. The shock of this was highlighted by television bringing the events into the sitting-room of every household. For the first time many people realised that, but for the grace of God, such power could have been used against them, or might be in the future. And this might well have been one of the objectives of the exercise. Some Maori are already saying that the event is a clear warning to other Maori protest groups of what to expect if they do not do as they are told: the present government intends to be tough.

It could well be that the Maori people had more reason to cry than the Pakeha. As a people in our situation we have always been sensitive to injustice, aware of our lack of unity and frustrated by the power that the majority group in New Zealand wields. Our people were psychologically crushed and symbolically defeated—again—on the battle ground by the almighty Pakeha. The tears were to add to those shed for Parihaka, for Rua the prophet and many others who were destroyed when Pakeha of an earlier day called the law in.

All of the events culminating in the spectacular clearing of Bastion Point highlighted poignantly the vulnerable and weak position of the Maori people in our New Zealand society. Ngati Whatua, who happened to be caught in the centre of the action, symbolised our weaknesses—our disunity, our confused thinking, our lack of expertise and our lack of effective power. All of this, the bitter truth, was brought out into the open for all to see.

The ease with which the Prime Minister exploited these weaknesses and his eager willingness to do so cut deeply. His subsequent denial to the Maori of a role in the protest and his attempt to blame it all on the Socialist Unity Party and the communists only added to the hurt. We are so ineffective and insignificant in the government's thinking that the Prime Minister can proclaim that we did not even exist at Bastion Point!

It might be said, with some justice, that Ngati Whatua did not seem to sense the importance of the moment in which history placed them, that they did not realise the issue was larger than they. But the same can be said of many other tribes and of many Maori individuals, including myself. The full significance of the Bastion Point protest did not emerge until the eve of the big police operation. For some people it was not until 25 May actually dawned that they stopped sitting on the fence. By then it was too late to help.

Support from other tribes—I believe very substantial support—could have been obtained had Ngati Whatua united and acted as a solid group. Their lack of unity played into the government's hands and made the issue a relatively easy one to win. Influential groups that might have helped were deftly sidelined by the political manipulations of the government. The King movement, the New Zealand Maori Council, the Maori Women's Welfare League, the churches, were kept out of the protest.

Some of our old people could well have cried out of exasperation and anger at the elders of Ngati Whatua. They stubbornly refused to come together as a group. Instead we saw the spectacle of one faction making a separate deal with the government, and confusing rather than resolving the issue. One might cry at the continuation of the 'divide and rule' strategy which put people into the categories of loyalists and renegades. It is time we saw an end to this sort of policy. History has a habit of later showing the renegades to be right and the loyalists to be wrong, so that both groups lose.

We might have witnessed either a partial or a total eclipse of the elders as an influential group in Maori affairs in the future. The example of Ngati Whatua elders will not go unnoticed among today's youth. Yet we might be expecting far too much of our elders, because they are as vulnerable and as weak as any other group of people. We expect them to be wise in handling the political problems of the day. An issue like Bastion Point, however, is a large and complex one. Some of the best land in New Zealand is at stake. This land happens also to be in the Prime Minister's electorate. As prime land it is bound to be coveted by powerful interests. We expect, perhaps unreasonably, that the elders can cope with the forces aligned against them. How would the elders of other tribes have fared against such odds? Probably not much better.

Anyone familiar with our history knows that tribal one-upmanship has played a part not only in our relations with other tribes but also, unfortunately, in our relations with the Pakeha. In the not-so-distant past some tribes were only too willing to take up arms against our own people and side with the Pakeha. This sort of thing has not helped our cause. Today we see an example of whanau one-upmanship and this cannot help the cause of the Maori people either.

There was indeed a lot to cry about, and much to think about. Yet, there was also something to be thankful for. A large number of Pakeha were equally upset by the events which television portrayed before us. The Maori people can take comfort from the fact that they were not alone, that there were hundreds of Pakeha who cried with us. This important fact must not be forgotten now, in the immediate future, or ever.

The Bastion Point Lesson

But what of the future? What has Bastion Point taught us? Again, I cannot deal with all of the implications or of the possible lines of action which might be taken.

We need to take a good look at our Maori organisations with a view towards making them more effective and cohesive. Different tribes might, for example, find out whether their present organisational structures permit a tribal point of view to be stated, whether one person can on certain occasions speak for the whole tribe. At a higher level, we might find a way of expressing the solidarity of a group of tribes associated with a particular canoe, such as Mataatua and Te Arawa. If we lack the organisation to permit such unity and solidarity, we need to explore ways of making this possible.

We need, too, to make the New Zealand Maori Council a more effective organisation—to strengthen, if necessary restructure, and give it new purpose so that it can represent the Maori people with confidence. There are many other organisations, such as those associated with the churches, which might look again at their structures and their objectives.

I see a need for Maori and Pakeha organisations to come together, to co-operate with certain tasks and to help one another. A stand-off stance serves no useful purpose.

We might also look at the manner in which we conduct protests. Here we might take some hints from Muldoon's operational code, as described by John T. Henderson in a recent article. I do this not because I really want to give advice to protesters, but rather to make a point that ought to be made.

'Politics is a "tough game"—a battle where only the strong succeed' is the first belief in the Prime Minister's operational code. Applied to the Bastion Point protest, it suggests that only the strong should take part—that is, those who are tough enough to see the thing through no matter what the odds may be. Harry Truman's saying is to be taken to heart, 'if you can't stand the heat get out of the kitchen'!

Another hint is contained in the second belief. This says that the moment you let your guard down someone slips one underneath it. The suggestion here is to adopt an aggressive 'counter-punching' style in all negotiations. There is also the suggestion that one should not listen too carefully to the other side because one's guard might be let down.

Yet another of the Prime Minister's beliefs has to do with strong leadership. Notions such as sincerity coupled with firmness, taking a strong stand, leading from the front, speaking your mind and challenging all incorrect statements are important features of leadership. Included here are other matters such as facing up to issues, never dodging a question nor turning down an interview. But an important one is 'determination not to be pressured into submission'.

Probably, then, a well-led protest is one which never admits or compromises what it set out to do.

There are obvious hints in the beliefs which say 'the best time to act is now' and 'say what's on your mind when it comes to mind'. But the trickiest one advises that 'politics is a high-risk profession, and success demands a willingness to accept these risks'. When this is accepted as a principle for protesters to follow, the possibilities are enormous and horrendous.

It could go on in this vein: taking ideas from the Prime Minister, and applying them not only to the Bastion Point protest but to all Maori organisations. If these as well as other ideas of his were adopted with enthusiasm, the result would be an unprecedented increase in confrontation politics in New Zealand. This style of politics would severely strain the rather fragile edifice which represents our race relations.

It would also, I believe, result in moving us closer towards inter-ethnic violence. The realism and pragmatism which our Prime Minister advocates and which involves facing up to issues and identifying the facts may in the arena of inter-ethnic affairs point towards an inappropriate solution. One cannot trust people to act with common sense in such a situation. Facing up to the issues and identifying the facts associated with Bastion Point might lead the more militant Maori to draw conclusions which might be realistic and yet, from the country's point of view, totally unacceptable and amoral.

The conclusion I draw from looking at the Prime Minister's style and manner of politics is that it is highly dangerous. What took place at Bastion Point produced far too much anger and disgust. It put our race relations in jeopardy, it damaged our national reputation and our self-esteem. It compromised our armed forces and our police. It humiliated Maori and Pakeha alike, and it hurt. An action taken supposedly to uphold the law must have been wrong if it made many of our people cry.

We should see to it that an operation such as that mounted at Bastion Point is not repeated. Clearly our national security was not at stake, nor was Auckland city threatened. The land was not being raped and it is certainly not the only spot on which land squatters were and are in occupation.

One positive move which we can initiate almost immediately—as a way of preventing a recurrence of a Bastion Point situation and as a way of providing more information for everyone, but especially for aggrieved Maori—is to institute a Maori Affairs Research Unit which is semi-autonomous and not attached to any government department. The function of such a unit would be to provide the best possible information which a Maori group requires in order to bring a grievance before government or before the courts. Its intention would be to provide equality of information and expertise to a group which has rarely ever enjoyed such equality. This would ensure fairness to the aggrieved parties and provide them with competent advice. It should go some distance to preventing the sort of misunderstanding and misinformation which threatened the Bastion Point protest.

In addition, I believe it is essential to provide the Maori with a different sort of equality—namely, equality of access to the mass media, or equality of expression. It took the Bastion Point issue to point out to me how tightly controlled the newspapers, radio and television are by the Pakeha. I realised that there was no true freedom of Maori expression in New Zealand except at Maori hui. Of the communication systems in our country, only the telephone allows true freedom of expression. The rest are so dominated by the Pakeha that at most times we are permitted to say only those things which the editors allow.

To correct this situation, I ask that the *Te Ao Hou* magazine, which has been in limbo for some time, be revived immediately, that it permit the free expression of Maori opinion and that, if necessary, it be subsidised by government to ensure that there is at least one regular magazine in which the Maori can write with reasonable freedom.

We might also look again at the idea of a Radio Aotearoa in order that some degree of equality of access to the mass media can be obtained. Te Reo Maori's petition for a Maori television production unit also needs to be looked at seriously, for it, too, is aimed at providing more equal access than is the case now. The result of all these measures I am suggesting is to ensure that we are all better informed, so that in the long run we can be more understanding of one another. A lot of aroha exists already. Why don't we build on to what we have so that we can all enjoy being citizens of New Zealand?

11. Two Blankets and a Puff of Tobacco
The Struggle to Build Bridges of Understanding

As events around the world have shown, misunderstandings, distrust and violence are common indicators of failure in ethnic relationships. Living together is difficult and, if problems are not addressed openly and fairly, conflict can arise, as we have seen in Bosnia and several parts of Africa. Ethnic conflict leads to slaughter of thousands of people.

Therefore every effort should be made to build bridges between the different ethnic groups and encourage understanding. A step towards understanding requires some honest appraisals of what has happened, what is causing problems, and what can be done to improve the quality of life for all. The 'one people' concept has been promoted by the dominant group as its answer for the future good. On the other hand, Maori want a degree of separation and of self-government as a necessary step towards greater understanding. Being submerged under a dominant group does not foster good ethnic relations.

Each side talks about the other and says what it wants, but rarely do serious discussions occur between the two sides. This remains a problem. Racism is the great divider and source of extremist anti-Maori sentiments. It leads the two sides to confrontations. This paper addresses the problems of racism.

Published in University of Auckland News, August 1984.

My main thesis in this talk is that the chief means of controlling the behaviour of the Maori population and of denying cultural freedom to them is through the operation of the ideology of racism. A basic tenet of this ideology is that all members of the white race, regardless of status or intelligence quotient, are superior in mental and emotional qualities to all members of other races. It often finds expression in a felt need to be superior and to act in a superior manner, called whakahihi by the Maori. Such an attitude gives to Pakeha New Zealanders a psychological advantage in all of their dealings with Maori people, because it is supported by the control and manipulation of government and all of its institutions and agencies, as well as the control of the supply of money and the activities of the mass media. It is an almost impossible task for individuals who want to be Maori ever to be equal with the Pakeha, let alone gain the upper hand.

In order to explain our predicament I go back to the past, to the Treaty of Waitangi, to the period of friendly accommodation when each side was prepared to listen to the other. I move on to the wars of domination and show how decisions made in this period reflect unrestrained racism. Many of these decisions are now a matter of great shame. Then I deal with the myth-making stage, which buries the past and creates false images in rosy-coloured mirrors. These myths, and there are many of them, become the prisons of the Maori people, affecting our behaviour, confusing us, leading us astray, frustrating our aspirations and forcing upon us a sentence that is already over 100 years long. But it is the ideology of racism that is behind the myths. Thus, I believe that freedom for the Maori requires the overthrow of this ideology.

Two Blankets

On Thursday, 6 February 1840, during the second day of the big meeting at Waitangi, Lieutenant-Governor William Hobson is reported to have said forty-five times: 'He iwi tahi tatou' (We are (now) one people) (Colenso 1890, p.35). As each chief came to the table to sign his name to the Treaty of Waitangi, Hobson murmured this famous invocation in Maori, smiled and then shook hands warmly. Later, each signatory received two blankets and a quantity of tobacco because the Queen was pleased with them. Then at the end of the day this motley group of tattooed chiefs gave 'three cheers for the Governor' in a manner which suggested that the missionaries had coached them well. The next day, Friday, 7 February 1840, it rained all day (ibid).

At this stage in Maori–Pakeha relations we were going through the friendly accommodating phase of the colonial experience. In countries selected by the British for settlement, a pattern had emerged. In the United States, for example, the accommodating stage lasted only as long as it took to increase numbers and fire power among the European settlers (Froman 1972, p.31). During this time the ideology of white supremacy, based on the belief 'that all members of what is called the white race are superior in mental and emotional qualities to all members of other races' (Froman 1972, p.23), was suspended. In fact, the ideology was found wanting, because the new settlers could not survive as well as the local Indians in an environment they understood from centuries of past experience. So the settlers were forced by the needs of survival to learn what they could from the Indians and consequently maintained cordial social relations with them. Some intermarriage occurred, and some interchange of ideas. For example, the basic idea of democracy—that is, of government 'by the consent of the governed'—came from the Cherokee Indians of the United States (Froman 1972, p.30).

In countries such as America, Canada, Australia and New Zealand, wherever there existed an indigenous population, incoming settlers from Britain and Europe followed a familiar pattern of seeking to dominate the new land and its people and of transforming both after the image of their homeland. Froman (1972, p.31) argued that there was a need to feel superior and indeed to be superior over the native people. Thus what happened after the initial period of friendliness was an inevitable result of thinking in a certain way and of acting in accordance with attitudes and beliefs that were consistent with the ideology of white superiority. Hence, in the United States scalping was introduced, with various sums of money being offered as rewards to bounty hunters or hunting parties being established by legislative means; wars of extermination were directed against the Indians and in the end millions were killed. Dead Indians were regarded as good Indians, while the living were bad because they got in the way of white progress. The result was that the land was cleared for occupation by white settlers, and this was very quickly followed by the establishment of government which typically excluded any participation by the indigenous population. At this stage, the native people are virtually denied the status of being human.

Rationalised

While the details of the experience might differ from one country to another, the results were very similar. The tribes lost the land, their sovereignty, their cultural self-esteem, their language and so on, while the settlers assumed complete control over the whole country and especially over the people they overran. Actions taken to dispossess the indigenous population were rationalised in terms of an ideology of racism.

At Waitangi in February 1840, British racism had already taken hold and permeated all other ideologies, such as religion (where the Church of Rome and Maori culture together were despised), commerce (which made it acceptable to overcharge and underpay Maori clients—an accusation made at Waitangi), trade, schooling and law. It is noteworthy, for example, that in drafting the Treaty of Waitangi and in writing it in Maori, only Pakeha advisers were called by the Lieutenant-Governor. No Maori was deemed adequate or appropriate for the task. It is also evident that, in the thinking current at the time, the role of the Maori was to sign, smile, give three cheers and listen to the advice of the British settlers, traders and missionaries.

An intriguing question is what Hobson had in mind when he said: 'He iwi tahi tatou.' He may have been applauding the fact that through the signing of the treaty the Maori people had become British citizens and hence at one with him and the symbols of British power. Moreover, he may have been thinking at the level of high idealism and of symbolic unity with the Empire. But Tareha, chief of Ngati Rehia, spoke of the realities as he perceived them. Among other things, Colenso (1890, pp.24–5) reports him as having said at Waitangi:

> Thou high, and I, Tareha, the great chief of the Ngapuhi tribes, low!
> To think of tempting men—us Natives—with baits of clothing and of food.
> Yes, I say we are the chiefs.
> If all were to be alike, all equal in rank with thee—but thou, the Governor up high—up, up, as this tall paddle . . . and I down, under, beneath!

He was well aware that the ideal of equality was up in the clouds while on the ground the attitudes of the British put the chiefs and their people low down in the social hierarchy. Tareha Kawiti of Ngati Hine, Te Kemara of Ngati Kawa and Rewa of Ngati Tawake were also keenly aware of the European practice of elevating themselves. They could not see how the promise of equality or of oneness with the British could be honoured. Their experience with the missionaries had already confirmed the difficulties of equality. What the missionaries wanted was for the Maori to be like them and to accept not only their religion but also their civilisation, guidance and leadership.

No Past

But, if one accepted their recipe for salvation, it required that even very old Maori men and women act like children in the presence of Europeans—that is, to behave as though they had no social or political position, no culture or economy, no traditions and above all no past. By adopting this strategy, which is still practised today by some religious groups, the missionaries became the fathers who could then assume roles of dominance over the native converts.

Some chiefs at Waitangi described themselves as mere children—Hoani Heke, for example (Colenso 1890, p.26)—while others acknowledged the dominant position of the governor and the missionaries. So some were referring to the missionaries and all the other Europeans present as father, judge and peacemaker (Colenso 1890, p.27), which prompts one to consider whether some Maori chiefs thought of the words 'which art in Heaven', for the models provided by the Bible probably had a strong influence on Maori thinking at that time. The Reverend Henry Williams made it clear to the Europeans gathered at Waitangi the debt they owed to the missionaries when he said to them in English: 'People should recollect that were it not for the missionaries they would not be here this day, nor be in possession of a foot of land in New Zealand' (Colenso 1890, pp.20–1).

For the missionaries, being one people probably did not mean equality or a partnership in government. What it meant was white dominance over a child-like population of natives, with all roles of authority held especially by the missionaries. I think they had a theocracy in mind. For the Maori, it meant on the one hand denying the reality of their ethnic existence in the presence of the superior Europeans, and on the other hand showing off their newly acquired Western technology and knowledge in the presence of other tribal groups. It was the beginning of a love–hate relationship with Pakeha culture.

The evidence of the day indicated that Hobson's views regarding the Maori were not very different from those of the British people present and that, while his words in Maori held out the promise of equality and partnership, he himself was not a champion of native rights. Thus what he really meant in 1840 was perhaps very close to what is currently understood by hundreds of New Zealand citizens who still believe in white superiority. To them one people, one nation means essentially a denial of the presence and reality of Maori culture on the one hand, and overt monopolistic support of European or Pakeha interests and values on the other.

The low opinion of Maori culture is expressed in *Race Against Time*, in such statements as:

> Maori culture has nothing to offer.
> It is a simple tribal illiterate culture.
> The Maori contributed nothing to world culture.
> They have nothing but some carvings and some legends.
> European culture is bigger and stronger and this is a law of nature that the stronger takes over the weaker (Tauroa 1982, pp.30–3).

In their desire to feel superior, the Pakeha want the Maori minority to remain docile, as in this lovely statement:

> Get rid of the stirrers and allow our wonderful Maoris to be themselves, dignified, courteous and with a great pride of race. Not the dirty, degraded, dishonest, lazy dole bludgers that our stirrers are turning into, because they think they are being 'got at' (Tauroa 1982, p.34).

Or they want Maori citizens to feel guilty, as in these statements:

> The use of the land/language/culture as a symbol of ethnic identity is not only spurious, it is also potentially dangerous.
> So long as racial emnity is encouraged and allowed in a country so racial disharmony to a greater or lesser degree is inevitable (Tauroa 1982, pp.33, 28).

Or they demand ethnic denial, as suggested in these statements:

> There should be no cultural differences, all races in New Zealand should be fully integrated so we can live in harmony.
> In New Zealand, we are all New Zealanders, whether Maori or European.
> As one people we must strenuously resist anything that divides the races (Tauroa 1982, pp.22, 23).

10,000 Troops

Views such as these are held by hundreds of people in positions of authority in New Zealand. In the nineteenth century many shameful acts were authorised by legislative means and carried out without too many pangs of guilt by persons in positions of power who held similar views to the racists of today. What happened in the United States happened here, too. For example, bounties were offered in Taranaki—£10 for a chief's head and £5 for others (Scott 1981, p.34)—villages were systematically looted and burnt, others bombarded into smithereens; pitched battles were fought at such places as Orakau or at Kakaramea (Taranaki), where 200 warriors faced a British force of 1000 men (Scott 1981, p.22). We would not want to remember that in the 1860s there were 10,000 British troops here (Scott 1981, p.22) and that Britain played a key role in the subjugation of the Maori people so that British settlers could take and rule the land with a free hand.

Some of the military operations approved locally and by the Colonial Office involved extermination, as when Von Tempsky and Major McDonnell in December 1866 left Wanganui and marched for 260 miles to New Plymouth and back, killing every Maori in sight. No prisoners were taken from the seven fortified pa and twenty-one open villages (Scott 1981, p.23) that were destroyed.

Tom Adamson became a hero for decapitating a dying Maori warrior and for beating a kupapa to his prize (Scott 1981, p.34). Major Maillard Noake, military commander of Patea, acquired fame as the man who was responsible for enforcing the rule that no native fire was to be lit again in Patea county. Those who tried to get back onto their homeland were mercilessly shot down like animals. He was also the man (together with Bryce) who 'shipped off to Otago' over 100 men from Patea after they had surrendered in good faith to them. This was to teach them to respect Pakeha power.

The stories are horrific, and retelling them is not a pleasant experience for Maori or Pakeha. So I hope you all felt uncomfortable! The point I want to make, however, is that the combination of the ideology of racism, the need to be superior, and greed for land led persons in authority to commit crimes against humanity which now shame us. There are many Maori readers who cannot read a book such as *Ask that Mountain* by Dick Scott because they cannot get past the first few pages without either weeping for the victims of Pakeha aggression or becoming extremely angry at the animal-like behaviour of Pakeha officials and military personnel. These acts have to be put into the context of the times: the introduction of Christianity, the signing of the Treaty of Waitangi, the promise of law and order, and also the promise of the same rights as British citizens to Maori people as guaranteed by Great Britain. Instead of protecting us, however, Britain was here in the role of aggressor.

A Lesson

The land wars were a lesson to the Maori of Pakeha power, and their need to be superior, and to be dominant in the sense of exercising total control over everything and every Maori body. The Treaty of Waitangi could not mean anything to individuals who were racist, because the treaty is about equality and partnership and about human decency and hope. Maori chiefs appealed time and again to the treaty, but such appeals could not be heard by ears that were dominated by the ideology of white superiority. Even now, Pakeha New Zealanders are having great difficulty in understanding the Treaty of Waitangi.

In the accommodating phase of the colonial experience, the frontline troops of domination were the missionaries and the traders. They did not use force but relied instead on creating a need for their product and then being on the spot to supply it. Behind them, however, was the threat of British or French naval power, of reprisals from New South Wales. As the missionaries were the teachers of Western knowledge generally, as well as being the preachers, they were in a position to influence the behaviour and minds of people to perhaps a considerable extent, especially in dealings with the government.

The signing of the Treaty of Waitangi prepared the way for the establishment of settler government and, hence, for controlling the means to exercise power over the native population. Twenty years later, the next phase in colonisation began: the ten-year land wars. In this phase, the frontline people were soldiers, government officials and politicians who appeared to have interchangeable roles. Soldiers ended up in Parliament, so that colonels and majors were commonplace and Ministers of the Crown were not slow to lead war expeditions themselves, as in the case of John Bryce, Native Minister, who rode into Parihaka on a white charger at the head of an army of 2500 men to be met by 200 children singing, spinning tops and skipping (Scott 1981, p.113).

The whole Parihaka incident illustrates only too clearly the irrationality of racist officials and the sort of absurdity that believers in white superiority can bring upon a nation. In one view, Bryce's attack on Parihaka was nothing more than resentment against the prophets Te Whiti and Tohu because they organised a community on the principle of self-government and produced marvellous results, such as orderliness, good work habits, happiness, no drunkenness and good housing. Such organised orderliness, however, was not in the interests of the land-grabbers. The prophets had to be cut down to size in order to satisfy Bryce's and others' need to be superior. In the aftermath, however, came some of the worst examples of the abuse of parliamentary power in New Zealand. These cases also resulted in the abuse of the judicial system by the Crown. It is such a shameful episode in our history that most people would prefer not to know about it.

Nonetheless, we should look at a few examples. After holding the warrior Titokowaru for six months, Judge Gillies found that there was no case against him and released him from jail (Scott 1981, p.138). In fact, Gillies ruled that Bryce did not have authority to remove from Parihaka people who 'merely sat still'. As a result, the government passed legislation to turn the Parihaka people into criminals, and with regard to Te Whiti and Tohu an act was passed that they were not to be tried, they were to be jailed indefinitely, and if released they could be rearrested without charge at any time. It did not end there. There is a litany of unjust legislation that was proposed by ministers suffering a bad case of racism. However, the voice opposing racism was always present in New Zealand, and I want to make that point quite clearly. It was weakened by the ready accusation of being 'one of them' and hence of being a traitor. It was actually very difficult openly to oppose racist politicians, soldiers and land agents during this time.

Gifts and Bribes

From the start, bribery and the political use of the takoha, or gift, had always been a tool for modifying Maori behaviour. For example, as already mentioned, chiefs who signed the treaty received two blankets and some tobacco. While under custody in Lyttelton, Te Whiti and Tohu were taken to see the sights of the town, and for six weeks they were escorted around the South Island in an effort to win them over to the Pakeha side (Scott 1981, p.141). Te Whiti was offered 'a handsome yearly income, besides making him perhaps a Legislative Councillor' (ibid). Eight months later, they were offered the chance of seeing their wives if they would repudiate their followers at Parihaka. Because they would not accept bribery, they remained in jail without trial from November 1881 to March 1883. And, just to reinforce Pakeha power, on 2 May 1883 some off-duty policemen assaulted Te Whiti (Scott 1981, pp.145–6). It is worth noting as an aside that the practice of policemen assaulting Maori citizens as a way of asserting Pakeha dominance goes back to the period of the land wars, and continues today.

Maori land speculators who were able to get signatures for the government got special gifts from land agents who wanted names on a document, even if they were of the wrong people. Anyone who was too friendly towards the tribes was likely to be silenced by a bribe or ridiculed, hounded and punished harshly by the courts, as in the case of George Rusden (Rusden 1974). Swords of honour and pensions were given to chiefs who rendered good service and killed on behalf of the government (Rusden 1974, p.141). Tribes that did not co-operate or take bribes of course received nothing.

Bribery and the use of the political gift still occur today, and can be seen in the way Maori leaders are chosen to join 'official' visits overseas or to participate in conferences here in New Zealand, in the selection of leaders to receive knighthoods and other highly rated honours, in the way Maori men and women who are seen to be pro-Pakeha are called upon to be the token Maori at Pakeha functions, and sometimes in the flow of funds into areas inhabited by so-called 'friendly' Maori.

According to Scott (1981, p.45), 'drink, bribery and a subsidized fifth column were the new forces enlisted for taking the land' in the 1880s. These were of course some of the same forces that were used for influencing the behaviour of Maori individuals or groups. Special mixes of alcohol, especially rum, were sold for consumption by Maori drinkers. Their sale in Taranaki was encouraged by the government. The selling of liquor to Maori people, though illegal, went on under the eyes of magistrates and police. Worse, much of the money used for such purchases was in large sums paid in secret to already demoralised chiefs who would betray their people for drink (Scott 1981, p.46).

The political gift and drink were also the means of establishing a subsidised or fully paid fifth column in the 1860s and 1880s. As Scott (1981, p.45) put it, 'the Government enrolled a horde of agents and informers in every Maori district in the country' and 'legal niceties for dispossessing an inexperienced people were reinforced by fraud, forgery and false interpreting'. Many innocent people lost their land and their lives as a result. Today, however, there is still the suspicion that 'a horde of agents' spy on Maori activities and that there is no shortage of the Iscariot-like figure among us who is ready to betray us.

Concealed

The confrontational, violent phase of the colonising experience ends once power is secured and the settlers really do feel superior. At that stage, two things happen. First, every effort is made to hide and forget the more unpleasant acts that were carried out under the mantle of government. This is relatively painless because the doctrine of white superiority provides convenient rationalisations for easing the conscience. Thus, it could be said, it was for the good of the Maori people themselves that civilisation and its benefits were brought to them. From this moment onwards all efforts made by aggrieved Maori tribesmen to seek justice for what was done to them are resented, played down or dismissed out of hand as false, or they are told that in the name of progress they should look into the future and not into the past. And it is interesting to contrast these different notions of the future for the Pakeha. It may be too simplistic, but it seems to me that Pakeha turn their backs on the past and walk into the future, while in the case of Maori our way is to keep the past before us all the time.

The second thing that happens is that the process of fabricating myths about the pioneers and the natives begins. This is familiar—the Americans did it, the Australians did it, and we did it too—and that is when the one-people, one-nation myth became important (Hohepa 1978). We have had myths about our wonderful, romantic and noble Maori; or about Kupe, Toi and the Fleet (Simmons 1982); or about our fine, upstanding, law-abiding and God-fearing settlers.

We seize upon such myths almost as a merciful branch to cling to so that we will not drown in the blood and misery of our past. They become the cover under which the doctrine of white superiority and domination is maintained. We, the Maori people, are imprisoned in the myths of the Pakeha and our prison walls are words and stories which appear to me to be as impenetrable as thick concrete walls.

Wherever Pakeha decision-makers are located, whether in television, radio, factories, offices, schools, universities, buses, aeroplanes and trains, or at cocktail parties, the myths supported by the doctrine of racism still dominate their minds. Pakeha people seem not to be happy unless they are in total charge of the country and in a dominant position.

By Force

If we as the minority native population become too assertive, as at Bastion Point, the need for the Pakeha to be superior is more likely to find expression in a Bryce-like mobilisation of overwhelming military or police forces to put the Maori back into a position of subservience. This is preferred to the simpler, cheaper and more brotherly solution of acknowledging a wrong and then handing over a relatively small portion of land as a way of providing justice for the people. Pakeha decision-makers seem to find it hard to make decisions on the basis of equality. Many are afraid they will be accused of being soft on Maori.

When a Bryce manoeuvre does take place, a large number of Pakeha New Zealanders applaud because it confirms the doctrine of white superiority which has never really left our country, though it might have fewer ardent followers than previously. Recent efforts by organisations such as HART show that the Pakeha attitude towards eradicating racism is about the same as men's attitudes towards stopping the rape of women. There is no great enthusiasm to change it. Yet it is plain, even as recently as the 'kia ora' incident with Mrs Naida Povey in May 1984, that the racist attitudes of decision-makers result in the intimidation of Maori citizens and in the prevention of the exercise of the right to use their own language as promised not only by the Treaty of Waitangi but also by the International Covenant on Economic, Social and Cultural Rights. Fortunately in this case exposure by the media resulted in public ridicule of the decision-makers. However, many other cases go unnoticed and as a result some Maori individual or group suffers an injustice. In fact, the suppression of the Maori language is a huge 'buried' issue that surfaced only briefly with the excitement over 'kia ora' and then afterwards was quickly buried again.

Perhaps it is time to lift from our country the veil of silence that was placed over the events of our colonial experience. The Pakeha of today, and indeed the present Maori generation, have become the 'Children of the Myths' because their great-grandparents and grandparents and the education system did not want to tell them the truth about how this country was colonised and founded. Instead, they wove myths which romanticised their role as pioneers and enshrined us as noble savages who keeled over and died when these wonderful pioneers from Britain came here.

Scholars and writers, among them soldiers, judges and land agents, began to write about the brave Maoris as being of a higher mental order than the Aborigines of Australia or the Blacks of Africa, of them being among the highest-ranked of all savages, of their being the greatest of navigators and hence worthy of the term 'Viking', and of their legends being equal to the classics of the early Greeks. Early published material in the *School Journal*, issued by the Department of Education, reflected the changed attitudes and emphasised the heroic and classical character of the Maori (Beaglehole 1982, p.39). In its first forty years of publication, the *School Journal* concentrated on extolling the virtues and heroes of the British Empire and of writing about the Maori of the distant past (Beaglehole 1982, p.39), totally ignoring the experience of the land wars and their condition in the contemporary period. That was when the contemporary Maori 'died'.

If we are to liberate both the oppressor and the oppressed, as demanded by the Brazilian Paulo Freire (1982, p.32), and if we are to liberate the Treaty of Waitangi so that it can be seen as a noble pact between Maori and Pakeha, and if all of us are to be 'freed' from the myths of the settlers, then we must look at ourselves warts and all, and we must learn to examine, discuss and contemplate the events of our past. The key to a happier future has been locked up in our unhappy past. I believe it is time to release the past and let us see it on television.

Deep-seated

One of the main barriers to the release of our history from the tyranny of myths that were fabricated to conceal it is the spectre of racism that arises out of the need to be superior. This is a deep-seated, fundamental need of human beings. In many societies the need is expressed through competitive activities between social groups and teams, as in sport, singing and dancing competitions, in becoming top in one's field of endeavour and in collecting and displaying material things, such as motorcars and big houses. Unless controlled by social means, this same fundamental need is expressed through more aggressive and destructive forms such as rape, the practice of racism, either by a dominant group against a powerless minority or by a white group against a coloured one, the use of violence against individuals that results in acts such as lynching or murder, and war, as in the Falklands.

Clearly, the negative aspects of the need to be superior have to be controlled. As rape has to be openly discussed, admitted as a problem and then controlled by law, so must racism be treated in the same way. Those who suffer it must recognise the symptoms of their mate whakahihi (the sickness of suffering delusions of vanity and grandeur) which Maori people recognise as a disease. We must learn to talk about this disease more openly than at present and we must find ways of controlling it and treating it.

In the long run, we will have to consider seriously treating bad cases of racism in the same way as we treat murderers, rapists and child molesters. They should be locked up in jail so our society is more comfortable to live in, race relations are happier and more progress can be made in allowing the Maori people to enjoy their culture, maintain and develop it, live according to how they want to live and become free at last from the yoke of racism in New Zealand. Or they should be sent to hospital for treatment. Otherwise they will continue to do violence to the rights and freedoms of people who are different, the Treaty of Waitangi will remain an unfulfilled dream, and the blankets given out at Waitangi warm only the bones of tattooed chiefs who thought they knew what they were doing on our behalf.

Bibliography

Beaglehole, Diana, 1982. 'The Maori in the *School Journal* 1907–81'. *Education* 31, pp.38–41.
Colenso, W., 1890. *The Authentic and Genuine History of the Signing of the Treaty of Waitangi.* Wellington, Government Printer.
Freire, Paulo, 1982. *Pedagogy of the Oppressed.* Auckland, Penguin Books.
Froman, R., 1977. *Racism.* New York, Delacorte Press.
Hohepa, Pat, 1978. 'Maori and Pakeha: the One-People Myth', in *Tihe Mauriora Aspects of Maoritanga*, edited by Michael King. Auckland, Methuen, pp.98–111.
Mead, Sidney Moko, 1981. 'Te Kaupapa Mo Te Whakaako i Nga Tikanga a Te Maori: The Philosophy Underlying the Teaching of Maori Customs', paper given at first National Art Education Conference, Auckland, May 1981.

Rusden, G. W., 1974. *Aureretanga: Groans of the Maoris* (originally published 1888). Wellington, Hakaprint.

Scott, D., 1975. *Ask that Mountain: The Story of Parihaka* (reprinted 1981). Auckland, Heinemann Southern Cross.

Simmons, D.R., 1982. 'A New Zealand Myth: Kupe, Toi and the Fleet'. *New Zealand Journal of History* 3 (1), pp.14–31.

Tauroa, H., 1982. *Race Against Time*. Wellington, Human Rights Commission.

12. The Maori People Tomorrow

Notes from a speech delivered to the New Zealand Association of Philanthropic Trusts Conference, 3 October 1991.

The removal of a Minister of the Crown from office is always a serious matter. To remove Winston Peters from his office of Minister of Maori Affairs is a very serious matter. The whole affair highlights some of the issues that are ahead of us. The first point is that Winston Peters is a member of Ngati Wai. He is a Maori and was the only Maori in Cabinet. Now there is no Maori in Cabinet, and this needs to be looked at carefully. I am sure the women of the nation would not tolerate having no women in Cabinet. Why should we tolerate having no Maori voice in Cabinet?

Let's leave that issue aside for the moment. No matter what reasons are given for the sacking of Winston Peters, one fact that cannot be easily dismissed is the fact of him being a Maori and hence a member of the tangata whenua, of the indigenous population of our land, of the Maori minority.

When he was sacked, Maori people were personally shocked and hurt by this exercise of Pakeha power over a Maori. Maori people are hurting over this action, are annoyed by it, and want to do something to show their disapproval. While Pakeha observers may see the whole incident as being inevitable, this is not the case for us. Why?

First, we are in a power relationship where the Pakeha majority controls power, sovereignty, the budget and so on.

Second, it is difficult to separate out the Maori component of the New Zealand identity. We are Maori and New Zealanders. The Maori part is hurt and the other partner did the hurting.

Third, the Treaty of Waitangi is significant and does have meaning for many of us. Some of us focus upon Article 3 and stress our common citizenship under the British Crown. Others focus upon Article 2 and tino rangatiratanga, and this is where most Maori people are looking. The government focuses upon Article 1 and says that our ancestors handed the sovereignty of the nation to the British Crown, therefore we should let the government get on with the business of government.

It is worth mentioning that the chiefs did not assign kawanatanga to the settlers. Rather, it was to the British Crown. Britain engaged in some deft manoeuvres and devolved its responsibilities to the settlers, who keenly formed a government and sought to exclude Maori participation in it and proceeded to destroy the tino rangatiratanga of the Maori.

One of our big problems in this country is that the descendants of the settlers find it very difficult to devolve kawanatanga back to the Maori people. Even sharing in kawanatanga has been too much for them. So we were stuck with four Maori seats that were established over 100 years ago and only for the 1996 elections was the number increased, by one, to five. Why is this? The Pakeha seats have certainly been increased many times, but the Maori seats have become a problem for the protectors of kawanatanga who do not want to give up any of it, or share it. There must be a name for this kind of phobia.

Tino rangatiratanga is currently the issue with a large proportion of the Maori population. Discussions about the rights of indigenous peoples have not gone unnoticed, nor have the events of 1990, the Commonwealth Games, Waitangi and the waka taua. These events have had a powerful effect on the Maori mind and now we must speak of self-determination, self-sufficiency, self-government and so on.

Kohanga reo and kura kaupapa Maori are keenly supported by the people. Iwi development is a top priority for Maori people today. The ideology of the One New Zealand Foundation is outdated, totally unacceptable and runs against the thrust of modern development. Assimilation in our country has been forced upon the Maori by military action, by confiscations, by persecuting charismatic leaders who rose out of the chaos, by legislation, and by many other devious means. We have had over 100 years of it and it is a thoroughly discredited, self-serving and dishonest policy. Yet it was still being imposed upon us up to the 1996 election.

What I am leading towards is to signal that a number of important changes have occurred, and these are the realities of today. These have a bearing on where the philanthropic dollar might be directed.

The majority of Maori people support moves towards self-determination and tino rangatiratanga. Maori people want help in order to help themselves. They want to do their own research, write their own reports, set their own goals and achieve their own outcomes.

Iwi identity has re-emerged as a powerful force. While the government might want to support Maori enterprises that are non-iwi-specific, the majority of Maori want to work within and for their iwi. The tribal unit has always been a dynamic, descent-based group and will remain a meaningful unit for a long time.

The Treaty of Waitangi is here to stay. It is becoming increasingly a factor in legislation, something to be remembered, to be considered before decisions are made. Many treaty-related grievances are actually being addressed today and many others have been registered. Waitangi Tribunal claims are generating a wide range of research activity, much of it being done by enthusiastic Maori researchers. Whatever might be said about the claims, Maori activity in researching their own histories and traditions, and rediscovering that knowledge base, must be seen as educationally, philosophically and morally good. But this positive trend is being discouraged by lack of research funds and by the mean attitude of Cabinet Ministers that Maori should fund themselves to research their grievances. The Crown would provide funds only if iwi agree to enter into direct negotiations.

Undoubtedly there is an important role for philanthropic societies to play. Maori people are moving in directions of their choosing and for causes they want to espouse. Proposals that are assimilationist in philosophy and intent flow against the general trends in Maori thinking, and in my opinion should not be funded. Also, programmes run on behalf of Maori people by well-meaning advocates have become less popular. The trend is definitely towards Maori people doing things for themselves.

Finally, the Treaty of Waitangi remains a meaningful document which links people together in a caring relationship where good will towards the other treaty partner is a guiding principle. The same spirit is required in providing funding for initiatives that Maori people want to pursue and for reasons which address their concerns.

Sovereignty

13. A Pathway to the Future
He Ara Ki Te Ao Marama

This article first appeared in 1979 in He Matapuna: A Source—Some Maori Perspectives, *published by the New Zealand Planning Council (which no longer exists). The article was first written for the Maori section of the Labour Party, which had a meeting at Whakarewarewa in about 1977. The article as presented here was toned down by the Planning Council, which found some of my views too 'controversial'. Certainly some members of the Labour Party were shocked.*

At the time, any talk about Maori sovereignty was held to be the height of radicalism. In fact, it bordered on treason to the Pakeha state. Our former Governor-General, Paul Reeves, writing in the same publication (p.13), made this comment about my article:

> He, too, is conscious of a Pakeha veto over Maori affairs and he offers some alternatives. Full autonomy for Maoris is rejected as unrealistic. Instead he offers a model of 'two people one nation'. I am challenged by the logic and clarity of the argument. It forces me to look at my identity, the aspirations of my family and the choices I might be required to make. That article has made me sweat.[1]

Donna Awatere followed with her thoughtful contribution to the discussions on the issues of sovereignty, or tino rangatiratanga, or self-determination, which some people have now trivialised to 'self-management'. This last word is an attempt by some conservative Pakeha to remove ideas of constitutional arrangements and rights from discussion. After all, merely managing our own affairs is harmless. It is no different from Federated Farmers managing their affairs.

But there are constitutional issues which need to be addressed. Putting them off for yet another decade will not do. The sort of democracy practised in our country marginalises us and puts us into the category of a powerless indigenous group that is always reacting to what other people do to us. We need to keep up with our cousins, the Hawaiians, who are considering the issues of sovereignty seriously and are openly engaged in discussions about the issue.

When you read what I had to say about sovereignty in 1979 you will accuse me of being too soft in the head, too timid and too limited in my thinking. We have moved forward some distance since then and yet, for some people, talk of self-government for Maori is seen to be threatening, unreal and disloyal to the Pakeha. The question is: why should we be loyal to the Pakeha who have done so much damage to our culture? Loyal to the country, yes. This is our land.

According to myth, the old sun, Tama-nui-te-ra, traversed the sky in too big a hurry and he gave out more energy than mankind needed or appreciated. So Maui-tikitiki-a-Taranga, the planner supreme of Polynesian mythology, held a one-man meeting and decided on a plan by which order could be brought into the lives of long-suffering mortals. His plan required imagination, cunning and drastic action which, like other revolutionaries, he felt was entirely justified because of the benefits it brought to mankind. Out of the pain suffered by Tama-nui-te-ra was born a world of order and certainty, or so the myth would have us believe.

Today, as our ancestor looks down at us, he must shake his head in disbelief. Now it is mankind that is throwing confusion into the world. Man is using up the resources of the earth at too fast a rate. He is building a technology of war which is becoming too hot to handle, and a micro processing technology which is making man redundant. Now it is possible to visualise the total destruction of human civilisation. In addition, mankind is in a financial turmoil with the prospect now of a country such as ours becoming bankrupt. Order has been lost and there is little that is certain. It is time for Maui to come again into the world and bring a plan that would give us a new sense of direction.

Most commentators on the state of New Zealand would agree that our society is reeling under the impact of economic and social forces which occupy most of our thinking today. The actions of our politicians clearly indicate a deep concern, a frustration at their inability to improve conditions for the people, an impatience with those who dare to differ with them. Theirs is a frantic search for scapegoats, on the one hand, and for recipes for improvement, on the other. But the experts speak without confidence and their recipes, made to conform with the interests of the cooks, fail. What the people see and feel are continually rising prices, higher and higher costs for energy, more people unemployed and a downward turn in the standard of living. The social costs are also increasing, as manifest in broken homes, a high divorce rate, increasing crime and more violence in our society.

In such conditions, the Maori people are probably worse off economically, socially, politically and morally than the Pakeha of New Zealand. The fact that ours is a youthful population, bubbling with undirected energy, probably exacerbates the problem. We were not prepared to meet an emergency such as this. Moreover, no one thought that we would need to some day. Now that the unplanned moment has arrived, we are not in a strong position even to defend ourselves against competition for employment or for finance. Our failure as a nation to face up honestly to the problems of Maori–Pakeha relations is catching up on us. Their effects show up in sharp relief and sometimes almost as a caricature of our condition today. The behaviour of Maori gangs probably best exemplifies this.

As a direct reflection of the fact that the Maori population is now predominantly urban, the so-called 'Maori problem' is mainly an urban one. It is in the streets and alleys of the cities where the youth of Maoridom struggle to find a new order in the best way they can. They comprise probably the only section of the Maori population which is making an honest and full-scale attempt to come to terms with the realities and the contradictions of the times in which we live.

A good number of our urban Maori youth reject the ideals of New Zealand society; nor do they accept what Maori society stands for today. Among them are people who are unable to tolerate what they see as the glibness and shallowness of our cultural institutions. There is, of course, a dysfunction between the practices of our institutions and the present conditions of life in New Zealand. The gangs seem to be at the very frontiers of changing circumstances They react to changes of which the majority of the population is hardly aware. Yet we call the members of these groups drop-outs, social misfits, the dregs of society, yesterday's mistakes.

The urban Maori gangs actually deserve close study, because the human values on which they place great emphasis are often values which are lacking or in attenuated form in their home communities. Initiative, imagination and a disciplined way of life are examples. In the very act of manifesting these values, the youth groups point out some of the glaring faults in our society. There seems to be little room in New Zealand for the exercise of real Maori initiatives, let alone Pakeha ones. Every move runs up against unforeseeable barriers—for example, various acts of Parliament—whose main effects are to stifle all New Zealanders and annoy Maori in particular.

The great value placed on internal law and order alerts us to the fact that these conditions are sadly lacking in some Maori communities, which in many cases, appear to have been thoroughly subverted by the western notion of the sanctity of the individual. The chief, that grand figure from our romantic past, who is capable of exercising influence and power upon the community, has become almost extinct. Instead, the land is full of pretending chiefs of little or no influence, bent on personal aggrandisement. Every man wants to be his own chief and his own spokesman and to be simultaneously Maori and Pakeha. The result is the leaderless drifting community from which many of the gang members have come.

It is perhaps ironic that the adult members of the community seem hardly aware that such ideas as Maori aroha and aroha ki te tangata (love to all men) hardly exist in the rough and tumble of life. These are notions which are spoken about in ritual contexts and which are often regarded quite seriously in ceremonial life. But in real life the words have a hollow sound and we are found wanting.

A sad fact of life is that the foundations of Maoritanga are slipping away before our eyes. Consider the plight of the Maori language, which, according to the researches of Richard Benton (1978, 1979), is in danger of being lost as a living spoken language. Already, the results of the decline in the use of the language can be seen at various marae around the country and heard at numerous urban hui. Yet, though evidence of the problem is plain, the people seem not to know how to cope with it and appear not to care.

All of the problems which we are facing today and which are certainly not new to Maori society are making life very difficult. However, whereas Maori society over the years withstood with amazing resilience wave after wave of social and economic change, today the Maori part of Maori society is at its weakest and we can no longer leave to chance decisions which are vitally important to us in the next few decades. We need a Maui-like plan to help guide us into the twenty-first century, and we need to begin the search for such a plan now. It would be unrealistic merely to wait and hope that something from heaven will drop into our laps.

As a beginning, I will attempt to set out the requirements of a desirable plan—that is, one which takes cognisance of Maori aspirations and which best allows the people to live a life that is satisfying and dignified. The 'shopping list' described here is a first effort at trying to articulate Maori aspirations as manifested in the words, both written and spoken, of various Maori spokespersons. Not everyone will be satisfied with the list or agree with each item on it. But it is useful to say what people want and then try to find the political arrangement or idea which can best accommodate their goals.

A desirable plan is one which, with economy of effort and finance, makes it possible for the Maori people to:
1. retain and develop Maoritanga in order to maintain a continuity with the past and provide a foundation for life in the twenty-first century
2. establish Maori as an official language of New Zealand and use it more widely in contexts other than the marae
3. develop an education programme where Maori is the medium of instruction and with the possibility of development from primary to tertiary levels
4. have control over a bilingual television channel, a bilingual national radio network, and some newspapers and magazines where Maori is the dominant language

5. develop a banking system, perhaps based in the office of the Maori Trustee, and obtain finance (from overseas if necessary) to help Maori individuals or groups establish business enterprises
6. exercise a greater degree of control over decisions and enterprises which affect the lives of the Maori minority
7. establish a modern leadership system which is based partly on achieved and partly on ascribed status and which is founded upon Herbert Spencer's dictum that 'Society exists for the benefit of its members, not the members for the benefit of society'
8. have control over some units of the police force and of the armed services
9. prevent the export of 'Maori foods' such as paua, pipi, toheroa, karengo, muttonbirds and crayfish
10. allow for the development of a separate court system to handle all cases involving Maori and New Zealand Polynesian offenders
11. return all uneconomic shares in land to hapu ownership and re-establish the mana of the hapu
12. change the status of the Minister of Maori Affairs to that of Chief Minister of Maori Affairs and make this position subject to the Maori vote
13. establish a Maori and Polynesian unit within the Department of Health and so assume greater control over the health of Maori people
14. reorganise Maori participation in national politics by changing the basis of representation to tribal rather than geographic, and increasing the number of seats
15. enjoy, along with all citizens of New Zealand, an ordered and meaningful life, to respect cultural differences among the population, to help protect the heritage of the nation and to pass it on to the next generation; and, if necessary, to play our part in defending that heritage.

It should be observed that certain arrangements to accommodate special Maori interests are already in place in New Zealand. Examples are the Department of Maori Affairs, the Maori Land Court, the Maori Trustee, various Maori advisory committees, the Maori Education Foundation, the four Maori parliamentary seats, the Kingitanga at Waikato, and so on. There was also a fairly efficient Maori school system, which was dismantled only recently and a form of which we might well consider re-establishing.

Among nationwide organisations are the Maori Women's Welfare League, the Maori Wardens' Association, Maori Congress and the New Zealand Maori Council. The Ratana and Ringatu churches are theoretically, also nationwide in their coverage but their actual strength may be limited to fairly well-known districts. A new national organisation established only in 1978 is the Bishopric of Aotearoa with the Bishop of Aotearoa at its head, and a council made up of representatives from around New Zealand as the main administrative and decision-making body.

Another new arrangement worth looking at is the Maori and Pacific Island Radio Unit, established at Papatoetoe. In this arrangement, as with the Bishopric of Aotearoa, a parallel Maori structure is established within a larger New Zealand structure. What is interesting in both cases is that a major battle had to be won for their acceptance. But, once this was accomplished, there was little further difficulty in making the organisations work: only the usual difficulties of quality of mind, vision, dedication to the task, and adequate finance.

An interesting question is why these parallel structures are being requested by the people, now and in the past. I believe the most frequently quoted reason is the desire to have greater control and participation in decision-making which concerns the Maori. Another expression of the same concern is the initiative which underlies the Tu Tangata programme launched by the Department of Maori Affairs. Yet another concern has to do with the quality of presentation of Maori events: proper reporting, respect for Maori customs and institutions, and 'proper' behaviour on the marae. Underlying the façade of goodwill towards the Pakeha is a dissatisfaction and resentment against a sort of imprisonment of Maoritanga within the institutions of New Zealand.

A question which we should ask quite broadly is: what are the alternatives before us? For many New Zealanders, this is a dangerous question which was not asked seriously before, because to deal with it honestly is to invite the ire of an indignant population. There is likely to be talk of treason and urgent pleas of 'please do not rock the canoe'. Some will declare that we have the best race relations in the world; why, then, should we change anything? Yet, we must consider the matter and try to find a solution which will help us survive as a cultural entity into the next century and beyond. In saying this, you need to note that I am now thinking particularly of the survival of Maoritanga.

One obvious alternative is to opt for more of the same—that is, more of the one-people, one-nation concept which the Pakeha New Zealanders have pursued with single-minded purpose since Governor Hobson enunciated it in 1840. The policy worked out over 139 years, and with a determination hard to match, has been so 'successful' that today we contemplate the possibility of the Maori language becoming extinct, of there being no such thing as Maori culture or Maori art, and of the startling fact that choosing to be a Maori or not has become a matter of individual conscience. Yes, the shot-gun wedding demanded of us by the Pakeha people has been much too effective in alienating us from our own culture.

One can argue, however, that, despite all the shortcomings of the policy of assimilation or integration, many good things were accomplished, such as the fact that, generally speaking, Maori and Pakeha have lived together in relative harmony. For a while, the thing seemed to work, even though it was largely based on a myth. Under the present system, we were able to establish the Bishopric of Aotearoa and this, as well as the example of the radio unit, demonstrates that we can achieve a greater degree of self-government than would appear possible at first glance.

But there are many things wrong with the present arrangement. The biggest single fault is that the Maori people find it difficult to initiate any important moves without the prior approval of the Pakeha voters. It is an unfair and undemocratic burden upon the Maori and puts us in the position of having to persuade the voters of the dominant society first before any initiative can be launched. This is so frustrating. What this arrangement does is keep real power firmly in the hands of the Pakeha majority. There seems little doubt of this when looked at from a Maori point of view. For example, during the moments of great stress and anxiety associated with Bastion Point, we seemed unable to get our point of view published in the newspapers, heard on radio or shown on television: the mass media were very firmly controlled by the Pakeha. More recently, the case for making Maori an official language seems to be foundering on the issue of whether Maori parents can force Pakeha children to become bilingual—that is, it is a matter of who has power.

Bastion Point also demonstrated clearly our lack of political power and our vulnerability in the face of a determined, unscrupulous and no-aroha government. Of course, it showed up other things, such as the fragmented and still suspicious attitudes we have to other tribes. It revealed the readiness of some of our people to betray any cause that might be seen as Maori; this, in turn, pointed to the embarrassing weakness of wanting to ingratiate ourselves with the Pakeha. We are so hungry for praise and so scared of displeasing the Pakeha that we appear to be a little too willing to turn a blind eye to what is happening to our own people or to our culture. We have been rather too eager to take a hand in our own destruction as an ethnic group, and too ready when political pressure is applied to denounce our own people. This sort of Iscariot-like behaviour must cease if we are to make any real changes to our present condition.

Recent evidence indicates that the leaders of New Zealand are more ready now than ever before in our history to allow to the Maori people more say both in the decisions which affect them and in the manner of putting these decisions into effect. The reorganisation of the Department of Maori Affairs, and the various programmes it has put into operation since 1978, provide evidence of this. There is hope in the present political arrangement. For many of our people, however, the openness of the system has come rather too late. Faith in the system has already been lost, and the most telling evidence of the loss is the apathy of the Maori people, the absence of the happy sparkle in the eye.

A Maui would reject this alternative as lacking in imagination, too frustrating, too cumbersome to accommodate readily to Maori aspirations, and too slow to remedy the ills which face us now. It is worth pointing out, however, that many of our present leaders are not at all like Maui and would prefer more of the same. This is an easy way out for them, a way of avoiding unpleasant decisions, a way of not becoming responsible for our future. I should also point out that many Pakeha elders would applaud them for that attitude and offer them a Queen's honour badge.

A second alternative is to opt for full autonomy, following the example of Samoa, Tonga and the Cook Islands. With this plan we envisage being given the machinery required for self-government, so that we would have our own chief minister, our own parliament, court system, police and army. We would then be able to have most of the items mentioned in the shopping list of Maori aspirations and, even more, our political status would change from being a member of the Fourth World to that of the Third World. We would then be equal with the Tongans. In many ways, being equal to other Polynesian nations is far more important and significant than being equal to the Pakeha. But the importance of this fact has not yet entered the awareness of most Maori leaders.

At this point in the essay, a thousand people are ready to shout that there are major problems with this wonderful idea. On one side is the fact that our Pakeha voters who believe strongly in the one-people, one-nation policy, understanding of course what that really means in practice, will have none of it. Even the most persuasive oratory we can muster will do nothing to change anything. On the other hand is the ambiguous position of the Maori. Despite all that has happened since 1840, a lot of Maori people would not agree to driving the Pakeha out to sea, nor to creating a state without them. To a very large extent, our lives have become enmeshed, and our kinship system and our social, economic, political and religious networks criss-cross one another and overlap at many points. It is perhaps ironic that the Maori is more enmeshed in the Pakeha world than the other way round—the Pakeha can get by without us but we have become a dependent child unable to contemplate a future without the Pakeha. This, it is sad to reflect, is an expected result of the colonial experience.

One cannot see full autonomy being granted to us by the New Zealand Pakeha without a battle. Personally, I cannot see the North Island being partitioned so that we can have, say, the Auckland, Waikato, Bay of Plenty or East Coast–Poverty Bay regions as our territory, there to establish a Maori province. Nor do I see the Maori people being ready for a confrontation of the type necessary to make partition of the land an attractive solution. The action called for is too drastic at this time and too much like Maui's final exploit when he sought immortality for man. Notwithstanding the difficulties, there are nonetheless many Maori people who are attracted to this solution.

A third plan is a modification of the notion of full autonomy towards the idea of two people, one nation—an idea Hohepa (1978) discussed in detail. A name for it is 'limited autonomy', and it implies settling for an arrangement which is less than full self-government but which might be just as effective, or even better, given the economic difficulties facing the world today. Under this plan we capitalise on what is already happening in New Zealand as we explore the possibilities of a suitable accommodation with the Pakeha population.

There are two kinds of limited autonomy, the 'soft' and the 'hard'. The soft version seeks to introduce the notion with as little change as possible and relies on a great deal of infiltration of the present structures and organisations with the 'right' personnel. In this case, the aim would be to Maorify the institutions of New Zealand and set up Maori and Pacific Island units within them. The soft limited autonomists would argue that in the end you achieve what you want and you do so with little disruption to the system. The trouble with it is that we might never get to eat the carrot, and it takes too long to find out.

The hard version calls for more drastic reorganisation and demands some real changes. It could incorporate some of the additional goals linked above with full autonomy; for example, the creation of a new position, Chief Minister of Maori Affairs, and the setting up of a council with the functions of a parliament. This would be made up of representatives from the main tribes of New Zealand, and could include representatives from other Polynesians who have settled here. The Department of Maori Affairs might be reorganised into providing all public sector services. As part of the package, a hard limited autonomist will ask for a parallel court structure to deal with Maori and Polynesian offending, and a parallel police force to enforce the law—indeed, all of the goals listed in this essay could now become part of the package.

The United Nations and its various agencies and committees, such as UNESCO and the Decolonisation Committee, clearly recognise that ethnic groups such as the Maori have a right to determine their own future. They have a clear right, and indeed an obligation on behalf of the communities of the world, to maintain and develop cultural institutions consonant with their values and wishes. The Maori people have so far not exercised their rights, and have, in fact, fallen behind other ethnic groups such as the Eskimos and the North American Indians in reasserting and developing their culture. We have been Pakeha-watching for so long, and so busy defending our culture in one crisis after another, that we no longer know how to grasp the initiative. As a people, we are even scared to do so: defence has become a way of life.

Now we must rise from our despondency and lethargy and take the initiative by demanding limited autonomy for our people. I believe that we must commit ourselves to this ideal in a way that leaves no doubts as to our desire to grasp our destiny. I have said publicly that the sort of commitment we need is that of the religious convert who is prepared to suffer and even die for the faith. The task before us is to develop that sort of commitment as quickly as possible for, without it, we will never be able to achieve the goal of a fully functioning Maori parliament by the year 2000.

Our priorities are first to gain acceptance of the notion that we want autonomy or mana motuhake for our people. Then we need to define more precisely what we mean by the notion of two people, one nation which is implied in the notion of limited autonomy. Finally, there is the task of filling in the details and giving form to the idea so that we can actually live and experience limited autonomy. These are important tasks which have barely begun and which deserve our serious attention during the next few years.

Underlying the quest for a pathway to the future (he ara ki te ao marama) is the belief that to go on with what we are doing now is not really satisfactory from a Maori point of view. The responsibility for the future of Maoritanga and Maori culture is really ours, and has always been so. Our history and our very existence and identity as a people are bonded in Maoritanga. The fact that the Pakeha population sees its identity as being closely linked to Maoritanga as well should not side-track us. Nor should we wait any longer for the dominant population to sort out its problems.

In the end, because it involves our destiny and future in a world that is full of uncertainties, we are the people who must make the decision about whether we want limited autonomy or not. It is our decision and not that of the Pakeha population. It is a decision which is important to us and to the world community. We are not in a position to negotiate with others in New Zealand until we have made up our own minds—without the interference, but rather with the co-operation of the mass media, and with the understanding of the Pakeha population. This is the ultimate test of just how good we are as a nation and of whether our reputation for good race relations was deserved or not.

Many of our leaders longed for this day—for example, King Tawhiao, Te Ua Haumene, Te Whiti, Tohu, Te Kooti, Rua Kenana, Aperehama Taonui, and Te Heuheu Iwikau. This was a pathway on which they longed to tread but could not reach. Today it is possible to walk that path to the world of light that our ancestors dreamt of. It is up to us who walk on the breast of Papatuanuku to carry this cause through to its realisation. My hope is that by the year 2000 we will be at long last much nearer to the goal of being equal in a political sense to the Pakeha New Zealanders and that we will live together as two peoples but one nation.

> Tuia te kawe;
> Tairanga te kawe
> Ko te kawe o te haere!

> Make the shoulder pack,
> Take up the shoulder pack,
> And let us go!

References

Benton, Richard, 1978. 'An English–Maori Bilingual Education Programme in Selected Hawkes Bay Schools.' Background information on a research and development project prepared for NZCER.

Benton, Richard, 1979. 'Who Speaks Maori in New Zealand?' Paper prepared for the symposium 'New Zealand's Language Future', 49th ANZAAS Congress, Auckland, January 1979.

Hohepa, Pat, 1978. 'Maori and Pakeha: The One-People Myth', in *Tihe Mauri Ora*, edited by Michael King. Auckland, Methuen, pp.98–111.

Footnote

1. Reeves, Paul, 1979. 'Te Kupu Tuatahi: The First Word', in *He Matapuna*, p.13.

14. The Rebirth of a Dream

Maori are moving slowly but surely to greater political independence. This article argues that the exciting dream of the Maori need not be the threatening nightmare of the Pakeha. Published in the Evening Post, *12 June 1980.*

Last Saturday's Northern Maori by-election focuses attention once more on the Maori rolls. Discussions have been about tidying and cleansing, which is a peculiar term to apply to the Maori rolls. Inevitably the result of re-examination and 'cleansing' is to reduce the number of electors who are choosing to remain on the Maori roll. Hence there are 16,000 names on the Northern Maori roll—a reduction of 6000.

We ought to be quite clear in our minds that the law encourages defections from the roll. The great carrot held out to the Maori electors is the chance to become something larger and better than being a Maori—an honorary Pakeha, perhaps, or even a New Zealander. The long-term result is one which I am certain the legislators planned for. Through the exercise of their own free will, the Maori people will deny their own culture and give to the Pakeha the excuse they have wished for these many years, a chance to get rid of the four Maori seats. So strong is this wish that most Pakeha people fail to see that they are trying to make us disappear under the carpet.

The assumptions underlying the present law regarding the Maori roll are highly questionable, and most of them rest on that ancient Pakeha myth that the Maori people and their culture represent a sort of temporary disease. With time and suitable Pakeha medicine, they will pass away and never be seen again. Then the rolls will be clean, as will the nation, which will be transformed into a Pakeha utopia.

The myth is well entrenched. Examples of its falsity, as in the cases of the Welsh, the Irish and the Ainu of Japan, do little to change it. It ought to be clear that we will not disappear by genetic or cultural conquest and that we are here to stay. What we did in the past was to go underground and to hibernate until the moment was right to re-emerge. Others have done this, for example, the Ainu of Japan.

People around the country sense that the greywarbler (riroriro) has called and that the moment has come for the sleeping giant to arise. So it is time to question what is happening to the Maori roll, as well as many other matters concerning our future.

Why should our people be given a choice as to whether they will be counted as Maori or become Pakeha and be registered on the European roll? Surely this is a subversive measure which isn't even subtle. The principle our people should adopt is simple: born a Maori, die a Maori. Why spend a lifetime trying to be something you're not? The obvious message is to be true to yourself and your culture.

Our lives are complicated unnecessarily by the offer of a choice which is not given to anyone else. In my view the choice is a false one. There is no choice. Maori voters who are not already on the Maori roll should, in my view, get back to where they belong, and stay there. An opportunity to do this is being given for the next general election, and it should be seized.

Supposing, however, that critics will argue strongly for the choice. Then, to be logical, all Islanders should be invited to choose whether they will be on the Maori or the European roll. In fact, I am totally in favour of changing the law to allow all Polynesians this choice. There are lots of good reasons why we should oppose the use of divide-and-rule tactics to prevent the Polynesian people coming together as a political force in this country. It is timely to think seriously about an alliance.

For the sake of making a point, you can argue that Pakeha voters should be accorded the same privilege. Many Europeans who are deeply involved in Maori activities could very well welcome the opportunity to become involved in Maori politics. Changes to the law which will permit a similar choice to everyone might help many of our own people put a proper value on being a Maori.

One of the problems we face is how to create such a demand and an interest in Maoritanga that the defections to the European roll will cease and our people will come back again. There seems little doubt that Mr Matiu Rata's stand and the Mana Motuhake movement constitute the most important infusion of interest into Maori politics that we have witnessed for a long time. Despite losing, Mr Rata has begun something which will continue to excite the imagination for years to come. It is the prospect of governing ourselves, of becoming responsible once again for own destiny, of Maori values being able to survive and be useful to us, that is causing such interest. The chance to be equal and free in a real sense, the substance not the shadow, captivates the mind. An old familiar dream, given up as impossible to achieve, is now being dreamt again. There is hope ahead for the Maori people.

We are moving slowly and surely towards a greater degree of political independence for the Maori. This is one of the main themes in the Mana Motuhake movement. The pity of it is that the exciting dream of the Maori is seen as a threatening nightmare by the Pakeha. It surely need not be. What is happening is that relations between Maori and Pakeha, the most important for our nation, are changing, and we are about to enter a more mature phase. This phase is characterised by a greater degree of equality (we are not swept under the rug again), more honesty, sharing and working together than we have seen before.

To achieve this hallowed state of affairs we have to give up the fiction that a Maori can choose to be a Maori or Pakeha. On the other side, the Pakeha must give up the fiction that we are a temporary phenomenon. We might have to adopt other myths and other catchphrases, such as 'What is good for the Maori is good for New Zealand', 'Maori is beautiful'. Catchphrases have their place in raising morale.

There are many urgent matters which we need to negotiate and discuss. In examining the bases on which electors join the electoral roll for Maori voters is one such concern. This requires that we look at how best to meet the needs of the Maori in a democratic society such as ours is supposed to be. One need only look at how a Minister of Maori Affairs is elected for most of the time this century to realise that all is not well. I personally cannot accept as democratic a system which allows a candidate chosen by Pakeha voters to minister to the needs of the Maori people and do the job badly. Such a person is not answerable to the Maori vote and cannot therefore be a man of the people. This is not a personal criticism of the present minister. Rather I am against the system which permits this curious undemocratic practice to continue.

I believe that the changes occurring now are to be welcomed by the Pakeha and not feared. We must grow in our relationship and we must accept that our cultural differences are a positive asset to the nation (witness the tourist industry) and not a liability. Maori have become more vocal and able to articulate their own needs and aspirations. The era of the silent and docile Maori is gone forever.

15. Maori Representation

This submission to the Royal Commission on the Electoral System in 1992 was written before MMP was introduced and the first-past-the-post system put aside in 1996. A record number of Maori members of Parliament were chosen, some by winning a seat in open competition on election day and others by being on a party list. There are now fifteen Maori members in Parliament. Five of them consist of the five Maori seats, up one from the previous election. It took some 128 years for the Maori seats to be increased by one.

The MMP system of government does not lend itself to increasing the number of Maori seats from five. Instead, mainstreaming is relied upon to deliver positions for Maori men and women to become members of Parliament.

For the first time in years, the Maori voters swung away from Labour and supported instead New Zealand First, led by Winston Peters, who contested the Tauranga electorate and won. The election process has become more interesting for Maori. However, the present system, exciting though it may be, still does not address the questions in the following submission.

Preamble

In 1835 the chiefs of the north issued a declaration of independence and asked Britain to help maintain the integrity of Maori rangatiratanga or mana Maori in New Zealand. That declaration was called He Wakaputanga o te Rangatiratanga o Nu Tirene and the intention of the chiefs was clearly that they and they alone should have the power to pass laws in this country. The opening statement of Article 2 of the declaration reads: 'All sovereign power and authority within the territories of the United Tribes of New Zealand is hereby declared to reside entirely and exclusively in the hereditary chiefs and heads of tribes' (Orange 1987, p.256).

Only a few years later, Governor Hobson appeared with a different treaty that he wanted to negotiate with the sovereign chiefs of New Zealand. This treaty was clearly aimed at obtaining from the Maori people their consent to the imposition of British rule. Thus, in Article 1 of the 1840 Treaty of Waitangi, the chiefs were asked to give over to Britain something which the chiefs did not have and could not really understand, namely the governorship (kawanatanga) or government of the land as perceived in a European constitutional sense. The preamble to the Maori text of the treaty refers to a person sent by the Queen to treat with the Aborigines of New Zealand to 'kia wakaaetia e nga Rangatira Maori te Kawanatanga o te Kuini ki nga wahi katoa o te wenua . . .'—'persuade the Maori chiefs to agree to the government (or governorship) of the Queen to all parts of the land'. The official translation puts it this way: 'to treat with the Aborigines of New Zealand for the recognition of Her Majesty's sovereign authority over the whole or any part of those islands' (Orange 1987, pp.257–8).

In Article 2, however, something akin to home rule was guaranteed in exchange for the right given up in the first article. This was called tino rangatiratanga, which implied that the mana of a ruling chief over his people was to be maintained. Also implicit in the notion is that chieftainship would be exercised in a Maori way according to the rules of Maori society. Home rule was to be exercised over land, their villages and homes and all of their treasures and their heritage (o ratou whenua o ratou kainga me o ratou taonga katoa). For the Maori chiefs, this article clearly implied partnership in government and was probably the main reason they agreed to sign the treaty.

But there is also a clear reference in the preamble when it says, '. . . kia tohungia ki a ratou o ratou rangatiratanga me to ratou wenua . . .' A literal translation indicates that the Queen was anxious 'to preserve to them their chieftainship and their land' (my tanslation). Thus there is a question of what the chiefs were asked to give up.

Article 3 guaranteed to the Maori people the same rights and privileges as British subjects. Such rights would, of course, include the right to govern, which the settlers thought that they alone had as the natural heirs of the British Crown. Also implied is the right of the Maori people to use the law in the same way as all other British subjects did, namely to protect their property and their persons. Just as parliamentary power could be used by British subjects to safeguard their culture and language, so could the Maori people do the same. These rights, however, were not seen or recognised by the dominant settler population. Indeed, the present population has difficulties in recognising the integrity of Maori society.

At the Kohimarama hui in 1864, Paora Tuhaere of Ngati Whatua thought that the Treaty of Waitangi was supposed to have established a partnership of Maori and Pakeha in the government of the land, and he was bitter about the non-fulfilment of Maori expectations. As is already well known, the settlers had very effectively cheated the Maori people of any chance of self-government or of shared government in their implementation of the 1852 constitutional act. They excluded the Maori from having any real power and in fact took over responsibility for Native Affairs themselves in November 1863; this act effectively put the Maori people under the power of the Pakeha from that time right up until the present. The four Maori seats established in October 1867 were an afterthought and evidence of some conscience among the white population of New Zealand.

Over time, the number of general seats has increased while the Maori seats have remained static—and only just, because some determined efforts have been made to undermine them, including the provision made for Maori voters to leave the Maori roll and defect to a general seat. Over the last twenty years, strong Pakeha pressure has been mounted to create doubt in the minds of Maori voters regarding the legitimacy of Maori seats. Pakeha attitudes have created doubt about the wisdom of Maori people retaining the small measure of political power they possess.

Discussions about increasing the number of Maori seats have been limited by the overpowering and very self-serving interests of the power culture, namely those of the Pakeha people. The fact that some 140,000 Maori voters are on the general roll and only 77,564 on the Maori roll is taken as evidence of the lack of Maori interest in Maori politics, rather than as evidence of successful Pakeha interference in the political process.* Furthermore, we are continually limited by the arithmetic designed by Pakeha voters for the nation's electorates.

Obviously, there are some crucial questions to ask. The following are suggested.

1. *How can the Maori people, the indigenous population of New Zealand, be given a greater share in the government of their own land, and hence be given a measure of real power?*

This question is based on the assumption of sharing mentioned earlier and on the right of the Maori people to govern themselves. It is certainly reasonable to consider that, if they are not given power, they will rightly demand it in future and maybe fight for it.

2. *How can the political process be made more effective and exciting for the Maori people?*

At the moment, the Maori people have no real power, and this is true whether they vote on the Maori roll or the general roll. A good reason for the defections from the Maori roll is that there is no power, no excitement and no real contest among the political parties for the Maori seats. This is due mostly, if not wholly, to the ridiculously low number of Maori seats and the failure of successive governments to increase their number. Thus, the act of voting is a sham and is a show of justice for publicity purposes only. Maori voters have recognised the essential play-acting which they are asked to do on voting day. [MMP has now changed all of this.]

* The questions traditionally asked by Pakeha legislators have been the wrong ones.

3. *How can the political process be integrated into Maori social, economic and political interests?*

This question relates to the fact that the political process can be made much more relevant by linking it wherever possible to tribal interests. Moreover, it is possible for the system of national politics to make up and repair some of the considerable damage done over the last century to tribal organisations and to the culture itself. It has had a fair beating at the hands of the Pakeha and their parliamentary system.

With these questions in mind, it is plain that a major overhaul is necessary. Tinkering with the system will not do. Rather, some radical change is required in order to give to the Maori people the sort of political status in our own country which does not demean us in the eyes of fellow Polynesians—the Cook Islanders, Samoans, Tokelauans and Tongans—and which removes the stigma of being second-class citizens from us.

Treating everyone the same or regarding everyone as equal is not acceptable as a solution. That sort of policy has resulted in the 'domestication of Maori culture', the assimilation of it by the dominant culture, and its control and manipulation particularly by politicians of the major parties to a degree that is objectionable. The integrity of Maori culture and its institutions must be protected. Thus, it is most important that we find a way of sharing power in a manner which accomplishes this end. Maori people are here to stay as a distinctive ethnic identity and as the indigenous group in New Zealand. They are the tangata whenua, the people of the land. They and their culture are the basis of our national identity in the modern world.

Furthermore, we must be given a way of voting with dignity and with the knowledge that we do have power in Aotearoa. Lastly, it is time for honest dealing in regard to giving Maori people a real say in the government of this land.

The New Net

Ka pū te ruha ka hao te rangatahi.
The old net is cast ashore and a new net will be used.

The old net fixed the number of Maori seats at four in 1867 and for 128 years it remained the same. It increased to five in 1996. The ethnocentric nature of this incredible fact can be emphasised by asking the Pakeha population to consider how they would like having twenty seats in Parliament for 100 years.

It would be useful at this point to consider that 100 seats will be accepted as ideal for New Zealand for the next few decades. Alternatives for the future can then be listed as follows. Each option will be considered in turn.

Option	General roll	Maori roll
A	100	nil
B	90	10
C	50	50
D	80	20
E	75	25
F	20	80
G	nil	100

A. *The Assimilationist Option*

This is the option favoured by a large proportion of the dominant power group, but it is rejected as being essentially dishonest, self-serving and unjust to the subordinate Maori group. It gives the Pakeha population absolute control over the country and especially over the Maori people.

B. *The Statistical Option*

This option finds favour among those who accept that the Maori constitutes ten percent of the present population. It should be stated, however, that statistics on the Maori population are highly suspicious and tend to understate the real situation. If based on people having some Maori blood, the figure is higher and so entitles us to twelve seats instead of ten. This sort of reasoning is non-productive, tends to favour the dominant group, and does not prepare us adequately for the twenty-first century.

C. *The Idealist Option*

This alternative assumes that the most logical way to express a partnership in power is to allocate power on a 50:50 basis regardless of population figures. The dominant group has so far shown little inclination to give up any of the power they have, and it seems likely that only a war which results in a victory for the Maori side can bring about a 50:50 allocation of power. But, if war has to be the means of access to power, then it would depend on the mood at the time whether seats would be allocated fairly on a 50:50 basis.

D. *The Minimal Partnership Option*

This option allocates the seats on the basis of eighty seats as general and twenty as Maori or tangata whenua seats. The twenty tangata whenua seats should as far as possible be tribally based and have approximately 10,000 Maori voters in each electorate. (There are roughly 220,000 Maori voters at present.) Of all the options presented so far, this is by far the most attractive because it addresses the three questions raised earlier.

First, it goes some way (though not sufficient for some) to meeting the requirement of partnership and sharing, and of giving real power to Maori voters. Twenty votes in Parliament is a huge improvement on four. Second, increasing the number to twenty immediately makes the voting process more exciting and engaging for the Maori voter. It also forces the major political parties to try hard to win a share of these seats, and so their policies will be affected. This alone would produce a positive result in voting. At present the act of voting in a Maori or general seat is essentially a sham and a dishonest show of democracy, hence the apparent apathy of Maori voters.

The third question above, about integrating national politics into Maori culture, is met by defining the twenty seats tribally. How this might be done is indicated in the following list:

1. Taitokerau North
   Te Aupouri/Te Rarawa
   Ngati Hine/Ngati Kahu

2. Ngapuhi
   Ngati Wai

3. Ngati Whatua, Uri-o-hau

4. Akarana

5. Hauraki
   Ngati Tamatera, Ngati Te Ata, Ngati Paoa, Ngati Maru, Ngati Whanaunga

6. Waikato

7. Ngati Maniapoto–Tuwharetoa

8. Te Arawa

9. Tauranga Moana
   Ngai Te Rangi, Ngati Ranginui

10. Tairawhiti
    Te Whanau-a-Apanui, Whakatohea, Te Whanau-a-Te Ehutu, Ngai Tai

11. Mataatua
    Ngati Awa, Tuhoe, Ikawhenua

12. Ngati Porou

13. Turanga-nui (Gisborne)
    Aitanga-a-Mahaki, Rongowhakaata, Ngai Tutekohe, Ngai Tamanuhiri

14. Kahungunu

15. Taranaki
    Ngati Ruanui, Taranaki, Nga Rauru

16. Whanganui
    Ngati Haunui, Ngati Apa
17. Raukawa–Ngati Toa
    Muaupoko
18. Te Ati Awa (north and south)
    (in Taranaki, Wellington, South Island)
19. Te Waipounamu North
    Ngati Koata, Ngati Tama, Ngati Kuia, Ngati Rangitane, Ngati Apa, Chatham Islands
20. Te Waipounamu South
    Kai Tahu, Waitaha, Kati Mamoe.

A committee would be needed to work out the actual definitions and details of each seat.

E. *The Multicultural Option*

This option increases the Maori share of power to twenty-three seats, allocates two seats to the growing Polynesian community in New Zealand, and decreases the number of general seats to seventy-five. It is an attractive option, because it meets the criteria set out for increased Maori participation in national politics while recognising the need to do something for other Polynesian groups. It should be considered carefully. The twenty-three Maori seats can be distributed as shown below:

1. Taitokerau North
2. Ngapuhi
3. Ngati Whatua
4. Akarana North
5. Akarana South
6. Hauraki
7. Waikato
8. Ngati Maniapoto–Tuwharetoa
9. Te Arawa
10. Tauranga Moana
11. Tairawhiti
12. Mataatua
13. Ngati Porou North
14. Ngati Porou South
15. Turanga-nui (Gisborne)
16. Kahungunu North
17. Kahungunu South
18. Taranaki
19. Whanganui
20. Raukawa–Ngati Toa
21. Te Ati Awa (north and south)
22. Te Waipounamu North
23. Te Waipounamu South

F. *The Utu Option*

This proposes a reversal of Option D in recognition of the fact that the dominant group deserves to be punished for their usurpation of power and their enjoyment of its fruits for over 100 years. This option must include a stipulation of no change in the number of Pakeha seats for 100 years.

G. The Maori Assimilationist Option

As the opposite of Option A, this alternative is not practical. It would be considered only if there is a war which is won by the Maori side. But it is fair to add that the proponents of Maori sovereignty advocate this option.

Conclusions

Of the options presented here, two are attractive from a Maori point of view. The first is Option D, the Minimal Partnership Option, which offers some measure of limited autonomy. I discuss the aspect of giving more power to the Maori people later. Here I want to introduce a new principle into Maori politics and discuss the present principle of transfer from a Maori seat to a general seat.

An important principle is that a Maori voter (one who identifies as Maori) must be automatically registered on a Maori roll. Transferring from a Maori seat to a general seat will be made more difficult. Several forms will need to be filled out. One form is intention of transfer from a Maori roll to a general one, in which good reasons must be given for taking this drastic step. Next is to fill in a renunciation form, in which the voter gives up identity as a Maori and the rights of a Maori, including access to Maori grants, monies and so on. This must be signed by a responsible member of the petitioner's hapu or by the chairman of the relevant tribal trust board. Next is the land rights form, in which the petitioner transfers all individual shares in Maori land, Maori land incorporations, etc, to the relevant tribal trust board to hold for a period of five years before finally becoming tribal land. The right to return to a Maori roll and for full restoration of special rights as a Maori must be sought from the Minister of Maori Affairs and will normally be granted with little fuss.

The next important principle, is that a Maori can belong to a Maori seat either by residence or by whakapapa. That is, a person resident in Auckland can elect to belong to the Akarana seat. But if the voter wants to be involved in the politics of his/her own tribe, then the criterion of whakapapa can be used. Thus if the voter is Ngati Porou he/she can register on the Ngati Porou roll.

This is an important principle, because it helps to repair the tribe and maintain its integrity; it enables alienated and urbanised individuals to maintain links with their tribe; it provides a new and sophisticated way of maintaining turangawaewae or of establishing it for individuals who would otherwise have no further part to play in the welfare of the tribe; and it helps to make Maori individuals feel good about being a part of the national political system. The last point is perhaps the most important one.

Limited Autonomy

It would be a great step forward to have twenty members of Parliament who are all working for the welfare of the Maori people. This number would enable the burdens of looking after a minority people to be shared out and more time to be given to considering future plans.

The twenty elected members of Parliament would form the basis of a Runanga Matua o Aotearoa (Great Council of Aotearoa), which would be augmented by an equal number of representatives from tribal organisations such as trust boards. The council would meet at Parliament for a minimum of five days annually to consider matters that are vital to the future of the people. The council will not become a committee of the government but must represent all political parties and include a fair representation of tribal opinion and a fair division between the sexes. It will follow the Maori custom of talking through issues in order to profit from the collective wisdom of the group and to keep the future of our people in view.

Resolutions of the runanga will be tabled annually in Parliament by the Minister of Maori Affairs. Such bills as need to be presented will be introduced in the name of the runanga by the Minister of Maori Affairs. Where the House is clearly divided by cultural issues which it cannot or will not understand, the Minister of Maori Affairs can request of the Speaker that only runanga members of the house vote on such an issue. The House divides and only the Maori members vote on an issue concerning the vital interests of the Maori people.

This principle provides the measure of limited autonomy required to demonstrate to all that the Maori people do have power in their own land.

Runanga Matua

Legislative matters which can be seen to have an effect upon Maoridom or which have something to do with the Treaty of Waitangi or which are referred by various Maori organisations, such as the Maori Women's Welfare League, New Zealand Maori Council, tribal trust boards, Maori Congress, or other tribal authorities, or which can be described as Maori Affairs, shall be brought before the Runanga Matua for debate. Recommendations of the Waitangi Tribunal must be referred to the Runanga Matua for legislative action. As a general principle, all matters which can be seen to involve the welfare of Maoridom, or to influence or threaten its future, qualify for consideration by the Runanga Matua.

Tangata Whenua Autonomy

This section identifies those issues which qualify for a division of Parliament to be called and to be voted on by tangata whenua members only. Selection is based on the following criteria: (a) the vital interests of Maoridom as a society and culture are involved; (b) the matter affects the future of a recognisable segment of Maoridom (e.g. the language); and (c) the issue is a cultural one on which it is possible for the majority culture to outvote Maoridom over many years.

Examples are:

1. matters to do with maintaining, developing and raising the status of the Maori language
2. matters linked to or arising out of the deliberations of the Waitangi Tribunal
3. educational programmes involving participation of Maori educators and aimed specifically at Maori children
4. programmes in social welfare, health, law, employment and finance proposed for the benefit of Maori
5. Maori land grievances
6. immigration policies of the nation
7. aspects of foreign policy
8. Maori representation in Parliament, electorate boundaries, expression of partnership in government according to interpretations of the Treaty of Waitangi.

The Minister of Maori Affairs

In the Runanga Matua system, the role of the Minister of Maori Affairs is critical. This person must as a matter of democratic principle be elected into Parliament by the Maori vote and thus represent a tangata whenua seat. The Minister of Maori Affairs becomes the leader of the Runanga Matua and is, in fact, more like a chief minister of Maoridom. While in office the minister is the senior political spokesperson for Maori society.

Rights of Parliament

This new principle recognises the right of Maori people to make decisions for themselves. Once an issue has been thoroughly discussed by the Runanga Matua, and agreed by them, Parliament cannot be given a right of veto. They have a right to know and discuss, but the issue cannot be debated again as though the runanga debate was of no consequence. Parliament's function is to hear, ask for clarification and so on, and then assist in passing the measure into law. This is when it can be said that a partnership exists and is working.

My preference is that the Minimal Partnership Option become our first priority and we try it out for ten years, after which we have the option of introducing three more tangata whenua seats and then two seats for Polynesians and other minorities in New Zealand. The Multicultural Option logically should follow the Minimal Partnership one.

Postscript

In some ways the MMP system of voting has produced some of the results that I envisaged in my paper. Experience with MMP might be an answer although at this point I remain sceptical.

References

Orange, Claudia, 1987. *The Treaty of Waitangi*. Wellington, Allen and Unwin, Historical Publications Branch, Department of Internal Affairs.

16. Options for Self-Determination
Tino Rangatiratanga

A conference was held in Taumarunui on 30 September 1993 and several indigenous representatives were present. The topic was 'Indigenous Water Rights' and it was organised by the Maori Congress. I was invited to speak on sovereignty issues at the conference and gave the following paper.

On 14 September 1993, Israel and the Palestinians signed a peace accord. The Prime Minster of Israel, Mr Rabin, and the Palestinian leader, Mr Yassar Arafat, met at Washington and shook hands on a historic deal: limited autonomy for the Palestinians. This was a political arrangement that seemed impossible, an accommodation that yesterday appeared to be out of reach, a dream that seemed unachievable.

In December 1979, the New Zealand Planning Council published a book called *He Matapuna: A Source*. Several of us were asked to write about issues of importance at that time. The writers were: Paul Reeves, Kara Puketapu, Robert Mahuta, Rose Pere, Timoti Karetu, Ranginui Walker, Bruce Stewart, Hugh Kawharu, Whatarangi Winiata, Manuhuia Bennett and myself.

We are a generation of writers who, in a matter of fourteen years, have since become preoccupied with other matters. Only Ranginui is still writing and putting forward a Maori point of view; only he is openly criticising the government on a regular basis. Others occasionally do so, such as my colleague, Whatarangi Winiata, and my fellow tribesman, Manu Paul. Former Secretary of Maori Affairs, Dr Tamati Reedy, criticised the government overseas and, in so doing, exercised a fundamental human right: the right to criticise one's government without fear of being shot and buried in an unmarked grave. Dr Tamati Reedy was verbally crucified by members of the government, in a shocking display of racist attitudes, and by one prominent Maori, whose reasoning remains unclear. He was called a traitor, and that is a serious accusation.

Earlier in the year, a group of kaumatua and kuia were commissioned by Te Puni Kokiri, the Ministry of Maori Development, to write a report and booklet on Maori leadership which would assist iwi and the government to think about the issues which affect Maori. When this booklet was published and sent to iwi, we were publicly criticised by two very prominent and 'politically correct' Maori, and the Minster of Maori Affairs. The two Maori leaders heaped scorn on our report and did their best to stop other iwi from benefiting from the ideas in the book. As you all know, the book was banned, and this act marked a low point in race relations, in freedom of speech and in the right of Maori to be informed by their own people without being censored by the government. The previous government did not censor a 1990 report by the same group of elders.

Voices critical of the government and its policies have largely been silenced, and talk of self-determination and tino rangatiratanga has been muted. This is the climate of the present time, in the early 1990s.

My 1979 paper began as an address to the Maori Policy Committee of the Labour Party, who met at Whakarewarewa in 1977. I put before the members an analysis of the situation as I saw it, and the political options that we as a people had to consider. Notions of autonomy and limited autonomy were discussed, and this sort of talk was regarded as 'revolutionary'. One person in particular went to the newspaper so as to distance himself from the discussion, which seemed like treason to him.

What I did was analyse the situation, identify our aspirations and wants as defined by us, and then look at what political arrangements best suited our position. Basic to the approach was the assumption that we must retain our cultural identity as Maori and that our future was our business and our responsibility. No other ethnic group could be trusted with our future and especially with our heritage. History had shown that the various governments and their policies could not be trusted. One has to assume that the Pakeha electorates which put the governments in power condoned the actions of their politicians. Many problems we face today are attributed to decades of deliberate undermining of our culture.

A lot of damage has been done to us as a people over the last few years. Thus there is a great need to reaffirm our Maori identity and our culture. There is a need to ignore the negative press and the rather arrogant discussions that Pakeha racists are having among themselves; it is as though we do not exist.

Today it is important to reaffirm certain indivisible articles of faith. These are:

1. We believe in our culture, our heritage and in our distinctive identity as Maori.
2. We believe in taking whatever steps are necessary to protect the integrity of our society, culture and heritage.
3. We believe that we are the tangata whenua and the indigenous people of Aotearoa.

4. We believe in the Treaty of Waitangi and its promise of tino rangatiratanga in Article 2.

5. We believe in a democracy whereby the government is not only of us and for us but is run by us.

6. We believe that our people should enjoy the fruits of good health, of education, of modern science and technology, and of economic development.

7. We believe in the principles of self-development, self-management and self-determination.

8. We believe in the right to tino rangatiratanga.

The questions asked in the late 1970s were relatively straightforward and sensible. The wonder is that we took so long to take an honest look at our political future and at our constitutional position. Three questions were asked:

1. What did we want?

2. How could we best achieve those wants?

3. What sort of political arrangement would best ensure our future?

The first question elicited a shopping-list of wants, aspirations and dreams that were being discussed at the time, and an assessment is made of progress since.

i. *Retain and develop Maoritanga as a foundation for life in the twenty-first century.*
   We are still committed to Maoritanga.

ii. *Establish Maori as an official language of New Zealand and use it more widely in contexts other than marae.*
   The language has been made an official language of Aotearoa but the majority culture stopped short of equal status with the language of the settlers: English.

iii. *Develop a bilingual education programme from primary to tertiary.*
   The bilingual thrust has been largely discredited, and kura kaupapa Maori is the more popular choice.

iv. *Have control over a bilingual television channel and bilingual national radio network (even I was too timid at the time to ask for a total Maori one).*
   Maori iwi radio stations are now in place and a few of them actually broadcast totally in Maori. They are mostly bilingual.

v. *Have control over some newspapers and magazines.*
   Many iwi newspapers have appeared over the last few years and *Mana* is the only well-produced magazine in place.

vi. *Develop a banking system, perhaps based on the Maori Trustee, and obtain finance from overseas if necessary to help Maori individuals and groups establish business enterprises.*

No progress has been made.

vii. *Exercise a greater degree of control over decisions and enterprises which affect the lives of Maori people.*

There has been some success in this aspiration, but overall a feeling of powerlessness and of being alienated in our own country remains the dominant theme.

viii. *Establish a modern leadership system that is based partly on the traditional and partly on achieved status, i.e. on expertise and experience in the modern world.*

A move was made to help achieve this want in 1992, but as already noted the only book produced so far which addresses the issues was banned.

ix. *Return uneconomic shares in land to hapu ownership.*

The Maori Trustee has made efforts to find the beneficiaries and deliver money owing to them. This happened in the early 1990s.

x. *Re-establish the mana of hapu.*

A great deal was done in the 1980s to lift the mana of hapu.

xi. *Increase the number of Maori seats and change the basis of representation from arbitrary geographical zones to tribal groupings.*

Maori are still largely disadvantaged by the Electoral Act 1993 and by acts before it. The seats remaining frozen by successive governments has undermined both the Maori rolls and the Maori seats, which as electorates are hopeless, largely meaningless and impossible zones. [Note: In 1996 another seat was added to make a total of five.]

xii. *Enjoy an ordered and meaningful life and respect cultural difference in the nation.*

In fourteen years, we have achieved about five out of twelve. On the most important issue on the list—the constitutional issue of better access to the benefits of democracy and a better reflection of the agreement in the Treaty of Waitangi—there has been no progress. What we have are more barriers, such as the difficulty of coming back to the Maori roll, and no real positive moves to strengthen and tidy up the rolls and increase the number of Maori seats. One has to ask: where is the fairness in all of this? Why the denial for 126 years? An increase of one seat in 126 years of Pakeha government is hardly progress.

Only four options of self-determination were put forward in 1979 for us to think about. Here they are:

1. More of the same. One people, one nation—assimilation, or mainstreaming today. The Pakeha are firmly in power and we subdue our identity as tangata whenua and join the Pakeha scrum and hold their hands as we march into the sunset. This was firmly rejected as being too frustrating, too cumbersome, too slow and based too much on an ideology of assimilation and of cultural and constitutional denial.

2. Full autonomy, following the example of Tonga, Samoa and the Cook Islands. We would have full self-government. This was seen as quite a good way of achieving the things we wanted. There would be no gate-keeping Pakeha holding up our development as they have been doing all along. But I could not see how we could achieve independence and self-government with a huge Pakeha population and other ethnic groups in the country. I put this option to the side, not because I thought it was wrong, but rather because it was too difficult to achieve.

3. Limited autonomy—the soft version. Two kinds of limited autonomy were offered, soft and hard. The soft option called for as little change as possible and could be achieved by Maori infiltrating the system and so gradually influencing the decisions made by government. However, the present government has shown us all that the soft version of limited autonomy is unworkable because the Pakeha majority still retains essential control over political and economic matters. It is even noticeable today that a process of 'ethnic cleansing' has been occurring in the job market, where jobs which were carried out by mainly Maori crews have become virtually all white.

4. Limited autonomy—hard version. This version is more like the political deal obtained by the Palestinians. It calls for more radical re-organisation and demands some real changes. Examples are:
   i. setting up a council with the functions of a parliament
   ii. establishing a parallel court system
   iii. having a parallel police force to maintain law and order, but foreign policy and defence would remain the responsibility of the New Zealand Government.

Obviously, kohanga reo, kura kaupapa Maori and whare wananga are examples of limited autonomy, which for most people do not go far enough. The rules of registration, operation and the allocation of funds are still controlled by government agencies.

These were the options put before the people at the end of the 1970s. I opted for limited autonomy and preferred the hard version, which is what the Palestinians have been granted by the Israelis and is supported now by the world community. They won this political accommodation through bloodshed—hundreds of their people died for it. They struggled for many years to achieve it. Do we have to follow their example or is there a more sensible way of reaching an agreement?

We are now in the 1990s and we are joined in the quest for sovereignty by the Hawaiians. They, too, are looking at sovereignty options, which are explored in a book entitled *A Call for Hawaiian Sovereignty* by Michael Kioni Dudley and Keoni Kealoha Agard and published in 1990. They consider the following options, which are interesting:

1. Nation within a nation. This is the Native American Indian model. The tribe is a nation and exercises some of the powers of local government. Applied to our situation, an iwi authority would define itself as a nation and would exercise controls over its people in education, health, law and order, over its tribal territory. The Hawaiian writers rejected this model as being too limited.

2. The Iroquois model of sovereignty (nation within a federation). The Iroquois have their own status in the United Nations, their citizens travel on their own passports and they are recognised as a sovereign nation in their own right. The Hawaiian writers looked at this option as a first step to what they really wanted.

3. Restoration of the Hawaiian nation. This calls for separation from the US and for restoration of the sovereign Hawaiian nation. The proponents argue (p.135) that 'the overthrow of the Hawaiian monarchy was an illegal act of the United States government'. Supporters of this option include doctors, lawyers, professors, corporations, executives, small business people, labourers, farmers and fishermen (p.135). The instrument to accomplish this option is a treaty with the United States Congress.

What does this mean for us here? It needs to be said that, when I proposed limited autonomy in 1979, my ideas were condemned as being too radical and the shopping-list of goals as being unreasonable. Today, with hindsight, the proposals were really timid and most of them turned out to be soft options. A measure that appeared to be straightforward, such as making the Maori language an official language, turned out to be difficult and what emerged was a watered down version of what the people really wanted. Pakeha gate-keepers ensured that Maori was not made equal to English.

The difficult issues, then, remain difficult today. For example, the Maori parliamentary seats remain a difficult issue for Pakeha voters and governments. They fear to let us enjoy life without them being the boss and having control over what we do. Also, I did not canvass all of the possibilities—some ideas did not occur to me at the time.

One of the assumptions we now have to consider is that there is no level playing-field for iwi. We are not all starting from the same position of political awareness. This means that iwi should consider the option that best suits them and their needs. However, no iwi should deliberately spoil the chances of another to achieve a measure of self-determination. There has been a history of pulling one another down, and this practice of 'crab-antics' must stop.

All iwi should be aware that in 1993 the government of New Zealand announced at a United Nations meeting at Geneva that they opposed the right of indigenous people to self-determination. They mean to hold us captive and they want to hold the key. Apparently, the government does not agree to allowing us to enjoy or practise the right of self-determination. That 1993 happened to be the International Year of Indigenous Peoples, and we are meeting to celebrate our survival as the tangata whenua, highlights our dilemma. The government is not about to assist us achieve the degree of self-determination that we seek; it will put many obstacles in our way and it will actively block us.

But what do we really want? My reading of the situation we are in today is that other options or sets of options need to be offered. We have become more sophisticated in what we perceive and accept as solutions.

Tino Rangatiratanga: Plan A

The package is capable of being introduced in stages and some iwi might choose to accept only a portion of it.

STEP 1: A Nation Within a Nation in Parliament

The Maori nation will have its own seats in parliament and its own Chief Minister. The proportion of Maori to general seats will recognise the growing importance of the Maori population, which is already half a million. Legislation will move ahead of the trends to make up for 126 years of neglect. The proportion of seats is yet to be determined, and should recognise the importance of our constitutional position in this country and provide a larger measure of constitutional equity than we have enjoyed over the years. It reflects the partnership inherent in the Treaty of Waitangi. This measure ensures that we have a real part to play in the Parliament of the country.

STEP 2: Limited Autonomy at Local Level

Previous policies of devolution to iwi authorities raised the image of iwi enjoying their own form of local government and existing side by side with present structures. Revenue would come from sharing rates and sharing the revenue of parking meters and so on. The Maori Trust Board Act 1955 would be amended to accommodate the change and to give to existing boards the powers of local government. This action accords to Maori people not only the right of self-determination but also the right to participate in and enjoy the benefits of democracy at local government level. Readers will remember that the idea of restructuring the Department of Maori Affairs was to devolve some of its programmes and funds to tribal authorities. We have lost out in both areas. It is necessary, however, to revisit the whole idea of tino rangatiratanga at a local level.

STEP 3: A Ruling Council of Maori Congress

Some iwi are already pressing for the appointment of a ruling council of elders to act as a policy-making and policy-deciding body. Some are pressing for a separate Maori parliament so that democracy can work effectively for Maori people. The idea is that we make our own laws and make important decisions regarding our future as Maori. This is not a solution by itself, but rather is a part of a larger package of measures to give to Maori a greater degree of self-determination. Basically, there is no reason why the Maori Congress cannot implement this step now.

Tino Rangatiratanga: Plan B

The Restoration Model

The Hawaiians advanced the idea of restoring their sovereignty. A similar idea can be pursued here on the basis that the Treaty of Waitangi did not give exclusive rights of sovereignty to the settlers. Under Article 2 of the treaty, sovereignty was never surrendered to the Queen; only kawanatanga was granted to Great Britain in order to bring law and order into the country. The treaty did not at any time give the settlers the right to govern or the right of sovereignty. These powers were devolved from Britain without the agreement of the treaty partners and using an authority which our people could not really understand. Who gave Britain the power to do this and which Maori leaders did they consult?

Thus there is an argument for restoration of sovereignty and for constitutional power to be restored to us or, at the least, shared on a more equitable basis than over the last 100 years.

Tino Rangatiratanga: Plan C

The Ngati Te Ata Model

Ngati Te Ata have written their own tino rangatiratanga charter and they have adopted their own measures of self-determination and self-government and have imposed them upon themselves and the agencies of government that want to do business with their iwi

The lesson from Ngati Te Ata is that, rather than talk with the government or ask for its permission, the iwi should adopt tino rangatiratanga in their organisation and dealings with others. Sovereignty is to 'be', some have said, or a state of mind. Its presence is detected not by what one says but rather by what one does. Thus, if you want self-determination for your iwi, do it and act as though you have it.

The restoration model calls for full autonomy and for a radical change in the political relationships among the ethnic groups in the country. Maori would then dominate Parliament, and it would be the Pakeha majority who would be scrambling to enjoy the fruits of democracy which they have denied to Maori.

Summary

Even as far back as fourteen years ago, most Maori agreed that the present system of democracy in Aotearoa was flawed and did not deliver the benefits expected. It was unsatisfactory and not fair to Maori, and yet we seem to go along with it. Why? Is it, as Nganeko Minhinnick accuses, that we have become accustomed to our oppression and we are not questioning its obvious unfairness? Do we agree with what they are doing? Do we feel that we must agree with the policies of Pakeha governments even when we know they are damaging our people and our culture? Have we lost the will to stand up and oppose? Is it, as some Pakeha commentator said on TV, 'the Maori have no fight'? Do we concede that the Pakeha under the present government have won the self-determination issue? Have they won by simply announcing that they will not allow it? Have they won the issue of our constitutional rights as embodied in the 'frozen' Maori seats by allowing us one more? Are we allowing them to win these battles without a fight, without the voices of the iwi being heard?

The year 2000 is fast approaching, and by then we should have a better measure of self-determination and autonomy that we enjoy at present. Here are some options to think about. These options are not the only ones possible, nor is it absolutely necessary that every iwi adopts the same option or combination of options. If your iwi is a nation, it follows that the policy of one iwi does not necessarily duplicate exactly that of another.

Iwi interested in pursuing the issues of self-determination should consult the book edited by William Renwick (1991) which looks at sovereignty and indigenous rights. There are many articles and comments on the concept of sovereignty.

Summary of the Options

1. The status quo—more of the same.
2. Full autonomy—Cook Islands model.
3. Restored sovereignty—Hawaiian model.
4. Nation within a nation—American Indian model.
5. Sovereign nation within a confederation—Iroquois model.
6. Limited autonomy: soft version—very little change.
7. Limited autonomy: hard version—the Palestinian model.

8. Limited autonomy—the three-step package:
   i. more seats in Parliament
   ii. iwi authorities and trust boards given status of local government
   iii. ruling council of congress.
9. The Ngati Te Ata model—get up and do it.

Iwi should consider where they are, what they want to achieve and what self-determination model best suits them. The choice is yours.

References

Awaroa ki Manuka, 1991. *Ngaa Tikanga o Ngaati Te Ata: Tribal Policy Statement*. Ngati Te Ata, Ngararapapa, Awhitu.

Fox, Derek (ed.), 1993. *Mana: The Maori News Magazine for All New Zealanders*, 2, April/May. Papatoetoe, Mana Publications.

Nga Tuara, 1990. 'He Tahuhu mo te Tau Ruamano: Discussion Paper for the Year 2000'. Wellington, Iwi Transition Agency.

Nga Tuara, 1992. 'Nga Toka Tu Moana: Maori Leadership and Decision Making'. Wellington, Te Puni Kokiri.

New Zealand Planning Council, 1979. *He Matapuna: A Source—Some Maori Perspectives*. Wellington, New Zealand Planning Council.

Renwick, William (ed.), 1991. *Sovereignty and Indigenous Rights: The Treaty of Waitangi in International Contexts*. Wellington, Victoria University Press.

Aspects of Culture

17. Dimensions of Meaning in Maori Art

A photographic exhibition of Maori art entitled Tangata *was held at the Australian Museum in Sydney in 1981. It featured the work of the celebrated photographer Brian Brake. I was invited to address members of the Australian Museum Society in June. This is the text of my address.*

This evening you will see a photographic exhibition entitled *Tangata*, a word which means man, human being, serf, slave or simply mankind. A calendar produced in 1979 by our New Zealand Ministry of Foreign Affairs, and featuring some of the same photographs which you are about to see, provided more explanation of what was intended by adding the phrases 'The Maori Vision of Man', 'Child of the Gods', 'Master of the World'. One can detect in the choice of words a search for appropriate descriptive labels to try to match Brian Brake's superlative photography.

At the outset we need to be very clear on one point: this is not an exhibition of Maori art which features actual examples for you to touch, feel and see with your own eyes! Rather, it is a collection of photographs of a very select portion of the visual arts of the Maori. Moreover, the style of photography employed by Brian Brake presents particular glimpses and moments in the existence of the art objects he chose. These moments, as captured by the camera, are contrived for artistic effect. The result, which is visually exciting and beautiful, can be described quite fairly as Brian Brake's vision of Maori art. He uses the medium of photography to reshape and recreate the works of artists of another culture and of another age. The thirty-three photographs in the exhibition feature items made in the eighteenth and nineteenth centuries.

In a sense Brian Brake is translating Maori art for you by focusing on each work in a particular way. By doing so he brings to the fore a kind of meaning which you can understand and accept even though you may know little or nothing about Maori culture. What he is doing is bring you to the point of accepting actual historical examples of the craftsmanship of Maori artists as true works of genius and as fine examples of art. The message you should take away is not only that Brian Brake is a very good photographer, but also that Maori artists of the Classical and Post-European period, say up to the close of the nineteenth century, were also superb artists in their own right.

My task is not so much to explain the exhibition as to provide a general background of information which might then help to broaden your understanding of Maori art. My address has been given the title 'Dimensions of Meaning in Maori Art', and I shall be talking in very general terms about some meaningful aspects of the art and culture of the people. These aspects, taken together, describe some of the attitudes and values which the Maori people have towards their art, and so provide tone and colour to an exhibition that is already colourful.

There is an importance to this exhibition which goes beyond aesthetics. You are all probably aware that some 30,000 of my cousins, nephews and nieces live in Sydney. You must also be aware that this is not the first time our people have come to Sydney in droves. It happened first in the early decades of the nineteenth century. As you know, we were governed from New South Wales at one time, so there are early links between the Maori of New Zealand and the people of this state. Now you are hosts to many of our people who chose to live here because they say conditions of living are better here and the wages bigger than at home in New Zealand.

It is their art that we are discussing this evening, it is their heritage, of which they should be very proud, and it is the work of their ancestors that is the focus of Brian Brake's camera.

A level of meaning called contextual meaning can be gained by simply providing some background information against which the art of the Maori can be appreciated. The Maori people occupy the largest country in Polynesia. They've been in Aotearoa, The Land of the Long White Cloud, for about 1000 years and came originally from central Polynesia. Our language is distinctly Polynesian and is very closely related to the languages of the Cook Islands, Tahiti and Hawaii. In fact, it does not take very long to reach an understanding of the languages of Easter Island and of tiny Tikopia to the north of you.

Our culture as a whole is a variety of Polynesian. There is thus no hesitation whatever in classifying Maori art as Polynesian art. Within Polynesia itself the great art-producing cultures were those of Easter Island (its stone statues), the Marquesas, Hawaii, Tahiti, the Cook Islands and New Zealand. Besides the luxury of sheer size, one of the advantages of living in New Zealand was the availability of rich resources of timber, various stones, including the highly valued greenstone, obsidian, and big bones, such as those of the giant moa and of whales. The country was teeming with bird life but there was a paucity of four-footed animals—we could boast only the dog and rat.

Through the centuries the Maori developed a distinctive art tradition. Examples of the work of Maori artists are scattered among the museums of the

Western world. Fortunately, many early examples remained in the country. Some of our most prized possessions were lost in swamps and then recovered in recent times.

If you visit the museums of New Zealand you will be able to see a variety of objects ranging from large decorated meeting-houses and their various pieces such as centre-post figures; storehouses and some distinctive carvings that are associated with them; canoes and especially canoe prows and stern pieces; fish-hooks; personal ornaments such as the well-known tiki, dog-shaped pendants and combs of various shapes and sizes; weapons of bone, stone and wood; items of costume such as dogskin cloaks from the 1844 period, kaitaka cloaks with their taniko borders or decorated thrums; hafted adzes especially the toki-pou-tangata; burial coffins; bowls shaped like dogs; treasure boxes, both oval and oblong in outline; and so on. These examples indicate briefly what the art is like.

When you tour New Zealand you will note an outstanding fact. Some of the traditional arts of the Maori are alive and functioning. Carved meeting-houses dot the countryside and are beginning now to appear in the large cities, such as Auckland, Wellington and Christchurch. For several decades they have been a part of our smaller towns. The meeting-house of my subtribe, Ngati Pahipoto, dates to 1882. It has been used continuously since that time. This continuity with the traditions and art styles of the Classical period is, however, not characteristic of all tribes, and this point needs to be emphasised.

Maori woodcarving was already well developed at the time Captain Cook first visited New Zealand, in 1769. A drawing of a carved slab belonging to the interior of a house indicates that the architectural form of the meeting-house was already established at the time Cook came. But the meeting-house became more common after the introduction of steel tools, and they became larger structures. Probably of more importance, however, was the increasing wealth of the tribes in the 1850s and 1860s which came from servicing the needs of the European settlers in both Australia and New Zealand. This was when tribes grew large areas of wheat, established their own flour mills and generally participated in local and international trade with vigour and enthusiasm. As an example, one of my ancestors is reputed to have operated his own trading ship.

These prosperous and exciting days did not last too long, however. Our people came into competition with the land sharks and business tycoons of Australasia. Soon we were embroiled in bitter land wars which ended in many of the tribes having their lands confiscated. With a lot of their land taken, our people lost their grip on agriculture and hence on trade. They became the poor of New Zealand, a position many of us still occupy today.

After the land wars, our people became dispirited and blamed their plight on being Maori. Many repudiated their culture, their art and their language. For a time the visual arts were in limbo, being despised by a majority of the white settlers and ignored by several tribes. Existing houses took on a neglected appearance and new houses were not carved elaborately but merely painted. To be fair to the Maori side, however, many of them were scattered to the four winds, their lands gone and, with the land, their villages, burial sites and historical landmarks. They were unable to continue as effective communities and unable to maintain their traditions.

Several epidemics also swept through the land, such as the flu epidemic of 1919. One can say that European politics, economics, warfare and disease together spelt ruin for the Maori. The wonder of it all is that the people survived and that our culture is still alive. But it should be pointed out that no people can come through such experiences without some bruises, and without feeling keenly the injustices they suffered. It would thus be a mistake to think that the Maori people of New Zealand are happy, guitar-playing individuals who sing and dance every day. Nor are we the fearsome primitive cannibals of the early nineteenth century. That has all gone, and we have been pacified, tamed, converted to Christianity and educated, and we are still not very confident in speaking out for our rights as a minority group.

A hopeful sign today is that the Maori people are reasserting their ethnic identity. The arts play a very large part in their rising nationalism. The phenomenon is not unusual, for one may go to the United States, to Canada and here to Australia and see evidence of the same use of the indigenous arts as symbols of social identity. It is difficult to express one's ethnic identity without art. For example, how can I express my identity as a Maori to you this evening? To say that I am Maori on my mother's side may not mean much to you. I can speak Maori to you, but that is more important in the presence of other Maori, where the ability to speak the language is an obvious sign of belonging.

However, I may be able to convince you by singing a Maori song, wearing Maori costume, by dancing for you, by playing a koauau (a wind instrument) or by wearing a Maori ornament. I need the arts to express in a nice way how I want to be regarded. The last item I mentioned is probably more convincing than anything else, for who would wear an ornament such as the one I have here unless there was strong positive commitment to the art and to the culture?

And what better evidence is there for commitment than the meeting-house I spoke of earlier and the fact that new ones continue to be built, such as Nga Tokowaru, which opened in 1979. There is, of course, other evidence of positive commitment besides the popularity of Maori ornaments, such as the increasing interest being shown in learning to carve wood, learning to weave and plait, the great popularity of art festivals and exhibitions of Maori art, and the large number of what are called culture groups but are really dance teams. There is an Institute of Maori Art at Rotorua, three carving schools in the Wellington region alone, and a nationwide Maori Writers and Artists Association. These are the signs of commitment and of increased activity.

Anthony Forge (1979) has provided some clues as to why the arts are so important in situations such as the present one for the Maori, as well as for the Aborigines. We are witnessing worldwide a movement towards seeking our roots and reaffirming a link with our origins. Our traditional arts provide a direct link to our ancestors. We can say that these are the symbols our ancestors created, these are the motifs which they thought important for us, here are the techniques they used to create these objects, and here are the materials they used. By reattaching ourselves to our traditional arts, we are communicating to the population at large that we have already made some important decisions—for example, I am Maori, I like being a Maori and I believe in our traditions.

Most people do not analyse the steps taken in affirming and reaffirming an attachment to one's cultural roots. It is only the writers, poets and students of one's own culture who tend to verbalise the fact of commitment. The usual thing is simply to do it, and get into the culture and become a committed member. To believe in the social identity one adopts, and in the customs and traditions belonging to it, is very similar to the act of faith required in religious conversion. We believe in Maoritanga, and that's that. No verbalised justification is necessary.

So now we can look at the Hauraki lintel and try to understand the story the artist has retold here. Here is a level of meaning that is referred to in the literature as iconographical, if you believe in Panosky, or exegetical, if you follow Victor Turner, or iconic, if you prefer Charles S. Pierce. The practising artist is likely to refer to this kind of meaning as being, simply, the story. So here is a story to tell. First, we have to view another door lintel, the one that helped unlock the story for many other lintels. The composition is read from centre to left and is repeated from centre to right. The whole forms a balanced artistic composition in woodcarving.

This is the story of Maui's quest for immortality for mankind (tangata). The key to immortality lay in the control of the goddess of death, Hine-nui-te-po. Maui had accomplished other great deeds before attempting this final feat. He had fished up the North Island, slowed down the sun and obtained fire for the use of man. Now he had to contend with the goddess of death. His plan was to catch her asleep and then enter her and so find immortality by reversing the process of birth. For did not life begin in the womb of woman? His companions were birds, especially fantails. He commanded them not to twitter and laugh when he commenced his re-entry to the source of life.

The day came and he found Hine-nui-te-po stretched out asleep with her thighs apart. Here she is at the centre of the lintel. He approached her quietly and began to enter. He had just managed to get his head in when the birds twittered and laughed. The noise woke up the goddess of death, who suddenly closed her great thighs. Maui died and so failed in his great quest for our benefit.

The story of Maui and Hine-nui-te-po is illustrated in this pare from the Whanganui Regional Museum. Hine-nui-te-po is represented in the centre and Maui's head is shown between her thighs.
(Athol McCredie)

The goddess of death is shown with thighs apart in the centre of the lintel. The twittering birds flank her on either side. Because Maui failed, the artist has ended his story with the statement that the lot of man, henceforth, is to contend with death: to tease its tail, as is the case here, or to challenge it face to face. Undoubtedly, this is one of the great stories of the Maori world that is told over and over again. Here is a part of the same story on an adze handle. It is a story that one accepts without question and without trying to apply to it tests of logic or scientific plausibility which are inappropriate. Myths provide a way of expressing universal truths. Forge (1979, p.285) identifies some of them as being 'fundamental assumptions about the bases of society, the real nature of men and women, the nature of power, the place of man in the universe which surrounds him'. These sorts of underlying meanings can be inferred from the many stories that are illustrated on house-posts—for example, the Te Kuiti house built in 1873. There is Tamatekapua and his stilts, a self-portrait of the carver, Rukupo, Paoa and his spotted dog, Whaene, who slapped his brother Kahungunu across the face with a fish, and Maahu, the great collector of food, with fish, dog, kiwi, stingray and tawhara leaves.

Around the world there is evidence of a return to the simple truths of myth. We are suspicious of science and technology, which have become the sophisticated tools of business and modern warfare. While it is true that together they have improved the quality of life enormously for much of mankind around the world, it is equally true that they have not solved the problems of our vulnerability to famine, earthquakes, landslides, tornadoes, floods and droughts, and other acts of God. In fact, we face new dangers of nuclear fall-out and of contamination of our food sources. We also face high levels of unemployment, which are being caused by allowing science and technology too important a place in our society.

The uncertainties of the moment, in addition to the problems of being a minority in our own country, conspire to transform Maori art into something close to the heart, beautiful, and meaningful. It is fair to say that our ancestors were artistic and aesthetically aware people. Art was all around them, in their clothing, their weapons and tools, in their modes of transport and in their buildings. There was no separation between the people and the art, and no effort made to keep it out of the sight of the common people. The artist was not a recluse but, apart from his or her undoubted expertise in some aspect of art, was probably indistinguishable from anyone else in society. Those of lowly birth could rise to become great artists. An example is the great tattooist Rangi, whose works on the faces of great warriors were actively sought out on the battlefield as spoils of war.

Today, communities which have a marae complex which includes a carved meeting-house still have their art around and near them. They are envied for having such an important amenity and for being able to control, maintain and defend the symbols of their cultural identity. The meeting-house now becomes the most powerful symbol of Maoritanga. It has rich meaning, not all of which is understood by the modern Maori because of the constantly changing social, economic and political climate in New Zealand.

Many meeting-houses are named after a particular ancestor who may be portrayed on the tekoteko, at the apex of the house, or as the foremost figure of the ridge-pole. The latter is often not visible from the front but must be viewed by looking up to the ceiling. The house is a symbol of that ancestor and in a practical sense is the ancestor itself. It has the power to bring the past to the present and to make the future comprehensible. The house thus becomes a focus of identity and a point of reference in one's genealogy.

It is a place of welcome, where one's guests are ceremonially received, and it is a place of farewell. The tribe's dead are usually brought to the marae. They lie in state, either in the meeting-house, the porch or in a special house of death which is located to the right of the meeting-house. For three days the dead lie with face uncovered so as to be seen by all who come to mourn. In the speeches made by the orators, both the meeting-house and the corpse are addressed as though they are alive and can hear what is being said.

The meeting-house is like an art gallery. It contains the best that the tribe can afford: of woodcarvings, paintings, lattice work and decorated mats on the floor. Photographs of the dead either hang permanently on the walls or are brought to the house when there is a death to mourn. It is also a history book, for on the walls are depicted an array of illustrious ancestors who are chosen for a number of reasons. First, they are recognisable leaders of neighbouring tribes or of the major tribes of New Zealand, such as Tuwharetoa and Hoturoa. Second, they are associated with some important event that has become a part of the traditions of the people. Third, they occupy an important part in the social order and are thus points of genealogical reference which are very important to their descendants. One's link to the house thus may be a general one through the main ancestor, or a more particular one through connection to an ancestor figure inside the house.

One cannot be indifferent to one's meeting-house because of all that the house stands for. The individual benefits by the reflected glory of the structure itself and by the gallery of ancestors it contains. All of the events that have occurred at the marae—the birthday parties, the weddings, the deaths, the important meetings to discuss land matters, the occasions when vice-regal persons were welcomed or when the Minister of Maori Affairs visited the locality to hear submissions from the people—help give to the individual a sense of participation in the social history of the tribe. My identity as an individual is associated very closely with the house. My forebears passed through the house and now all that is left are their headstones in the neighbouring cemetery. But I know who I am because of them.

A meeting-house also means obligations to the marae, such as building amenities such as a shelter for visitors. Now that our young people are scattered through the cities of New Zealand and Australia, it is difficult both to receive the benefits of identity with the house and to give it one's labour, time and financial support. By not being associated with the marae, young people are being alienated. They are not learning their traditions, their songs and their customs. Moreover, they do not know anyone else but their immediate families. The longer they stay away, the worse the problem becomes—this is probably the predicament of those living in Australia at the present time.

They also become alienated from the art styles of their particular region. So the people and their art are being separated. For example, I do not know how familiar with their own art forms are the thousands of Maori living here in Sydney. They suffer by not having a marae to go to and by not having a carved meeting-house here. In the end more than the arts suffer: the very ability to carry through the rituals associated with a marae are threatened. Ultimately, the whole culture is at risk, and this is the situation among many tribes today.

Sometimes, however, alienation can have a positive influence, when it

The meeting-house Hinetapora at Mangahanea, Ruatoria, which celebrated its centennial in October 1996.

(S. M. Mead)

becomes a motivating force in the arts. Most of the outstanding Maori artists of today are people who were educated in the Western tradition. Many of them went to Western-type art schools in New Zealand, which taught them much about Western art but little about their traditional art forms. So here were Maori artists more at home with European art forms and techniques than with their own culture. They were educated to become uncomfortable and guilty about their lack of knowledge about themselves. One can see in their innovative work evidence of a struggle to come to terms with their Maori identity. Selwyn Muru illustrates the struggle with his Parihaka series, Para Matchitt seeks to incorporate Maori motifs, as do Sandy Adsett and Buck Nin. For many of them the struggle has taken some twenty or more years to partly resolve. From a Maori point of view, they were dangerous people because they wanted to introduce radical change into the art of the marae and hence of the masses. Hapai Winiata did this in the meeting-house which he carved, and his innovations caused a great deal of agony at the time.

Some have chosen to work exclusively in the halls of Western art, where there is room for innovative ethnic art produced through well-understood media such as the painted canvas or sculpture.

These new artists are in a sense mediators because, on the one hand, they bring new artistic techniques and materials to the marae and, on the other, they introduce more Maori artistic influences into the national art of New Zealand. Alongside them are many artists who are beginning their artistic training by turning directly to the traditional arts. These artists learn the older forms that are connected with the past and hence with the ancestors. They tend to be less well educated in a Western sense and, in comparison with the first group, appear to be less innovative. But I believe they must be judged by different criteria. The latter group are definitely less threatening, are more aware of the symbols that mean something to their people, and are less concerned with pleasing Pakeha spectators. Many of them are very innovative.

But the whole field of Maori art is complicated by the fact that New Zealanders of European and British origins are now identifying with it. Just as the Maori people on their part are seeking and defining a new identity, so are the Pakeha people who see New Zealand as their homeland. But they come to the task with different backgrounds, loyalties and histories. There is, I believe, a considerable body of Pakeha opinion in New Zealand which sees Maori art as New Zealand art, which makes it their art as well. It has meaning for them especially when they are abroad, and also at home, according to different social contexts. Many who have married into the Maori world have little difficulty identifying with Maori art. Similarly, those who work in situations which bring them in close contact with Maori. Others may not yet be aware of their attachment to Maori art, and for others the moment of truth has simply not yet arrived—and may never do so.

The *Tangata* exhibition which you will see this evening is, in fact, inspired by Pakeha interest. It was commissioned by Pakeha, photographed by a European photographer and arranged almost exclusively by non-Maori people. It is actually more than Brian Brake's vision of Maori art: it is a vision of many Pakeha New Zealanders who want to do things with our art and express something of their own feelings through it, but who really do not know much about it. And so this exhibition and the way it has been put together illustrate one of our dilemmas. It is a dilemma which you must face, too, in relation to the art of the indigenous tribes of Australia. You are not spared from the agony of learning how to handle this problem.

As in your case, so too in ours, the native arts have a meaning for the whole population. Outside our domestic squabbles at home, all New Zealanders relate more deeply to Maori art than they realise. It is the art of the country. It belongs exclusively to New Zealand. Despite its similarities to the arts of other Polynesian peoples, it is a distinctive art which is part of the proud heritage of the Maori people. You see examples of this art on the tails of our planes, on business logos and in many public buildings. There is little doubt that commercial interests are well aware of the utility of Maori art as symbols of a New Zealand identity.

The *Tangata* exhibition is brought to you with goodwill and with aroha. I suspect that the meanings you see in it will depend in large measure on your own personal attitudes towards New Zealand as a nation and towards us as a people. One thing is sure: Maori art is among the great arts in that category which the experts of the West have called 'primitive art'. We are one group in that vast mass we call tangata, and our art is an expression of our humanity, of our fears and our hopes, our joy and of our desire for a place under the sun.

18. The Rahui and its Applications

Customs are like art styles. They can be set aside for long periods of time and then revived and used again. A custom cannot be dismissed as a 'thing of the past' that belonged to a past age and has no relevance today. Customs are part of our heritage. They represent solutions to certain problems, solutions that our ancestors employed.

There is no reason why old solutions cannot be revisited and adapted to the problems of the present. The custom of the rahui was revisited in 1979 and caused a furious debate because it was to be applied to one of our 'sacred cows', rugby football. The author led the charge and became the target of abuse. One of my relatives, a keen rugby man at the time, threatened to beat me up for daring to upset him and his team mates.

But, having declared my hand, I had to continue with the debate. At that time neither the government nor the Rugby Football Union would consider any cultural argument, least of all one based on the rahui.

While the rugby tour went ahead, the debate continued. The debate opened the doors of universities to courses on tikanga Maori. Victoria University was the first to offer a course within the BA degree, entitled Customary Concepts of the Maori. Courses on tikanga Maori are now commonplace. This paper could therefore be considered a landmark for tikanga Maori.

Published in Customary Concepts of the Maori, *compiled by S. M. Mead, Department of Maori Studies, Victoria University of Wellington, pp.125–37, 1984.*

Preamble to original paper

Late in February 1979, I proposed the use of the rahui as a means of trying to stop a party of rugby football players and administrators from going to South Africa in March of that year. The intention was to persuade the Maori people, through one of their own customary rituals, to disengage from rugby football and so provide a way of exerting political pressure on the New Zealand Rugby Football Union to call off the visit. The persuader was to be the rahui, which was to be applied to football fields, hence putting a taboo on them.

This was a novel way of applying the rahui, and the suggestion immediately began a furious debate as to its appropriateness in this instance. Some angry supporters of rugby questioned the idea, and others laughed at it. But over the next few weeks the laughing ceased and serious discussion began.

Various experts on the rahui gave their considered opinions as to both the meaning of the concept and its application to sport. Although often given with the weight of Maori authority behind them, many of the pronouncements were incorrect, not based on sound knowledge and, at best, just personal opinions. However, the important thing is that the people began to think about the notion of rahui and wanted to know more about it.

On 2 December 1979, the Bishop of Aotearoa, the Right Reverend Manuhuia Bennett, supported by other church leaders, instituted a rahui on taru kino (bad weeds). This action once more forced the people to focus attention upon the rahui as a traditional tool of control and ponder again its appropriateness in the modern world. This time there was no furious denial or debate, but quite the reverse—widespread support. Discussion centred on the possibilities of success or failure, and upon whether the youth of the Maori world would pay any attention to it.

Support for the rahui on taru kino does not necessarily mean that the concept is now better understood than before. What it might indicate is that the idea of emphasising a Maori way of acting has become more acceptable in our society.

With the aim of encouraging more understanding of the rahui as a customary concept and of informing our thinking about it, I offer this paper.

Definition of Rahui

Basically, the rahui is a means of prohibiting a specific human activity from occurring or from continuing. It might be directed at a group of people or focused on a single individual. There might be a visible signal, such as a post, to let people know that a rahui has been 'stood up' (whakatu—to cause to stand). There may be a special ceremony to introduce it or it may be simply announced or proclaimed. Similarly, its conclusion might be marked by ritually pulling down something—the post, or the leaves or cloth tied around it—or by an appropriate announcement, or by everyone noting that the time of restriction agreed upon at the commencement had expired.

Rahui may be categorised in various ways, such as those with 'teeth' and the others without, as suggested in Best's (1904) writings, or as severe and mild, a distinction which Firth (1929, p.259–60) learnt from Best. Probably the most useful way of beginning to differentiate between various examples of rahui is by examining the reasons (take) or the sequences of events when a rahui was regarded as an appropriate response.

The most common types of rahui are those associated with pollution and hence tapu (the pollution rahui), and those related to conservation of resources (the conservation rahui). These two are closely interlinked and, in fact, one implies the other. A third type might be referred to as the 'political rahui' or the 'punitive rahui'.

In the first type, the cause which warrants imposition of the rahui is that the land or the water, or both, have become polluted by the tapu of death. This might be described as the more common model of rahui: it is the one remembered by the elders and is still applied in modern times.

Tapu Rahui (Pollution Rahui)

The examples given by Best (1904, p.84) cover a range of take. In one case, a rahui was placed on the land and water of Okahu at Te Whaiti (Urewera) when the children of the chief died. According to Best, this 'was simply a ban placed upon the food products of that district'. The ban was lifted in 1847. Unfortunately, Best did not give the precise cause of death (we can only guess that it was by misadventure) or how long the rahui lasted. But he did say that no post was put up and no special ceremony was performed. This was a rahui by proclamation.

In another example from the same area, Best says that the Whirinaki River was made tapu when the blood of warriors slain at the defence of Okarei Pa stained its usually clear waters. In this case, Best (1904, p.84) noted that a special whakanoa (tapu negating) ritual was performed in order to return the river to normal use. A human sacrifice, a slave named Taupoki (lid), was killed, cooked at Waikotikoti Pa, Te Whaiti, and eaten by the people. No reason is given as to why the rahui was terminated in this way.

The intensity of the pollution varies according to the rank of the victims. For example, when several Arawa chiefs, Tionga, Te Wahakaikapua, Te Hurinui and Te Rangikatukua, were killed near Mount Tarawera, a large area, which included Lake Rerewhakaitu, was placed under a rahui for several years. So intense was the pollution that the land and water in the area were completely avoided. I estimate on genealogical evidence that the rahui was placed around the 1830s. It was not lifted until 1869 (Stafford 1967, p.174—but the information is attributed to Best).

A widely known example is the Tuwharetoa case, when the paramount chief, Te Heuheu Tukino, and his people were buried in a landslide at Mount Kakaramea on the shores of Lake Taupo in May 1846 (Ngata 1959, p.191). As in the previous case, land and water in the immediate vicinity were made out of bounds and no food resources of any sort could be taken. The rahui lasted for five years. This is the length of time that was thought necessary for the 'radioactive' nature of the pollution to dissipate into the atmosphere and become harmless.

As soon as the rahui was lifted, the first fish caught in Lake Taupo were taken to the high priest, Te Takinga, cooked and eaten ritually by him alone (Buller 1895, p.152). In this case, too, Buller notes that the chief of the land, Te Heuheu Iwakau, exercised his right both to apply the rahui and to lift it.

Drowning Rahui

A classic example of the rahui following a drowning is provided by James Cowan (1930, p.70–1). The incident occurred in August 1900, when a party of school children from Omaio were drowned near the mouth of the Motu River while attempting to cross it in a canoe. The Whanau-a-Apanui tribe immediately applied a rahui upon the land and water near the site of the disaster. The outer regions of the polluted area, from Te Kaha to Opape, were under restriction for one year, while the central area was banned for four years. The restriction was observed and any one out of bounds was likely to find himself the target of yet another means of social control, the muru (ritual plunder). A neighbouring chief of Maraenui 'trampled on' the rahui quite unwittingly when he took a drink from the restricted portion of the river. Cowan (1930, p.71) informs us that a taua muru (plundering group) from 100 miles away (Gisborne) paid him a visit and the drink cost him an estimated £50. This type of rahui is still used today.

Rahui with 'Teeth'

The last examples given above would be regarded by contemporary Maori elders as the most severe form of rahui. However, it is very doubtful whether this is true. What Best (1904, p.84) regarded as 'the kind which is endowed with magic or supernatural powers' is certainly not the Christian rahui of modern times. Rather, it is the one which has 'teeth' and is believed capable of 'biting' those who challenge it.

A tohunga versed in the karakia required for establishing the power of the rahui is needed to provide the 'teeth'. He must also know the incantations for 'sharpening the teeth' and for reinforcing its biting power (turuki i te kapu rahui).

Best (1904, p.85) explains that there is a post (pou rahui) to which is attached a maro (apron) consisting of a few fronds, leaves or a fragment of cloth. In the incantations, the maro is added to a stone, and these together form the whatu of the rahui. According to Best, it is the whatu which contains the 'true power' and the 'life destroying, magic power' that is put there in the first place by the tohunga, when he calls upon Tangaroa, god of the sea, to sharpen his teeth and cause the flies to swarm and the maggots to crawl.

These material symbols of the power of the rahui are concealed some distance away from the rahui post. A false maro is attached to replace the one over which special karakia have been recited. Kapu, a term which applies to the charmed tokens hidden away in this manner, is the same as whatu. It is the kapu which inflicts punishment upon anyone challenging its effectiveness. However, it is not guaranteed to act in all circumstances, because the kapu is believed to lose power and 'go to sleep'. That power has to be brought to full strength by periodic karakia turuki, as described above.

Conservation Rahui

This type of rahui is usually described as the mild one, the one with no teeth or the one over which the karakia whakaoho (incantations to awaken) are recited. Its purpose is apparently not to destroy but rather to restore the productivity of the land (Best 1904, p.86). In this case, the kapu together with the mauri of the land are taken periodically to a sacred fire (ahi taitai) and there special invocations are recited 'in order to restore and retain the productiveness, health, welfare etc. of the food products, as also of the land and people'.

To my knowledge, no one in recent times performs the rituals which restore to a tired and misused earth and water their vitality and essence. We do know, however, of efforts to reduce not the pollution of death but that caused by the living—but this is a different situation altogether.

The conservation rahui was used to protect the products of the land and water. Best (1904, p.83) mentions forest products (berries), birds, fish, cultivated crops, fern root, flax and places where red ochre was obtained. What is interesting is that the list is not confined to food resources alone but includes other products.

An example described by Best (1904, p.88) concerns the Ngati Apa (of Murupara) chief Tukuha, who set up a rahui post at Te Rautawhiri. The post remained in the same position but, whenever the chief wanted to rahui the eels of his part of the Rangitaiki River, he would hang 'one of his old garments' on it. That would signal a complete ban on that one resource—eels. In this instance, the name of the place, Te Rautawhiri (the leaves twisted on), indicates that it was used by custom as a place to signal a rahui. Other stories told about Tukuha (Best 1904) also suggest that one of his particular tasks was controlling the supply of eels.

This seems to have been the case in other localities. For example, Piri Sciascia recalls that their chief at Porangahau always controlled the karengo (seaweed) season. No one could take any until he had obtained the 'first fruits'. Richard Taylor (1870, pp.171–2) mentioned that kiekie (used in tukutuku work) would be put under a rahui until the fruit was properly ripe. A young man would be sent by the chief to check the fruit until it was deemed ready. At that point, the rahui post was pulled down and, according to Taylor, 'the entire population go to "takahi" or "trample the wood" '. In this instance, too, the first fruit was presented to the chief.

It seems that in most cases involving a conservation rahui a post is 'put up'. In the Murupara example a garment was hung on the post. First (1929, pp.260–1), however, mentioned that in a case involving the conservation of the fish and bird life of the three lakes Tara, Kiwa and Poukawa, the posts were smeared with red ochre and this, apparently, was equivalent to tying an apron on each one. It is interesting in this instance that a challenger came along later and not only pulled out the rahui posts but also burnt them.

The No-Trespass Rahui, or Aukati

Most of the early ethnographers draw attention to the no-trespass rahui that was put up in a place where it would be seen—on a tree, across a track, and so on. This type of rahui can also be regarded as a conservation rahui when it is used to protect resources. Best (1904, p.84) suggests, however, that, more often than not, its purpose was to stop people from using a particular pathway. Best regarded this type as a 'minor form of tapu or rahui' but he was mistaken in his opinion.

Interestingly, this sort of rahui is widely known in the Pacific and seems to have been used by both Melanesians and Polynesians. It is evidently an ancient cultural trait that might go back to the Lapita people who were the ancestors of the Poynesians.

The no-trespass rahui is more commonly known as an aukati. The word means to block and prevent one from passing over or through a defined line, or it may refer to the line across which one may not pass (Williams 1971, p.22). Examples of the application of the aukati are many, but it is possible that its frequent use became necessary in the culture-contact situation, especially during the 1860s when the sale of land to Pakeha buyers became a burning issue.

An aukati was established by a variety of means. A person who is an 'owner' or guardian of a property might declare an aukati without reference to anybody else. In this instance, rights of use or of occupation, say, over a block of land are firmly established and not in dispute. A more usual way was for a meeting of the hapu or iwi to be called. The issue was then discussed and a decision agreed upon. Then the aukati would be established by public declaration and by the use of appropriate ritual. The tohunga would add the element of tapu to the aukati.

In all types of rahui, power relations come into play and leaders put their reputations at risk. However, the political nature of the rahui is most obvious when neither conservation nor pollution is the main reason for its application. Thus, it follows that the no-trespass rahui or aukati is perhaps the most vulnerable to political use. There are, in fact, several examples of the rahui being used as a weapon to punish or to thwart for political reasons. On occasion, the rahui may be used as a reaction to hearing something offensive.

For example, the Ngati Apa chief mentioned earlier put a rahui on the eels of the Rangitaiki River because someone passed a disparaging remark about a hapu to which he belonged (Best 1904, p.88). The same sort of reaction was recorded in the Taranaki area by Richard Taylor (1870, pp.168–9). At a pa up the Mokau River lived the chief, Te Kuri, and his community. They were all Roman Catholics. Into their group came a German Protestant missionary, whom the chief's head wife liked very much: she became his patron and his convert. Later, when the priest called into the village at Motu Karamu on his regular rounds, he scolded Te Kuri 'for suffering a heretical missionary to be located in his district' and he apparently called the intruder some insulting names. This infuriated the chief's wife, who next morning put a rahui on the river. The priest could not continue his journey because no one would take a canoe out. Eventually he was forced to go back.

The best example of a case involving high politics is the Ngati Pikiao incident in the Rotorua area (Stafford 1967, p.368–70). In 1864, in an endeavour to get to Orakau to help Rewi Maniapoto, a party of volunteers made up of Ngati Porou, Te Whanau-a-Apanui, Whakatohea and Ngati Awa men tried to cross Te Arawa territory. The chiefs of Ngati Pikiao, a sub-tribe of Te Arawa, put a rahui on their land and prevented the volunteers from going any further. They declared an aukati and established a line which was not to be crossed by the others. To understand the full significance of the action, the

This pare (door lintel) from Galatea and Murupara was put up on the pou rahui whenever a rahui was established.

National Museum, ME 1472. Photo: National Museum.

reader needs to know that at this time Te Arawa was fighting on the government side. This rahui, therefore, was to aid the Pakeha settlers and the government. The volunteers tried to breach the line but Te Arawa defended it successfully on their own.

Later, when the volunteers tried to go via Maketu, they were blocked again by the aukati, which had been extended to the coast, and once more a battle followed. This time the hand of the government was much more evident and the full political implications were not lost on those who participated.

This is a case where the rahui idea was used to delay reinforcements to Waikato and so help the Pakeha win the battle. The example is not remembered with any relish or pride, but it should be noted that Ngati Pikiao, who put up the rahui, also sent 100 men to help Rewi Maniapoto. This fact is worth stressing, if only to show that the chief might move in one direction while the people go in another.

An interesting example is recorded in a letter by Wiremu Kingi and several other Maori chiefs from Taranaki to Walter Buller, Resident Magistrate in Wanganui. The chiefs complained about the government trying to assert its mana over their land at Waikawa. ('Kaore matou e pai kia eke mai te mana o te Kawanetanga ki runga.') They had heard that the government had put a rahui on their land which removed from the Maori any right to go on to the land. ('Kua rongo hoki mātou ka rāhuitia e Kāwanatanga kia kore ai he mana a nga Maori ki runga.') No date is given for the letter but it was probably in the 1840s. The incident referred to might have occurred on 4 November 1842, as the Williams refer in their diaries to Wiremu Kingi being upset over a rahui (Porter 1974, p.226).

As one might expect, the rahui has been used in land disputes quite often. The Waikawa incident illustrates the use of the trespass or aukati concept in a manner so like the rahui that the owners saw it as such. It is possible that the resident magistrates and land agents actually modelled some of their land legislation on Maori concepts of control. There is little doubt that the Maori used the rahui when they thought it was the right thing to do.

For example, Taylor White (1892, p.275) draws attention to a court case in Hastings on 25 February 1892. In the evidence, it was revealed that two men, Te Rangikamangungu and Hawea, had possession of a block of land extending from Te Whanga to Puketitiri and Titiokura at Mohaka. Ownership of the block was disputed by Ngai Te Upokoiri. The occupiers of the block 'put up rahuis all over it'. At Puketitiri, it was said that the rahui was Piko, while Oinga or Hauhau it was Kauhoarangi, but it was not made clear whether these were dead men or living men. White asked: 'How could men be "put up as rahuis"?' This question followed his discussion of the fact that at Hauhau, on the Omahu block, the chief Te Hauwaho impaled a woman on a rahui post. Apparently she gave mana not only to the rahui but also to the claim of ownership. Perhaps a further question could be asked: was a person belonging to the tribe (and not necessarily of the tribe) sacrificed in order to transform a political rahui in to a pollution rahui?

To conclude this section on political uses of the rahui, it is as well to report again the words of Richard Taylor (1870, p.172), who said that a chief 'laid a ban upon whatever he felt disposed'. Continuing, he said: 'It was a great power, which could at all times be exercised for his own advantage, and the maintenance of his mana or dignity, which in some respects corresponded with manorial rights; frequently he would make some trifling circumstance the reason for putting a whole community to great inconvenience, rendering a road to the pa, perhaps the most direct and frequented, a grove, fountain or anything else, tapu, by his arbitrary will.'

Kairamua, or Eating the Day Before

When a rahui is challenged or breached, it is expected that there will be utu. An offence against a rahui is called kairamua (Best 1904, p.86), which refers to eating before the right time. The person who commits the offence is also called by the same name. On the authority of a Mataaua informant, H. W. Williams' *Dictionary* (1971, p.89) says that the punishment for a kairamua was to be killed, cooked and eaten. I have not so far found any reported case of this actually happening, but the threat was probably an effective deterrent.

Referring to either a conservation or a political rahui applied on this basis of mana tangata (personal prestige) alone, Best (1904, p.87) says that 'witchcraft might be resorted to, in order to punish the offenders'. However, it is part of contemporary folk knowledge that some form of witchcraft is always associated with rahui, but especially with a pollution rahui. It is believed, for instance, that if you commit a kairamua some form of aitua will follow. Typically, it is expected that some members of the offender's family will die, and it is not until the third death has occurred that full utu is believed to have been made.

In earlier times, the punishment was apparently some wasting disease (Firth 1972, p.262) which infected the culprit. In this case, the notion of punishment by aitua still holds. The significant difference is that formerly the culprit alone was the target of utu, whereas in more modern times it is the whanau or hapu.

There is little doubt that 'meddling with a rahui', as Firth (1972, p.262) put it, was dangerous and foolish because, if magic failed then the kairamua was open to reprisals of various sorts. The use of muru has already been referred to. Another instance of the muru being used as utu is recorded by Taylor (1870, p.166). In the Taranaki area, a rahui was placed on an unnamed river for a reason not given in the record. A mission group, which one suspects included the Reverend Richard Taylor himself, was annoyed by the rahui and, thinking the Pakeha to be 'above' all this, set off in defiance of it. But they had not gone far when members of the local community pursued them, dragged their canoe to shore and seized everything they had—bottles of medicine, pots of preserves included. However, the Pakeha group defied the rahui a second time and got through. As Taylor put it, 'they found they could not meddle with Europeans with impunity'. A more likely explanation is that, because there was nothing else left to muru, the only alternative to exact was death. At that point, Pakeha power won the day for the mission group.

Probably the most important deterrent to breaching any rahui, but especially the aukati, was fear of confrontation and violence. Firth (1972, p.262) drew attention to the Rangitane case when that group applied a rahui on their land in order to prevent another from occupying it. They erected a post called Puahi-te-ao. When the opposing tribe cut down the post, war between the tribes began in earnest.

The Arawa rahui mentioned earlier resulted in confrontation between opposing groups and ultimately men were killed. Defending the rahui was clearly linked to defending the integrity of the group. This was so at Lake Rotoiti, when Ngati Pikaio applied the rahui and had to defend it. Later, when the confrontation shifted to the Maketu end of Arawa territory, the result was the same: confrontation, loss of life, the rahui post remains standing, the integrity of the tribe is upheld, the confronting group retreats. There must be numerous instances, however, of the sequence ending in the triumph of the challengers. An infamous case is that of Ngati Awa, who, after declaring their aukati, were overrun by the New Zealand army and units of Te Arawa. Their property was taken or destroyed. In the end the tribe had 194,000 acres of its land confiscated by the government in 1865.

In 1929 Firth was clearly of the opinion that it was fear of reprisals and loss of life that restrained people from committing a kairamua. In his mind, the moral aspect, the justice or correctness of the rahui, was an issue of secondary importance. Today, however, it seems that the rahui is to be honoured more as a sacred ritual of the traditional past than because of the politics involved. And, perhaps, it is a reflection of the political powerlessness of the Maori people that utu by aitua has also become very important.

Conclusion

From this review of how the rahui was used as a means of social and political control in times past, it would seem to be a creative tool capable of being applied in a variety of situations for a wide variety of reasons. I grouped the reasons into three main categories—pollution, conservation and political—and regarded each as a type of rahui.

The first, the pollution rahui, was closely associated with the religious beliefs of the Maori and with the traditional notion that death pollutes land, water and people. A rahui was a device for separating people from contaminated land, water and the products thereof. After an agreed lapse of time, formerly several years and now about three months for drownings, the community is free once more to exploit the resources of land and water.

Conservation rahui seem to have been associated not only with control of resources for the good of the whole community but also with the political use of resources. In the former, common sense regulation of bird, fish and plant life seems to have been a consideration. It might even have been a survival technique, which enabled a group to act for the good of all members rather than allowing the greedy and the powerful to take all.

Nonetheless, it is evident that the conservation rahui was used by the chiefs for political reasons, which might be related to the 'foreign policy' of the tribe or might be for the personal aggrandisement of the rulers. In every case, however, the object was to separate the resources from the people and allow them to grow unmolested. In Grey's overland journey in 1841, mentioned by Firth (1972, p.260), the party arrived at Lake Rotomahana and found it under a conservation rahui. It was teeming with ducks and it was the breeding season. When the appropriate time came to take down the rahui, the community hunted as a group.

In the third type of rahui, the political factions were ritually separated, and this provided an opportunity for the target group to consider its position and decide whether it was strong enough to challenge the defending group. The political advantage remained with the group that ordered the separation, put up the pou rahui, and stood by ready to defend it. Nonetheless, it needed to assess its strength relative to the other side and to calculate the political benefits that would accrue from such action.

How the rahui was used in its various forms suggests that the Maori of former times were not the political innocents that we of today might believe. They were able to act in a variety of ways and to act imaginatively and boldly on a number of issues. The instrument that they thought with, and with which they acted out their decisions and desires, was the rahui.

References

Best, E., 1904. 'Notes of the Custom of Rahui', *Journal of the Polynesian Society*, XIII, pp.83–8.
Best, E., 1924. *The Maori*, in two volumes. Wellington, Harry H. Tombs.
Best, E., 1924. *The Maori As He Was*. Wellington, Government Printer.
Buller, W., 1894. On Some Peculiar Maori Remains, Transaction of the New Zealand Institute, XXVII, pp.151–2.
Cowan, J., 1930. *The Maori Yesterday and Today*. Wellington, Whitcombe & Tombs.

Firth, R. 1929. *Economics of the New Zealand Maori*. Wellington, Government Printer.

Ngata, A. T., 1959. *Nga Moteatea*, Part I. Wellington, the Polynesian Society.

Oliver, D. L., 1974. *Ancient Tahitian Society*, in three volumes. Canberra, Australian National University Press.

Porter, Frances (ed.), 1974. *The Turanga Journals 1840-1850, Letters and Journals of William and Jane Williams, Missionaries to Poverty Bay*. Wellington, Price Milburn for Victoria University Press.

Stafford, D. M., 1967. *A History of the Arawa People*. Wellington, A. H. & A. W. Reed.

Taylor, R., 1870. *Te Ika A Maui*. London, MacIntosh and Jones.

White, T., 1892. 'The Rahui, Extracts from a paper by Taylor White'. *Journal of the Polynesian Society*, I, pp.275–6.

White, T., 1892. Polynesian Society Papers. MS Papers 1187, Folder 205, Alexander Turnbull Library, Wellington.

Williams, H. W., 1971. *A Dictionary of the Maori Language*. Wellington, Government Printer.

19. The Nature of Taonga

In this article a term commonly used these days is discussed. The term 'taonga' is applied to arts generally, and 'taonga tuku iho' is generally applied to heritage items handed down from the ancestors to the present generation.

There are debates within the community as to how this term is being used. For example, it is being applied to a tupapaku (deceased person) in the speeches of the orators when they say, 'Takoto mai e te taonga.' In this instance, the orator is using the term as a metaphor by calling the deceased a 'prized art object'. The translation would be, 'Lie before us, oh prized object.'

This is an unusual application of the term, but nonetheless it is being used. The discussion in this paper concentrates on the nature of taonga, on different aspects of the term and what is associated with taonga. By doing so the nature of art itself is discussed.

Published in Proceedings of the Taonga Maori Conference, *held 18–27 November 1990. Department of Internal Affairs, Wellington, pp.164-9, 1990.*

'Taonga' is a term that has crept recently into the general vocabulary of New Zealand museum staff and of scholars of Maori art. For example, there is the *Taonga Maori* exhibition currently showing at the National Museum. This exhibition was shown in three Australian cities—Sydney, Melbourne and Brisbane—and so the word 'taonga' has at least an Australasian currency. The catalogue entitled *Taonga Maori* (1989) ensures that the word has a place in the literature on art. In the context of the exhibition the word means 'treasures', which is quite a good slogan. It should be noted, however, that 'taonga' was also used very frequently in the United States from 1984 to 1986 during the time the *Te Maori* exhibition was showing, in New York, Saint Louis, San Francisco and Chicago. In the catalogue entitled *Te Maori* (1984, p.21), the concept of taonga was introduced and defined.

The spectacular success of *Te Maori* helped change a few attitudes towards

Maori art, and to certain Maori customs such as the rituals of opening and closing exhibitions. I do not intend to speak about the broad issues of change, but there is one area of particular interest to any discussion of taonga. This concerns social contexts such as our own, which some have described as a Fourth World situation. Nelson Graburn (1976), for example, includes us in his book *Ethnic and Tourist Arts Expressions from the Fourth World.* The Fourth World includes societies such as New Zealand, Australia, Canada, Japan, United States, Hawaii and Tahiti in which the indigenous culture has been reduced to minority status by a larger and later wave of settlers. This larger group controls all the resources of the nation; it controls government, imposes its law and its education system. Robert Staples (1984, p.15) lists some of the characteristics of Fourth World societies as follows:

1. non-whites are not in the social system voluntarily, but have it imposed upon them
2. their native culture is modified or destroyed
3. control is in the hands of people outside their community
4. racism prevails, i.e. a group seen as different or inferior in terms of alleged biological traits is exploited, controlled and oppressed socially and psychologically, by a group that defines itself as superior.

A pataka or decorated whata at Kaihinui Pa, Queen Charlotte Sound. The painting of the taonga by G. F. Angas in 1844 is itself a taonga. The pataka is an example of taonga of Te Puawaitanga period.

(*Victoria University*)

Eventually, the power society imposes such a mesh of controls upon the indigenous society that it virtually manipulates how the subject people are to think about themselves and most aspects of their culture. In fact, members of that society set out the rules, determine whether to give funds or not, and speak and write on behalf of the indigenous group.

Before *Te Maori* (1984), the study, protection and care of, and the speaking about Maori art were largely the province and domain of the dominant culture. Maori art was a captured art, and museums could be regarded as repositories of the trophies of capture. Up until very recently, there were no Maori curators or cultural officers employed at museums and art galleries. All staff were Pakeha, and there was a tradition of this dating back to Augustus Hamilton, author of the large book, *Maori Art* (1901). The scholars used the terminology, the categories and the theories of Western society to describe Maori art. This continued to be the case when Maori scholars entered the field, such as Te Rangi Hiroa in his day and even myself. The Maori people whose traditions were being studied were not an important part of the scholars' world, except in the limited sense of being informants. It was assumed that everyone belonged to and believed in the world of the dominant group. A particular mind-set gripped the scholarly community and it required an event such as *Te Maori* to challenge the old order and bring about a new, renegotiated working partnership between scholars, ethnologists, archaeologists, art historians and art critics on the one hand, and Maori people on the other. I am proud to have been one of the negotiators on the Maori side and to have played a part in redefining the terms we use.

An immediate issue is terms such as 'art objects' and 'artifacts', which appear to be straightforward but are in fact clouded by the larger label of 'primitive art'. Despite all efforts to strip this term of its negative connotations, as for example in Anderson (1989), Haselbergher (1961) and a host of others, the unfortunate primitives of the world refuse to accept a negative label of this sort. Thus, whatever artifacts or objects admitted as Maori art are held to be, they are tainted with primitivism and in this sense not quite proper, beautiful but quaint, part of the nation's heritage but certainly not to be regarded as equal in legitimacy to the Western forms of art associated with the Pakeha. This sort of thinking distorts the world view of the indigenous culture, and distorts Maori art for the very people who should be proud of it. A result is the alienation of Maori people from their own art, or at the very least a doubting of the legitimacy of their heritage. And doubt is a step towards cultural repudiation.

One way of recapturing one's culture is to take control of the language of definitions and descriptions, and to have members of the culture speak for themselves, and present their culture, such as their music, dances and various art forms, in a manner they consider appropriate to them. This is a very important educational, intellectual, psychological, social and self-esteem-raising exercise for members of captured cultures. Literally hundreds of young and old Maori people who acted as kaiarahi, or guides, for *Te Maori* in various locations around Aotearoa in 1986 and 1987 can testify to the truth of this statement. What they did was possess their art linguistically as well as by right of whakapapa, which brings with it a heritage right. They enjoyed the experience of being trustees of their art and speakers of their world.

The task of the guides was aided by providing for them a set of Maori terms they could use in talking to the visiting public about their art. An example is the development sequence, which is based on growth metaphors from Maori language.

Nga Kakano (The Seeds)	AD900 to 1200
Te Tipunga (The Growth)	1200 to 1500
Te Puawaitanga (The Flowering)	1500 to 1800
Te Huringa (The Turning)	1. 1800 to 1900
Te Huringa (The Turning)	2. 1900 to present

These terms allow Maori people to enter and participate in discussion on the development through time of early forms of art and technology, which were originally less Maori and more early Eastern Polynesian in character and gradually becoming more like what we accept as Maori art. The metaphors used above were meaningful as tools of explanation for kaiarahi, and, perhaps more importantly, opened up the doors of archaeology to them.

One can look at the word 'taonga' in a similar way. It is a tool of explanation which Maori people can use, and by using it scholars are able to understand a Maori perspective on art. This second function, however, is less important than the first, which is to enable the owners of the heritage to understand their art. So what is taonga?

Williams' *Dictionary* (1971, p.381) defines taonga as 'property, anything that is highly prized'. However, this is not very helpful except to emphasise a high value placed on such objects. In order to reach some understanding, it is necessary to introduce other Maori words, such as 'korero' and 'whakairo'. Korero means talk, but in the sense in which I am using the word it means the talk associated with creation and production of works of art, and particularly with the stories and explanations given by artists and patrons to such works. The Western word for this sort of talk is iconography. All objects that are called taonga have korero attached to them, and if the korero is lost the task of the scholars is to find it. The korero is a valuable aspect of any taonga and it is the korero that gives meaning and cultural significance to it. Korero enriches the taonga, enhances it, provides it with a history and links it very strongly to a particular social group, such as a whanau, hapu or iwi, who have cultural rights not only to the korero but also to the taonga itself. Providing korero is an expected part of the process of creating taonga.

However, it is clear that creation cannot be done in a sort of cultural vacuum.

The Nature of Taonga 183

Every society has accepted rules for altering the natural state of materials, such as wood, into cultural work. There is a transforming process and a set of guidelines which assist the public in making judgements about whether the artist has reached an acceptable standard or not.

Various domains of art are categorised as 'whakairo', which according to Williams (1971, p.80) means 'ornament with a pattern, used of carving, tattooing, painting, weaving'. I take this to mean that whakairo is the process of transforming something natural into something cultural called a taonga

An example of whakairo from Ruatahuna showing a Tuhoe style of carving. The poupou were acquired by A. M. Grant of Te Whaiti and sold to the National Museum, Wellington. The poupou would be dated the early Te Huringa period.
(National Musuem)

(highly valued object of culture) whakairo (to which the transforming process of art has been applied)—that is, a taonga whakairo. The use of the qualifying term enables us to try to differentiate between the taonga which is art and the taonga which is not.

A characteristic of most taonga is that they are passed down like heirlooms from one generation to the next. The more generations involved, the greater the mana of the object. Antiquity is valued because it implies association with the ancestors, who form the foundation of Maori identity. Old taonga are very definitely given greater value than those produced very recently. Objects passed down in this way are called 'taonga tuku iho'—that is, an heirloom object. One aspect of antiquity is the linking back in time to the founding ancestors of the iwi and linking forward to the descendants alive today. This means that the living descendants are trustees of the taonga by right of whakapapa, and this includes the youth of the tribe.

The most telling attribute of taonga is their spiritual essence or force. This quality is described in the korero associated with a taonga, and one accepts or rejects it according to one's experience and faith. Many people who visited *Te Maori* said that they could feel the spiritual force of some of the taonga. Over the four years of showing *Te Maori*, it soon became known which pieces in the exhibition were 'scary', which ones were always treated with great respect by the guides and the public alike, and which ones elicited strong responses from their tribal trustees. Today we speak of 'taha wairua'—that is, the spiritual aspect—and it is generally acknowledged that a major difference between 'artifact' and 'taonga' is that there is a taha wairua to the Maori concept.

One of the reasons there is a high spiritual aspect to some taonga is that they represent an ancestor who is related by whakapapa to a group of descendants. For the living relatives the taonga is more than a representation of their ancestor; the figure is their ancestor, and woe betide anyone who acts indifferently to their tipuna (ancestor). It became a common phenomenon during *Te Maori* to see Maori elders and many of the young guides embracing their ancestor, or bringing green leaves to place at their feet, or speaking to them. This sort of behaviour towards taonga whakairo indicates an entirely different attitude to art objects than is common in Western countries.

Discussions of spiritual power inevitably involved us in discussions of mana and tapu. The two terms are closely linked. When a taonga has high mana, as in the case of Uenuku—that is, it is a powerful taonga of great prestige—it is also very tapu—that is, sacred and charged with spiritual power. A taonga of low mana also has a low level of tapu associated with it. Thus taonga differ in the level of mana and tapu accorded to each one.

In a sense, all Maori art has increased in mana since *Te Maori* opened in New York in September 1984. This is a result of two factors. The more obvious one is international recognition, by entering the world art scene at the Metropolitan

A taonga of great mana stands proudly in the Field Museum of National History in Chicago in 1985. Rennie Ormsby and Te Waea Murray stand before Uenuku. *(Field Museum)*

Museum of Art. Maori art was launched into the consciousness of the art world and is now even better known than it was before. International recognition boosted the mana of the art at home, and this conference is a reflection of that. Many things have happened since *Te Maori* to provide evidence of increased mana. The presence of Maori staff in many of our museums today is an example.

The other factor, in my view, is as important as the art itself: Maori art is great art and it can take its place alongside other great art traditions. However, the magnificence of Maori art is related to the mana of the Maori people who created it. The launching at New York involved the launching of Maori culture, Maori society and Maori people, who gathered there to give their art the best support they could—ceremonial, spiritual and social. The Maori people who went to New York were themselves a great hit among the art community of that city. Art, culture and people were launched as a package, and this is actually the genius of *Te Maori*.

Thus the point I make is that Maori art today is held to be important by the international community because Maori culture and Maori society are held in high esteem by them.

The reasons are varied. It is partly that Te Rangi Hiroa prepared the way for us in the great works he published and in the mana he built up during his distinguished career. It is partly curiosity tinged with admiration and awe that such fierce cannibals could produce such beautiful art. It is partly sympathy for our captured state and for the great fight we are engaging in to save our language and our culture. That we retain so much is one of the wonders of the world, and is attributed to Maori persistence rather than to Pakeha benevolence and good will.

It is partly a result of various myths coming together, such as our supposedly superior status among the cannibals of the world, our supposed intelligence and initiative and so on. Whatever the reasons, the result is an acceptance of our importance as a people and as a culture. At the present time we have the good will of the international community. It may not always be so.

As mentioned earlier, some taonga have a greater level of mana and tapu than others. The difference may be put down to a few variables. The first is that there is a correlation between the mana of a taonga and the mana of the owning tribe or iwi. Uenuku is perhaps the best example of this: it belongs to the tribes of Tainui and is associated with Queen Ata. The korero associated with Uenuku is impressive. Thus the principle involved might be described as big tribe, big mana, hence high level of mana attached to its taonga. On the other hand, little tribe, little mana, and not much mana attached to its taonga. The level of mana is also correlated with the level of tapu. Uenuku is a taonga of great mana and great tapu, and there is little argument about this.

The next variable is the closeness of an association with death. Taonga such as bone chests are more tapu and have more mana than other taonga because they are part of the customs of burial. The bones of important people are scraped clean, deposited in one of these specially carved chests and then hidden away in some darkened cave. The bone chests in *Te Maori* were treated with great respect everywhere, and more so here at home, and again there is little argument that proximity to death renders taonga and people very tapu.

Another variable is genealogical connection to the owners and creators of the taonga. A taonga was accorded a higher level of mana and tapu by the descendants of the owning tribe than by all others. The genealogical link, once recognised, set in motion certain social obligations which the descendants felt it necessary to carry out. This might mean keeping close to their taonga, bringing an elder to clear away the tapu so they could interact with it safely, holding a church service to control the awesome powers of the ancestors, talking to the taonga as though it is their ancestor, bringing green leaves to lay at the feet, or generally behaving in a very affectionate manner to their taonga. Such behaviour indicates that the whakapapa principle is at work.

Another variable, mentioned already, is antiquity: the greater the antiquity associated with a taonga, the more mana and tapu adhered to it. A reason is that antiquity transforms ancestors into either tipua (awesome figures who are like taniwha or denizens of the ocean) or atua (godlike beings). An example of a tipua is my ancestor Te Tahi-o-te-rangi, who became a taniwha who is usually depicted as marakihau (sea monster) in carved meeting-houses in the Mataatua district. He remains today a highly respected ancestor of all the Mataatua tribes of Aotearoa. The Kaitaia lintel is clearly an example of an ancient taonga that has great mana and tapu. There are two regions in Aotearoa which have produced many very old taonga: the South Island, and the north of the North Island.

Another principle is the ihi, wehi and wana (the power, the awesomeness and the authority) of the created work. Some taonga are so beautiful that everyone agrees that the artist reached the ultimate heights of creativity, which our ancestors described as the three-in-one concept: ihi, wehi, wana. When antiquity is added to this quality, we have taonga of great mana and great tapu. Good examples are the storehouse carvings of Te Kaha, Te Potaka, the Patetonga lintel and many Te Ati Awa carvings recovered from the swamps at Waitara, Taranaki.

There are other variables, such as size and material, which play a part in differentiating taonga, and they do affect the judgements made regarding the mana and tapu of a taonga. Obviously, greenstone is highly valued, so that a greenstone patu is accorded a higher level of mana and tapu than a wooden one. Again, a whalebone patu is given a greater value than a wooden one, and so on. Such value judgements are bound to be affected by the size and quality of the material used.

Sometimes a taonga becomes very tapu and has high mana because of its particular korero and history. Ngati Kahungunu's Te Kauru-o-te-rangi is a fine example of this sort of taonga. Or it might be that the artist was a chief of great social position, or simply a great artist. Raharuhi Rukupo of Gisborne is a good example of a great artist. Other taonga are held to be great because of the mana and tapu of the original owner, as with a weapon associated with a particular chief. Obviously, such objects have a high heirloom value.

Conclusions

It is obvious from what I have written that taonga whakairo are a fascinating topic. They are complex creations of the human spirit which come out of Aotearoa, our particular corner of the Pacific Ocean and of the world. The results reach across generations and across national frontiers and are to be found in the museums and art galleries of the world. While they are a source of great pride to all people of Maori descent, they are at the same time open to being admired by the tini me te mano—that is, by the millions of people around the world. Maori artists have made, and are continuing to make, a contribution to human creativity which has a cultural mark of its own, a quality which is distinctively Maori.

Taonga whakairo has entered the consciousness not only of the scholars represented at this conference, but also of the Maori owners of the heritage, and particularly of Maori youth. This is a new phenomenon: a move towards repossessing part of one's cultural heritage and, by owning it, making a move

An example of the work of Raharuhi Rukupo, the great carver of Gisborne, who built and carved Te Hau-ki-Turanga, 1842. Now in the National Museum.

(National Museum)

towards controlling it. Repossession, however, entails learning, sometimes a painful re-education, and at other times an exciting experience of education and schooling working within the culture and for the benefit of the culture. Maori art has become a means of enculturation, of education in one's own culture.

In this context the terms we use become very powerful instruments of thought and of entry into the considerable literature on art. I have written about taonga; of korero associated with taonga; of whakairo, the art transforming process; of ihi, wehi and wana, the ultimate goal of creativity in Maori terms. I wrote about mana, the prestige and power of taonga, and of tapu, the sacred quality which kept pace with the level of mana accorded a taonga. Principles by which taonga were given different levels of mana and tapu were discussed. All in all, I presented a way of discussing art objects which drew upon the concepts of own culture, and by doing so attempted to provide a picture of how our people regarded their art. Such a discussion should throw some light upon our understanding of taonga.

References

Anderson, Richard L., 1989. *Art in Small-Scale Societies* (2nd ed.). New Jersey, Prentice Hall.

Davidson, Janet (ed.), 1989. *Taonga Maori: Treasures of the New Zealand Maori People*. Sydney, Australian Museum.

Graburn, Nelson H. (ed.), 1976. *Ethnic and Tourist Arts Expressions from the Fourth World*. Berkeley, University of California.

Hamilton, Augustus, 1901. *Maori Art*. Dunedin, Fergusson and Mitchell.

Haselberger, Herta, 1961. 'Methods of Studying Ethnological Art', *Current Anthropology* 2 (4) (October), pp.341–84.

Mead, Sidney M. (ed.), 1984. *Te Maori: Maori Art from New Zealand Collections*. New York, Harry N. Abrams Inc. and The American Federation of Arts.

Mead, Hirini Moko, 1986. *Magnificent Te Maori: Te Maori Whakahirahira*. Auckland, Heinemann.

Staples, Robert, 1984. 'Maoris and Black Americans: Members of the Fourth World', *Tu Tangata* 17 (April/May), pp.24–5.

Williams, Herbert W., 1971. *A Dictionary of the Maori Language*. Wellington, Government Printer.

20. Traditional Maori Leadership

The report 'Nga Toka Tu Moana: Maori Leadership and Decision Making' is a remarkable document. It was prepared under instruction from the Ministry of Maori Development as a way of assisting iwi and various government departments to understand issues of Maori leadership and mandate.

The whole question of mandate became very important after the signing of the Memorandum of Understanding for the Sealords deal, by which the Crown invested $150 million on behalf of Maori in Sealords, a large fishing company. A debate followed about who had authority to sign, what was the basis of their mandate, and whether they were self-appointed or mandate leaders.

As a result of this debate, iwi now have to sign protocols of mandate outlining the basis of the mandate of appointed negotiators. In this sense, the Sealords deal was a landmark decision which opened up a large area of debate about Maori leaders.

It therefore came as a complete surprise when the Minister of Maori Affairs, Doug Kidd, banned the distribution of the report of Nga Tuara, the group of elders appointed by the chief executive of Te Puni Kokiri, Wira Gardiner. The elders were Sir Monita Delamere (deceased), Bishop Manuhuia Bennett, Te Makarini Temara (deceased), Kate Walker, Kawana Nepia and me. 'Nga Toka Tu Moana' must stand alone as the only report banned by a Minister of the Crown so that information prepared by Maori for distribution to Maori about leadership was banned. We were accused of criticising the Sealords deal.

I have taken out of the report a chapter on 'Traditional Maori Social Groups' which I wrote. The title has been altered to focus on leadership. The information is straightforward and hardly a matter to be banned.

Nga Toku Tu Moana: Maori Leadership and Decision Making. Prepared by Nga Tuara, Te Puni Kokiri, Ministry of Maori Development, pp.8–21, 1992.

Introduction

Leadership and decision-making are aspects of a social, economic and political organisation. They are parts of a cultural system and cannot be understood fully by isolating them from their proper context.

In this report, however, an attempt is not being made to explore all aspects of Maori leadership and decision-making. Rather, the aim is to sketch in the details of the traditional system as a starting-point for discussion.

In this section, therefore, an outline of the social organisation is given, because leaders are attached to groups. The information is distilled from various sources and the model described is not to be regarded as a universal one which appeared in ideal form all over the country. Rather, the picture which emerges from the studies of archaeologists is that some tribal groups were more mobile than others and ranged over a huge territory to harvest a wide range of food when the time was appropriate. Other tribal groups lived and worked within a more prescribed area and had crops such as the kumara which enabled the people to live in more settled villages.

Attention turns then to the leadership system and what was expected of those in positions of responsibility. Different levels of leadership become apparent, and these are described.

In traditional Maori society there were four principal social groups: waka, iwi, hapu and whanau. These groups are linked together by virtue of common ancestry and a common history.

Te Waka

It is an essential part of matauranga Maori that the ancestors came from Tawhitinui, from Tawhiti pamamao, that is from a place across the sea of Kiwa. Several waka journeyed from Polynesia, and reached the shores of Aotearoa. The waka that feature prominently in the stories are Tainui, Te Arawa, Mataatua, Kurahaupo, Takitimu, Aotea and Tokomaru. Many songs celebrate the coming of seven canoes but there are actually many more, such as 'Nga Toki Mata Whaorua' and 'Horouta', to mention but two.

Stories tell of navigators and sailors who landed in Aotearoa, surveyed the land, claimed a portion of the country, established their territories and then settled the land.

As a social group, the waka is made up of a loosely organised cluster of tribes which descend from the crew members of one of the canoes. It was best to show descent from the captain of the waka.

The relationships between the units within a canoe cluster of tribes were maintained by war as well as by marriage among persons of the highest ranks. When the waka did come together for war purposes, the leadership was

Sir Monita Delamere and Makarini Temara. *(Mead collection)*

Frequently members of Nga Tuara travelled with the staff of the Iwi Transition Agency to meet with the people. Here the group accompany Wira Gardiner on the way to Otiria. *(Mead collection)*

The other member of Nga Tuara Kawana Nepia, seen here with kaumatua of Te Arawa. *(Mead collection)*

Some members of Nga Tuara are seen here with the CEO for what was then the Iwi Transition Agency on a visit to Ngati Maniapoto in 1989. In the group are John Paki, Henry Pryor, Pokai Waiari, Makarini Temara, leader from Te Arawa, Hirini Mead, Wira Gardiner, Bishop Manuhuia Bennett. The group is approaching for the welcome. *(Mead collection)*

assumed by the most senior line of the descendants of the founding family or by which iwi was leading the war effort. The waka rarely acted in solid form of union for any length of time and was rarely a controlled and cohesive group.

Te Iwi

The iwi was the largest socio-political organisation in Maori society. Although the name of a canoe was applied to a cluster of related tribes, the name of an eponymous ancestor was used as the name of the iwi, although an incident in tribal history may also have provided the name. Special prefixes were attached to the name of the tribe, signifying descent from a common ancestor. These were Ati-, Ngati-, Aitanga-, Ngai- and Whanau-. Both female and male ancestors provided the names. The most important feature of iwi was the principle that members were all related by descent through either parent.

While the iwi was the largest group that showed distinct autonomy in its internal organisation, and in its external relations with other similar groups, the tribe itself was a loose federation of smaller constituent groups related by common descent. Iwi is commonly translated as tribe.

Te Hapu

The iwi was made up of several subtribes or hapu of varying numbers, often reaching some 200–300 people. Central to the hapu was the kinship which joined all members of the hapu to a common ancestor, who may have lived a number of generations back, and through this focal point to the eponymous ancestor of the iwi. The ancestor chosen to represent the hapu was usually junior to the founding ancestor of the iwi. If not, an incident of history was selected as the name of the group—for example, Ngati Patutatahi, that is, the hapu defeated on the seaside.

The hapu united family groups for purposes of work and military defence. Large-scale projects such as building an assembly house, clearing cultivations, fashioning important canoes, fishing expeditions and the conduct of war were carried out by the hapu.

The hapu lived on that part of the tribal land owned by the hapu, and this ownership was recognised by other hapu in the iwi. The group owned gardens, swamps and forested areas, as well as fishing grounds inland and out at sea.

In the early 1800s three institutions stood out as important community assets: the marae (storehouse) and the whare runanga (assembly house). These together represented the social core of the hapu. Where the hapu settled was determined by the availability of food supplies, and by considerations of security against attack by other iwi or hapu. There were generally two types of areas: the pa tuwatawata, a fortified place usually on a high prominence, and the kainga, down on the flat. Outside the kainga at a convenient distance were the cultivations, and not very far away were the sources of other food supplies, such as the bush, with its bird life and edible rats, the inland lakes and rivers and the coastline and bays, which were sources of seafood and fish. The hapu had specific rights of access from their kainga to these food sources as well as ownership of these resources.

In some villages there was another institution which was not obvious to outside viewers but was usually well known by everyone else. This was the whare wananga or house of learning. Some, like Rawheoro at Tolaga Bay, were like high-status universities. They were known well beyond the boundaries of the iwi. Most iwi had at least one whare wananga, which all hapu supported, but the building was part of the assets of the hapu that cared for it.

Descent and inheritance of hapu members passed through both the father's and the mother's lines. It was usual for the wife to live with her husband's hapu, so that the offspring grew up and maintained closer association with the father's hapu. Land rights were inherited through either the mother or the father. There was, however, an important stipulation. In order to make good one's claim to land, one was required to keep the lighted fires burning there. This was known as 'te ahi ka', and was achieved through occupation and cultivation. Otherwise the claim became mataotao, or cold, and the title was extinguished.

Te Whanau

The hapu consisted of extended or joint family groups called the whanau. The whanau was the basic group in the Maori socio-political system and comprised the most intimate circle of social relationships. The whanau consisted of three to four generation levels, which included grandparents, parents, children and grandchildren and numbered as many as thirty or more people. The whanau was the household unit in the village. Each household unit consisted of separate buildings for sleeping, cooking and storing food.

The whanau owned all its own household units as well as fishing nets, fowling gear and canoes for river fishing. There were, however, individually owned weapons, fishhooks and cloaks. Members of the whanau shared many of their things, although some personal articles were more attached to some individuals.

The whanau was the most convenient work unit, with both men and women sharing some tasks such as cultivation and the drying of certain produce. While the women were the main gatherers of shellfish, it was the men who did the fishing, fowling and hunting. Men and women shared the cooking. The making of mats and weaving of garments was women's work.

The whanau provided the leaders for positions higher up and provided the basic workforce for the leader.

Tribal Differences

The social groups described above were not always formally structured. In the South Island (Ngai Tahu), for example, different hapu mixed together and were often nomadic. It was not uncommon to find in one settlement members of several different hapu. Settlements were often occupied on a seasonal basis depending on the availability of food.

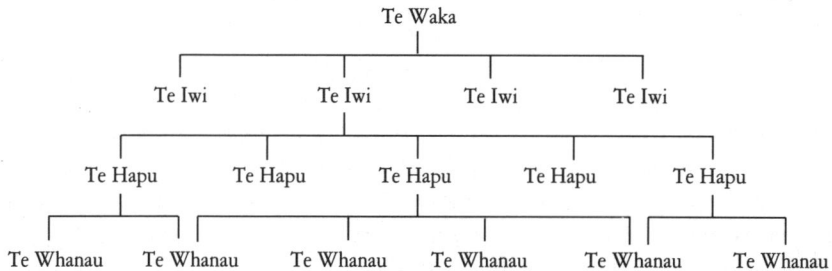

Figure 20.1
Te Waka, te Iwi, te Hapu, te Whanau

The Traditional Leaders

Within the defined social groups of waka, iwi, hapu and whanau were identifiable leaders who were chosen on their genealogy and personal qualities. These leaders were called ariki, rangatira, tohunga and kaumatua.

The Chiefs—Ariki and Rangatira

The chieftainship was held by two classes of leader. The more important was the ariki, or paramount chief. The ariki was the head of the iwi. The highest-ranking ariki, in whom the senior lines of the genealogy from tribal descents converged, was recognised as the head of the waka.

There was an ordering process according to whakapapa, and the variables are the matamua (first born) and the tuakana (seniority) preferences. The ariki is the person who was born out of a senior descent line (aho ariki, or chiefly thread), which ideally is a continuous line of first-born sons.

There was also the rangatira, or chief. The rangatira was the head of the hapu, and held a status slightly lower than that of the ariki to whom the rangatira was related, being a descendant of the original founding family along the junior line. The ariki and the rangatira were the social and political leaders in Maori society and they also played a part in economic affairs.

D. R. Simmons (1986, pp.129–30) suggested there was another ranking system in place and above the rank of rangatira—there were the taiopuru, the ahupiri, the noaia, the konini, the kaitahutahu arikinui and the kaitahutahu ariki—but there is little evidence to support such a fine grading of ranks or levels of leadership. The South Island iwi might have followed a different system, for there the social groups were much more dispersed; they tended to have few members, and were multi-hapu in nature (Anderson 1980). They had high chiefs and other chiefs.

The Elder—Kaumatua

Another class of leader was the kaumatua, or elder. The kaumatua was not necessarily a chief. The status of a kaumatua depended on whakapapa, age, wisdom and experience. The kaumatua was recognised by members of the extended family or whanau as their immediate leader. The kaumatua took part in all hapu and iwi discussions on behalf of the whanau.

The Ritual Leader—Tohunga

The tohunga was a specialist and gained a following from the expert knowledge he possessed. It is useful to focus on the general meaning of the word 'tohunga' because it appears on linguistic evidence that it was an inclusive term that admitted several persons, men and women, to leadership roles. This does not mean that it was easy to become a tohunga. The evidence of woodcarving and tattooing, tohunga whakairo and tohunga ta moko respectively, suggests that there was a long period of training and that a high standard of performance was demanded. Youths could not become tohunga and had to prove themselves over several years of performance to qualify. Sometimes the people to be trained as specialists were identified early and given special attention.

Leaders of the Maori world at Waitangi, 5 February 1990, at powhiri at lower marae. This was a day before the big events of Waitangi Day when the Queen was the guest of honour.

(Mead collection)

Most common was the religious expert or ritual leader. The tohunga as ritual leader was necessary throughout Maori society because of its strong religious orientation.

One of the features of the leaders we have outlined was the overlapping of many of the positions. the ariki, head of the waka, was also the head of an iwi, the rangatira of a hapu and the kaumatua of a whanau. A tohunga may also have been the head of a whanau but quite often was also a rangatira and an ariki.

In summary, there were chiefs, elders and specialists who covered a wide range of activities, from food production to fishing, preserving food, making fish nets, weaving cloaks, making doormats, shaping adzes, to making decorated kites. The various levels of leader acted within a structure of whanau, hapu and iwi.

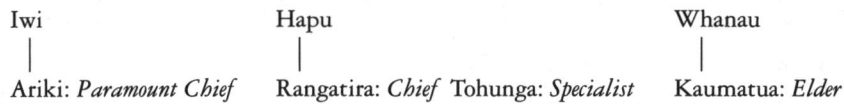

Iwi	Hapu		Whanau
Ariki: *Paramount Chief*	Rangatira: *Chief*	Tohunga: *Specialist*	Kaumatua: *Elder*

Figure 20.2
Traditional Maori Leaders

The Mandate of a Chief

In 1850 Te Rangikaheke asked: He aha te rangatiratanga o tena tangata? (What is the basis of that man's chieftainship?) (Grove 1985, p.11).

Rangatiratanga in Te Rangikaheke's terms was concerned with the mana and mandate of a leader, the basis upon which a leader was recognised as a chief.

Whakapapa—Moenga Rangatira

Te Rangikaheke believed that a rangatira came from a chiefly union of parents which he described as a 'moenga rangatira' (chiefly marriage bed). This was the most important aspect of the leader's mandate. Williams' *Dictionary* (1971, p.323) defines rangatiratanga as 'Evidence of breeding and greatness'. This definition certainly accords with Te Rangikaheke's views. Many writers since Te Rangikaheke have emphasised the importance of 'proper' birth credentials as an essential aspect of leadership.

A person coming from a moenga rangatira inherited certain 'pumanawa' or talents, and these are said to come from 'te koopu o toona whaea' (the womb of the mother), in Tikitu's opinion, or from te moenga rangatira, according to Te Rangikaheke (Grove 1985).

Nga Pumanawa o Te Rangatira—The Talents of a Leader

A leader was expected to possess certain talents: knowledge relating to some high-priority areas, and expertise to manage the affairs of the iwi. This is the second factor, after lineage. The two authorities, Tikitu and Te Rangikaheke, differ on the priorities and on the listing of talents. But they are agreed that expert knowledge is required. Firth (1959, p.12) described the particular talents as 'executive capacity'.

Tikitu was very clear about the attributes or talents of a chief and what they must be able to do in an ideal situation. He lists eight talents as follows:

1. He kaha ki te mahi kai.
   Has the knowledge of and is industrious in obtaining or cultivating food.
2. He kaha ki te whakahaere i ngā raruraru.
   Able to mediate, manage and settle disputes.
3. He toa.
   Is courageous in war.
4. He kaha ki te whakahaere i te riri.
   A good strategist and leader in war.
5. He mōhio ki te whakairo.
   Has knowledge of the arts of carving.
6. He atawhai tangata.
   Knows how to look after people.
7. Te hanga whare nunui, waka rānei.
   Has command of the knowledge and the technology to build large houses or canoes.
8. He mōhio ki nga rohe whenua.
   Has a sound knowledge of the boundaries of tribal lands. (Grove 1985, pp.6–7)

At the time that Tikitu gave his list of talents to Elsdon Best, the land wars were over and iwi were involved in a different sort of war: contesting ownership and entitlements to various land blocks in the Maori Land Court. In this context, it was essential that the leader representing an iwi in the Maori Land Court knew the boundaries, the history of battles, and sacred or significant places within blocks of land, and was familiar with the boundaries of other iwi. This level of knowledge had to be broader than knowing about one's own hapu or iwi.

Te Rangikaheke's list of 1850 was given at a time when traditional values were still strong and before the divisive and debilitating land wars of the 1860s had occurred. His list of six talents is set out below:

1. He mōhio ki te whakahaere i ngā kōrero o te mahi kai.
   Has command of the knowledge, science and technology of food acquisition and production.

2. He mōhio ki te whakahaere i ngā kōrero o te tangohanga whare, waka, pātaka, hereimu.

   Has command of the knowledge, technology, rituals and traditions pertaining to the construction and acquisition of houses, canoes, store-houses and cooking sheds.

3. Ka mōhio ia ki te whakahaere i ngā kōrero mo te whawhai, toa tonu ki te riri, hopu tūpāpaku tonu atu, whati rawa mai ka riri, nāna anō i whakahoki atu te whati.

   He knows how to conduct discussions on the strategies of warfare and is himself courageous in battle, is not afraid to kill and can turn adversities into victories.

4. Ko te kōrero manuhiri anō tētahi.

   Inviting and welcoming visitors is another (talent).

5. Ko te kōrero rūnanga anō tētahi.

   Conducting meetings of the people to discuss important issues is another.

6. Ko te atawhai anō tētahi.

   Yet another is being able to offer hospitality and to take care of people.

Te Rangikaheke puts a lot of stress on warfare, which, in his day and following the Ngapuhi raids, was an issue of paramount importance. He covers all aspects of warfare. The leader had to be a good fighter as well as a good manager and strategist.

Acceptance and Confirmation by the People

Thirdly, after the people have considered the whakapapa qualifications and the talents of the leader and seen some evidence of expertise, they will say 'Koia, kātahi nā nō te tino rangatira ko tēnā!' (There indeed is a true rangatira!) (Grove 1985, pp.150, 155). From this point Te Rangikaheke argues that, if the qualifications are right and the leader performs well, it all goes back to good breeding. It is because both the mother and the father were great people. Firth (1959, p.132) puts it another way: 'But birth alone did not suffice for chieftainship. Personality and executive capacity were also required to maintain rank and authority. An incapable ariki, as we already know, would be set aside in practical affairs and only called upon to perform certain religious rites.'

Identity of Leader Known by Other Iwi

The fourth aspect of a mandate is that the name of the leader is heard ('Ka rangona atu na tona ingoa') (Grove 1985, p.150). This means that, over time, other people become familiar with who the leader is for a particular iwi. A rangatira is not a surprise who appears from nowhere but is a person who is known to be a leader and whose name is associated over time with a specific group of people.

The Turangawaewae Principle

Just as it was important for the leader to have the appropriate birth credentials, it was equally important for the leader to be based in a rohe (territory). The leader's feet must be firmly grounded on land that is associated with the descent group to which the leader belongs. In the context of the land, the leader is able to call upon the symbols of the people that are part of the natural environment: the mountain, the river, the sacred places, the lake, the harbour. These symbols are part of the leader's aura or spiritual significance and are an important part of their credentials.

The Gender Aspect

Both Te Rangikaheke and Tikitu assumed that the leader, chief or ariki was male. Most chiefs were male, and being male imbued the mandate with the concerns of men, the style and nature of male leadership. Api Mahuika (1981), however, points out that there were many instances among Ngati Porou where the leaders were women and often leaders of ariki status. Women brought their own qualities to bear on leadership, but by and large the expectations of them were the same as for men.

Mana and Tapu

A leader who satisfies all of the qualifications and possesses the desired attributes is said to have mana tangata. According to Mahuika (1981, p.67), this gave the chief 'the authority to control and direct the activities of the tribe or sub-tribe'. The qualities of mana and tapu are an essential product of moenga rangatira and become attached to the person. How the qualities are expressed is subject to the personality of the leader and to performance over a period of time. Ihi, wehi and wana are qualities associated with mana tangata.

The Negation of Mandate

When a person fails to meet the criteria, the mandate is removed or, more typically, usurped by someone else. The next ideal choice is a more junior member of the same moenga rangatira, who might be the youngest brother.

Mahuika (1981, p.66) lists several ways by which the mandate of leadership can be acquired.

Briefly, these are:

1. by a younger sibling taking over the role of leader
2. by leaving the district and seeking promotion elsewhere
3. by forcing a division of the empire
4. by arranging a political marriage to improve one's prospects
5. by establishing a new leadership line and by inheriting the mandate from this moenga rangatira.

Research has revealed two other ways:

6. by waging war and occupying the land of another tribal group—that is, by raupatu (by the blade of a patu) or ringa kaha (the strong arm)
7. by cunning and sometimes outright murder.

Through time, the tendency is to return to the matamua or senior line but, whatever happens, the whakapapa credentials of a person cannot ever be extinguished. As Mahuika (1981, p.67) puts it, the right to be a leader can be forfeited but the privileges and rights of chiefly birth remain.

Leadership Responsibilities

A leader in traditional Maori society had a number of key responsibilities which were a direct reflection of the social and natural environments of the time.

1. Te mauriora (survival). This responsibility was paramount. Leaders had to concern themselves with the survival of the group despite the ravages of war, starvation and disease.
2. Tikanga (customs) and kawa (procedure). Leaders operated within a social system, and the group as well as the leader were guided by rules and precedents.
3. Moenga rangatira (the chiefly marriage bed). The chiefly lines had to be preserved and this was often achieved by arranged marriages between men and women of high birth.
4. Pa harakeke (continuity). As part of the responsibility of survival, it was considered important to ensure that birth rates were maintained at a level that ensured continuity of the social group. As a result, polygamy was not uncommon.
5. Tangohanga (acquisition of wealth). This responsibility concerns primarily the establishment of a sound economic base, e.g. plentiful sources and supplies of food, procurement of pounamu and taonga, etc. Economic wealth raised the status or mana of the group.

6. Tohatoha (fair distribution). It was important to ensure the fair and equitable distribution of resources within the social group. For example, the fishermen shared out the catch to all households in the village.

Decision-making

Executive Decision-making

In traditional Maori society decisions were made in various ways. There were times when leaders used their power to control and direct the people. Firth, as already mentioned, alludes to executive-type decisions. Where these were made, the leaders would know that their decisions would be accepted and supported. Their mana tangata would give them the authority and the confidence to make these types of decisions.

Decision by Runanga

At other times, decisions were reached by means of a runanga of the people. At such meetings, people could discuss the pros and cons of the issues and work towards a decision, through consensus. Where argument did not win the day, the word of a priest might. It was common practice to seek the advice of a matakite (seer) before embarking on any important activity. The seer was able to give confidence to a decision by predicting success, or to change a decision by predicting failure.

The role of the rangatira at a runanga was to listen to the discussion, summarise the main points and, if not apparent, indicate where the consensus view lay. Where necessary, the rangatira might participate in the discussion to persuade or convince people to a certain course of action.

Conflict Resolution

A good rangatira was expected to have the ability and expertise to settle a wide range of disputes. The rangatira achieved this by: keeping in mind an account of old scores that needed responses in the future; achieving utu successfully; having a store of precedents for handling internal disputes; and using judgement to apply the most appropriate precedent to fit a particular dispute.

Internal disputes could also be settled by means of the runanga. These were usually grievances that threatened the well-being of a hapu. The procedures were common to any runanga-type hui, with the people having the right to participate. The rangatira's main role was to ensure that the settlement was fair and that the runanga had properly judged how much public censure and whakama (the institution of shame) to apply.

Conclusion

The evidence indicates that there was a well-established leadership and decision-making system in traditional Maori society. The social groups of waka, iwi, hapu and whanau provided the traditional Maori with an established social and political structure within which various levels of leaders worked and where decisions were made.

Rangatira dressed differently from other people and were usually clearly defined in social gatherings. They wore superior cloaks, were well tattooed, and their hair was done in a topknot and adorned with a decorative comb and feathers of various birds.

There were many metaphors for rangatira, such as: te tumu herenga waka, the anchor-post for canoes; te rata whakaruruhau, the sheltering rata tree; te ta kotuku, the white heron feather.

The rangatira with a tattooed face vanished a long time ago, but tattooing is being revived and in the future the country could well see new tattooed leaders.

A hapu or iwi without a leader was held to be in danger of drifting like an abandoned canoe. The point is made in the proverb: Kia ai he ta kotuku ki roto o te nohoanga pahi, kia tau ai (Let there be a white heron feather in the assembly so the people are settled) (Williams 1971, p.354).

There were processes that involved decision-making by runanga or executive decisions made by the leaders.

Some leaders were ariki, others were rangatira and yet others were kaumatua.

Leadership personalities were acknowledged as a result of their whakapapa or chiefly qualities; they were not elected.

Leaders in traditional Maori society had the power and authority to punish and reward members of the various social groups. Their support was necessary for the well-being of the individual, but it was also true that the leader needed the support of the people.

The social system of traditional times is still in place, though greatly changed. Waka, iwi, hapu and whanau still exist despite years of government efforts to undermine them. There is still a Maori leadership system.

References

Anderson, Atholl J., 1980. 'Towards an Explanation of Protohistoric Social Organisation and Settlement Patterns Amongst the Southern Ngai Tahu', *New Zealand Journal of Archaeology*, Vol. 2, pp.3–23.

Firth, Raymond, 1959. *Economics of the New Zealand Maori*. Wellington, Government Printer.

Grove, Neil, 1985. 'Te Whatanui: Traditional Maori Leader', MA thesis, Victoria University, Wellington.

Mahuika, Api, 1981. 'Leadership: Inherited and Achieved', *Te Ao Hurihuri: The World Moves On*, edited by Michael King. Auckland, Longman Paul.

Simmons, D. R., 1986. *Ta Moko: The Art of Maori Tattoo*. Auckland, Reed Methuen

Williams, H. W., 1971. *A Dictionary of the Maori Language*. Wellington, Government Printer.

21. Tamaiti Whangai
The Adopted Child

A conference focusing on adoption, Adoption 1990, *was held at Victoria University on 10–13 May 1990. I was asked to give the keynote address. This is the text of that address.*

There are many Maori adults who were tamaiti whangai and understand the issues discussed. In most cases, they were brought up by a relative. There are cases, however, where adoption was cross-cultural and secret. Once the tamaiti whangai grows up, questions are asked which at first might be denied even by the adopted person. For example, it is possible for a Maori child brought up by Pakeha adopting parents to deny his or her identity as Maori and try to insist that he or she is Pakeha. This sort of adoption can become very troublesome. Openness presents the tamaiti whangai with fewer problems later in life.

After I presented this paper, many Maori told me they were tamaiti whangai and guessed that I was one, too. That is true.

Published in Adoption: Past, Present and Future, *edited by Pauline J. Morris, Proceedings of Conference, pp.85–95, 1994.*

According to our ancestors, the very first person to be adopted was Maui-tikitiki-a-Taranga (Grey 1953, pp.6–23). The circumstances were unusual, as one would expect. Maui was half-human and half-god, a demigod of Aotearoa and of greater Polynesia. The reasons a person is adopted can be good/positive or bad/negative. In Maui's case, his birth was unusual: he was so premature as to be classified as an abortion (he whakatahe). His mother wrapped him up in her hair and with seaweed and threw him in the sea. Maui was an aborted and rejected child (he tamaiti whakatahe) and his case is at one end of the spectrum.

Eventually the bundle was cast ashore, and by this time it had grown in size through becoming entangled with flotsam on the beach. There he was found by his tipuna or grandparent, Tama-nui-ki-te-Rangi (Great Son of the Sky). The tipuna wrapped him, cleaned him up, hung him over a fire, warmed his body and gave him life. From that moment the grandparent became Maui's matua whangai, his foster parent. No details are given of how he was brought up. We can assume, however, that because he was brought up by a grandparent he would have grown up in a caring environment.

When Maui grew up he did what is regarded as normal behaviour for a tamaiti whangai: he went in search of his parents. The story says he was drawn to the house of his family by the sounds of dancing and singing.

He found his parents but was grilled intensively by his mother to establish his claim that he was her youngest son, Maui-tikitiki-a-Taranga (Maui the topknot of Taranga). His mother was so pleased to be reunited with her son that she made him sleep beside her. This affectionate act caused great jealousy among the older brothers, who thereafter never really liked the intruder who just dropped in from nowhere.

Once his identity was properly established and his whakapapa clear to everyone, Maui went on to perform great deeds. He fished up the North Island, Te Ika-a-Maui, he slowed down the sun, he brought fire to the human population, and he challenged death itself but failed in this last task.

Another model of adoption is represented in the story of Tutanekai, who married Hinemoa, the princess of Tuhourangi, Rotorua (Biggs, Hohepa & Mead, 1967, pp.62–73). He was not born on the takapau hora nui (the spread-out mat) but was adopted as his own by the legitimate husband of Tutanekai's mother. This is a story of a forgiving husband, of a man who loved his wife's son as much as his own children. Tutanekai was brought up in a loving, caring environment and was nurtured by his own mother. His mana as a person was respected. To be sure, the other children were jealous of him, but the point of the story is that Tutanekai won the heart of Hinemoa. The pair married and founded a large hapu.

A third model of adoption is the case where two families meet over several months to discuss the sharing of a child. Eventually it is resolved that a child of Couple A will be given to Couple B to be brought up as their own, but without exclusion of the biological parents. An arrangement is worked out and while the child grows up there are frequent visits between the couples in order to keep the link between them warm. In fact, the couples co-operate in a number of social events, thus acknowledging a kinship link that has been made strong and warm by the sharing of the child.

I now discuss these three models in more detail. The analytical framework I use is derived from the Maui story, which points to the following aspects of adoption.

1. Te take (the cause). There is always a cause or a set of circumstances which are positive or negative and which lead to the child being adopted.
2. Te whanaungatanga (the relationship). There is a relationship, traditionally based on kinship, which marks the status of the adopting parent in relation to the child.

3. Te whangai (the nurturing). Once an adoption actually occurs, the adopting parents assume the responsibility to bring up the child as a member of the nuclear family and of the culture to which the parents belong.
4. Te kimihanga i te whakapapa (seeking the identity). This is the search for the correct whakapapa and real identity as a member of a social unit (hapu or whanau). The identity of the adopting parents is suspended while the search is on but is rarely rejected outright.
5. Te mana whanau (mana of the birth family). This is a result of the search when the individual is reinstated into the founding social unit—that is, one is reconnected with the roots of one's own identity as a person and wants to be recognised and accepted as belonging to that group.
6. Te mana whanau whangai (mana of the foster family). Once the search has been undertaken, answers found and the parents located, the tamaiti whangai is able to choose to stay with the matua whangai (adopting parents), to transfer to the other unit, or to simply act as a link between the two units.
7. Nga mahi (the deeds). Now the individual settles down to live their own life, to accept the challenge ahead in the manner of Maui, or marry and establish a whanau, as did Tutanekai, or follow an unremarkable but otherwise quite successful career.

1. Te Take

It needs to be stated at the outset that many adoptions are happy and are enjoyed by all concerned. In these cases the reason an adoption occurred was that precedents had already been established in Maori culture and thus there were models to follow. The precedents cover such cases as:

He whare ngaro (lost house)

Here the aim is to help a child survive because the parents' house has a 'ritual lien' on it and the family is classed as a whare ngaro. In such cases it is believed that the children will not survive and so must be given to other relatives to bring up. The children of a couple might be distributed widely in order to give the house a fighting chance of survival. Many older Maori people were brought up outside their nuclear families, and sometimes outside their locality, because of belonging to a whare ngaro.

He whakamahana i nga here whanaungatanga (warming the kinship links)

In this case two sets of parents negotiate over a long period of time for a child to become a link between them in order to keep the bonds of kinship between them warm. Such adoptions are open and the child has access to both sets of parents, between whom there is a close bond.

He wahine pukupa (barren woman)

In this case the wife is classified as barren and so the childless couple negotiates with relatives for a child for them to bring up. Sometimes a family can bring up many children, there might also be only one or two children. Such children enjoy an advantage of inheriting large land interests and of acquiring valuable taonga later in life.

He waka pakaru (broken canoe)

In this case the waka is broken and a parent, usually the mother, has died. The children are distributed among other relatives to bring up. This category of adoption is openly discussed, though hardly in circumstances in which free choices are available. Rather, it is more likely that kinship obligations apply and that relatives must try to share the children.

The precedents described above are traditional adoptions, which were recognised and practised extensively. There is a contrast between adoptions contracted Maori-style and according to custom, and the modern legal adoptions, which are bound by Western law, specify the obligations of the adopting parents, and give them legal 'ownership' of the child.

We come now to reasons which are regarded as bad, arising from some irregularities in the norms and values of society. Maui represents an extreme case of being born in an irregular way, of being whakatahe and not a regular human baby. So his mother rejected him and threw him into the sea.

In some countries, poverty might be cited as a strong reason for the abandonment of children. In New Zealand today, the most frequent cause of parental rejection is an unwanted pregnancy which occurs out of wedlock. In traditional times rejection was not an option: someone in the extended family would take the child.

Today, however, because of the movement of Maori populations to the cities, coupled with a tendency to adopt the Pakeha ethic of individuality, women are isolated from their whanau and hapu and sometimes from their nuclear families. In these circumstances, the unwanted child is distributed along a network of agencies and can end up in another country and often in another culture. It is done according to the law of the land. But these procedures are totally outside Maori customary law and would be regarded as a total abandonment of all cultural obligations and a denial of the whakapapa rights of the child.

The reason for being adopted is of pressing concern to a tamaiti whangai. Adoptions which follow customary practice are discussed often so that the reason someone was adopted is likely to be understood. But there are instances where everyone but the tamaiti whangai knew the circumstances of the adoption and understood the nature of the relationship between the two sets of parents.

The rejection model is the most difficult for the tamaiti whangai to cope with, and indeed for the parents to explain. The Maui story does not provide a ready excuse for modern cases of rejection.

2. Te Whanaungatanga

In traditional times a child given to an absolute stranger could end up being food for the oven. In this case the child loses all rights to the founding group, is vulnerable and open to abuse, and has no protection. In fact, the child becomes a non-person. The kinship principle is of paramount importance in Maori thinking, the closer the better, in order to protect the interests of the child. These interests include:

a. the social place of the child
b. the heritage, including physical property such as land
c. the culture and language
d. the self-esteem, mana and tapu of the child.

The child was considered to be a taonga or valuable human asset of the whanau and one day would become a participating adult. Thus it was in the interests of the whanau to protect its human assets.

From the child's point of view, the close relatives could generally be relied upon to help when needed, to give a commitment for the future and to provide a social nest in which to grow as an individual.

The three models of adoption described in this paper follow the whanaungatanga principle. To give a child to strangers is tantamount to throwing Maui out to sea, and to give a child into the hands of a stranger and alien culture amounts to the same thing. It was not done in traditional times.

It is worth saying that an individual parent does not have a right to sever the kinship cord or life-line of a child, nor to throw a child into another culture. If the whanaungatanga principle is followed, no cultural violence is done to the child.

3. Te Whangai

In all traditional models of adoption, the basic assumption is that the tamaiti whangai will be brought up as a member of the whanau, speaking Maori and behaving like an enculturated Maori. It was not quite like this for Maui. He was brought up by a god, and the activities he enjoyed and the manner in which he did them were altogether different from the way of his brothers. He did not really fit the family of his brothers. On the other hand, Tutanekai was brought up by Whakaue to be a Maori chief and to be acceptable as a husband and later as a father of Maori children. There was no dislocation or alienation from his culture.

In Maori terms, the important task of the foster parents is to feed the child, hence the term 'tamaiti whangai' (tamaiti = child, whangai = to feed). But whangai focused not only upon food but also upon nurturing, educating, providing opportunities to grow up as a healthy individual with one's mauri strong, one's mana secure and one's tapu intact. Eventually the tamaiti becomes adult and, though it seems that the job is done, in fact obligations have been established in the process of growing up and a bond is established for one's lifetime.

It is quite clear in the Maori mind that the task of whangai was to bring up the child in the culture of the parents. In the modern world, however, the expectation is complicated by mixed marriages and by a growing interest in a uniform international culture where everyone listens to the same pop music stars, eats hamburgers, drinks Coca-Cola and wears jeans. Let me discuss these different circumstances.

At Victoria University I have met several very obviously Maori people who were adopted by Pakeha parents and brought up as Pakeha. University is usually the time and place when young people face a crisis of identity. Maori students in this situation go through a traumatic re-entry process which is personally painful, difficult and terrible to witness. From cases I have seen at Victoria University, I am convinced that the practice of allowing Maori children to be brought up by Pakeha New Zealanders to be white New Zealanders is wrong and cannot be justified. What happens is that Pakeha parents follow the theory and practice of assimilation, they assimilate a Maori child, and in the process they alienate the child from its culture and its relatives. The failures of assimilation are then loaded onto the tamaiti whangai, who is then regarded as an ungrateful beast. A thornier problem is the case of a mixed marriage when the child in the middle becomes not a valuable link but rather a cultural football. One obvious answer is to whangai the child into both cultures, so that the child can be culturally comfortable with either parent.

The problem, however, is what happens in adoption. The Maori attitude is that a child born of a Maori parent, has a natural right to whakapapa, to the heritage of the Maori parent and to the culture. Denial of these rights by well-meaning adopting parents cause immense problems for the tamaiti whangai and often result in a life of guilt and a very slow path back into Maori culture. Maori communities lose the services of such people, and a way of making a contribution to one's culture is blocked or made difficult.

There is a tendency in the modern world towards an international ethic in which cultural differences are suppressed and everyone shares the same goods.

Following this tendency is the practice of adopting exotic babies who are treated like exotic pets. This practice does not accord with tikanga Maori, or Maori customary practice, and I for one do not approve of our babies being exported for adoption. It would be the ultimate insult to an indigenous group such as ourselves to be regarded as a supplier of unwanted children.

4. Te Kimihanga i te Whakapapa

Maui set out to find his parents because in his case a dislocation had occurred. As already pointed out, the search was rendered unnecessary by the traditional modes of adoption, which were negotiated and discussed openly. Moreover, in the growing-up phase, the links between the two sets of parents were kept warm and the whakapapa rights of the child were maintained. This aspect of traditional adoption ensured that the child enjoyed the attentions of more than one mother and father. And, since the kinship system itself classified all aunties as mothers and all uncles as fathers, there was no trauma attached to having two sets of parents. The point needs to be emphasised: the kinship system allows for many mothers and many fathers who traditionally are all part of the family support system. Thus it is not unusual to have, for example, several mothers. In fact, it was an advantage to the child to have many mothers and fathers.

The strong value placed by our Maori ancestors on maintaining the whakapapa rights of any child, and especially those of the tamaiti whangai, is worth keeping today. If this right of the child is protected, then the troublesome phase of having to search for that whakapapa is made unnecessary. For the tamaiti whangai who was adopted in secrecy, the searching phase is difficult and it may take years to break through the veil of secrecy.

5. Te Mana Whanau

In Maui's case, when he found his parents he turned against his foster parent, Tama-nui-te-Rangi, who represented the warmth-giving sun. He beat him and slowed him down so that all humans could enjoy longer and warmer days. This is one model, and it could be that many adopted sons and daughters return to the whanau and derive their mana and their identity from that group. It becomes the social unit within which they live out their lives as adults.

It could also be that the more traumatic the search process is, the more likely the fostering family will be rejected. This would be because the matua whangai oppose efforts to find the other parents and do not approve of the tamaiti whangai going back to their own culture. New Zealand can provide some examples of awkward and difficult foster parents who disapprove of Maori culture and object to 'their' child going 'back to the bush'.

6. Te Mana Whanau Whangai

In many cases discovery of the real parents does not result in a change of residence. The tamaiti whangai remains an important member of the whanau whangai (foster family) and acts out the various roles of adulthood from that social unit and its place of residence. Discovery of the whakapapa links satisfies the hunger to know and understand one's self. As long as the adopting parents remain open and understanding, so will the mana of adopting whanau remain.

7. Nga Mahi

In the three models I described, the tamaiti whangai was able to lead a successful life. Because Maui was a demigod, we cannot really regard him as an appropriate model. One expects a demigod to accomplish phenomenal deeds, such as fishing up the Great Fish, the North Island. But the point to be made in the story is that being an adopted child is not necessarily a handicap. It can be, if principles to safeguard the interests of the child are neglected and set aside. By and large, however, there is every reason to expect that being a tamaiti whangai can be and should be a good positive experience which will help to bring out the pu-manawa (talents) of the individual. Using the model of Maui, one can predict that most tamaiti whangai will try harder to succeed than others. Many successful men and women spent their childhood as a tamaiti whangai.

Conclusions

Modern adoption practices which are sanctioned by law mean well, but from a Maori perspective do not really protect all the fundamental rights of the child. No matter what the circumstances of the birth, a child is born with a unique set of attributes and qualities. A Maori child is born with a whakapapa—that is, with a place in a set of social relationships within the context of a hapu or of several hapu. The whakapapa defines the child, both as an individual and as a member of a social unit. One provides an individual name and the other gives hapu designation—for example, Ngati Pahipoto. The child is also born with a personal mauri (essence of life), tapu (a sacred quality inherited from the parents) and mana (a position in the social universe). Finally, the child is born into a culture which provides another designation, Maori, by which a person is identified. With the culture comes access to a rich heritage of art, history, language and special things known as taonga tuku iho (heirlooms), and today access to tribal aspects and programmes of assistance is of vital importance to a person who might qualify to be a beneficiary of a particular tribe. Recent settlements of tribal grievances—Tainui, Ngai Tahu, Whakatohea and others—highlight the importance of whakapapa.

The package of attributes and qualities which belongs to a child at birth needs protection. While it is true that some natural parents fail to protect and nurture a child properly, a great majority of parents do bring up their children well and do attend, more or less, to the cultural needs of their offspring. Adoption customs pose a threat to the package. Changes to legislation should specify the rights of a child which need to be protected and which the matua whangai have to address.

First is the right to know about the circumstances of the adoption. This means that, at a suitable time, a disclosure has to be made to the child and the appropriate documents handed over. If made informally at an early stage, and so the child already knows, a formal disclosure procedure can be waived.

Second is the right to know one's whakapapa. This follows logically from the right to know. The tamaiti whangai knows who the biological parents are and is able to get in touch when a need is felt.

Third is the right of whanaungatanga. Here the child has the right to expect that the adopting parent belongs to the same hapu or iwi and that there is some relationship between them. And, if this is not the case, special measures need to be built into the agreement to make visiting rights to the whanau mandatory and regular.

Fourth is the right of cultural integrity. Present legislation is weak on this point. The child must be brought up in a way which makes entry into Maori culture comfortable and welcoming. Adoption must not result in cultural alienation. The ideal situation is for Maori children to be brought up by Maori foster parents, Chinese children to be fostered by Chinese parents, and Australian Aborigine children to be brought up by Aborigine matua whangai. This is an issue of primary concern to minority groups.

Finally, the bottom-line position is that the person, the child, is the most important taonga to be considered. The question is asked: He aha te mea nui? Maku e ki atu, he tangata, he tangata, he tangata. What is the most important thing? I answer it is the child, the child, the person.

References

Biggs, B., P. Hohepa & S. M. Mead, 1967. *Selected Readings in Maori*. Wellington, A. H. & A. W. Reed.

Grey, Sir George, 1953. *Nga Mahi a Nga Tupuna*. Wellington, Maori Purposes Fund Board.

Recommended Reading

Else, Anne, 1991. *A Question of Adoption*. Wellington, Bridget Williams Books.

22. Haere, Haere, Haere
Maori Ideas about Death and Grieving

This article was published in a series dealing with Perspectives on Death and Dying. It appeared in the book Coping with the Final Tragedy: Cultural Variation in Dying and Grieving, *edited by David R. Counts and Dorothy A. Counts, friends I met at McMaster University in Hamilton, Ontario. The book was published in 1991 by Baywood Publishing Company, Amityville, New York.*

I trained as an anthropologist and served as professor of Maori Studies at Victoria University. But I am also an active participant in my own culture. This article springs largely from direct experience in attending many tangihanga, both as a member of the bereaved family and as a visitor. I write also as one who has had to play the role of elder and speaker on many of these occasions. There is a considerable difference between being a participant observer and being an actual in-group member.

Proverbial Sayings

It is a truism that human life is but a brief moment in the stream of history, that life is transitory, is measured and, being limited in duration, is highly valued. The wise men of the Maori world had many proverbial sayings about the nature of life and death. An example is:

Rārangi maunga tū te pō tū te ao: rārangi tangata ka ngaro, ka ngaro, ka ngaro.
A range of mountains remains standing night and day but a group of people is lost, is lost, is lost.

Sayings such as this continue to have an important place in the mourning ceremony called tangihanga (the weeping) because people want to know what their ancestors thought about death and what wisdom and good advice there is for them. Although proverbial commentaries on death might be repeated again and again, members of a Maori community do not tire of hearing them.

Likewise, the story of Maui's attempt to seek immortality for us humans can be told many times without boring the audience. This is because the stories have a spiritual and mystical dimension to them which is additional to the knowledge carried by the words.

Significance of Traditions

There is, in fact, more to the so-called myths of tribal society than scientifically trained educators realise. Moreover, the explanations for death given by scientists or by Christian teachers are not inherently superior to those that belong to indigenous cultures, nor are they more comforting to the bereaved. For the Maori people of New Zealand, it was their culture hero Maui-tikitiki-a-Taranga (Maui the topknot of Taranga) who provided the model of death. He was the first to die and, since he died, we must all follow him. There is no escape from the path prepared by Maui.

How he died provides one cultural model of behaviour for the modern-day Maori. He attempted to expand the frontiers of immortality by challenging the goddess of death. The theory the sages proposed for the confrontation was that death is the opposite of birth, that the spark of life lies in the womb of woman, and that the way to secure immortality was to reverse the process of birth, grasp the spark of life and remove it from the goddess, Hine-nui-te-Po (Great Maid of the Night). Maui failed. His accomplice, the twittering fantail, laughed at the spectacle of the man-god Maui re-entering the womb. Consequently, the goddess woke up with a fright and crushed Maui, and that was how he died. He did not wait for death to claim him. Rather, he tried to outwit the goddess but failed in his attempt. Thus life can be viewed as an active pursuit of the spark of life. To give up this struggle is to succumb to the goddess of death.

Explanations of Death

During a tangihanga a lot of talking and explaining is done. The ceremony usually lasts three days and formal speech-making (whaikorero) is a standard requirement. It is during these speeches that people remember and talk about Maui. Explanations of death are of paramount importance to the mourners, to the relatives of the deceased, to the friends who are touched by the sense of tragedy which death always causes, and to those who are summoned together to attend the tangihanga. The tragedy of the situation affects the immediate family perhaps more than others, and they especially want to hear the explanations, the proverbs and the comforting words of the ancestors. This is not to denigrate other explanations such as Christian ones, which are frequently heard at tangihanga in New Zealand today.

It is also fair to say that not all modern Maori families are attuned to and trained in their culture. Many are not familiar with Maui's deeds and their association with the tangihanga ceremony. This is due to the nature of New Zealand society, dominated by an English-speaking, largely British-oriented majority and their values and customs. Some Maori families are persuaded to follow the mourning customs of the Pakeha and not their own. Nonetheless, there is a strong ethic among Maori people to conduct the ceremonies of mourning properly and in the proper cultural context.

Public and Private Grieving

There are some obvious reasons for people wanting to talk about death. First is the human need to share the tragedy and draw support from around the immediate kin. The next is to express grief through tears and talk, and by these means come to accept the death of their relative.

Maori practice favours open grieving but, as happens in other cultures, there are patterns to this apparent free-for-all weeping. The culture does not expect mourners to weep copiously for three or four days. Rather, there are public and private moments for grieving. The public times are signalled either by the arrival of visiting mourners or by significant changes in the ceremony. In the former, the manuhiri and the tangata whenua or home side engage in loud wailing, sometimes exacerbated by the presence among the visitors of a close relative. Such concentrated wailing and weeping among the women may last about five minutes.

It stops when the home orator gets up to make his formal oration. The wailing may start again half an hour or more later, when the visitors come to meet the tangata whenua and the kiri mate (dead skin) or immediate family. In between the arrival of visitors, and late at night, there are comparatively private times for the family. They are free to weep on their own, and many do.

Points of Intensity in Mourning

Other times when weeping is likely to become intense are when some irreversible stage is reached in the ceremony. The arrival of the corpse on to the marae to lie in state is one of those moments. Another is when the coffin is finally closed and the face of the deceased is never seen by human eyes again. Yet another moment is when the body leaves the marae for the cemetery. Often the most dramatic and poignant occasion for the mourners is when the coffin is finally lowered into the ground. At this point, all physical signs of the deceased are lost and this is the final farewell, the final closure on a life. The words 'haere, haere, haere' (depart, depart, depart) take on a special finality.

After the funeral, the kiri mate might be required to go as a group to other tangihanga ceremonies to take their mate (death) to the other marae. Some visits are a long way from home but this part of the mourning process is called 'kawa mate' (taking the death) when some commentators have noted that the spirit of the deceased is called back and then farewelled again.

A year later, when the memorial stone is unveiled, the kin gather again at the marae to go through an abbreviated form of the tangihanga. Weeping is less intense at this time but, as before, custom allows loud weeping at set times—at the very beginning of the unveiling ceremony and again beside the grave at the cemetery. This is callled 'hura kohatu' (unveiling the stone). Outside these prescribed times the bereaved family is free to weep privately in their own way.

The Leading Role of Women

What characterises the tangihanga ceremony is the respect paid to those who are weeping and the care taken not to stem the flow of tears. The mourners have the right to weep in public. There are no limits set on age or sex, but there is a clear expectation that it is the old women who lead the mourning and who set the cultural standards for the occasion. The British value placed on the stiff upper lip in the face of adversity has no place in the tangihanga. Instead, grief is given expression in tears, wailing and talking. In former times women used to

The kohatu or memorial stones at the cemetery at Kokohinau Marae. These have to be unveiled at a hura kohatu ceremony.
(S. M. Mead)

A poignant moment at a tangihanga is the actual burial. Here tohunga of the Ringatu church are conducting the burial service.
(S. M. Mead)

cut themselves with obsidian, but this is no longer done. What remains from the past is a form of weeping which is like a dance. The mourner employs the quivering hand movements of dance and weeps to a sort of dirge. It is a very beautiful form of mourning which is becoming less common.

Reviewing the Life of the Deceased

There is no shame in tears and there is great comfort in words. Visitors tell their memories of the deceased, and sometimes recount their shared experiences. At times the life's work of the deceased is subject to criticism or praise. Often an orator draws attention to the loss to the community as well as to the family. A person is lauded for the activities they performed for the common good, for the tribe or for Maori society generally. Or the deceased might be condemned for not doing enough. But it is a time which can be used to bury the hatchet and allow conflicts to be resolved.

Sharing Traditional Knowledge

During the formal speeches, speakers frequently allude to traditional Maori knowledge. This occurs when the exploits of Maui are interpreted to make them relevant to the bereaved. People talk about Maui as though his encounter with the goddess of death occurred only yesterday. The speaker mentions those already departed, and may talk about the journey of the deceased to Te Reinga, at the northern tip of the country, and the ocean journey to Hawaiki-nui (Big Hawaiki), Hawaiki-roa (Long Hawaiki) and Hawaiki pamamao (Distant Hawaiki), the mythical homeland of the Maori (Oppenheim, 1973, p.94). We share with many other Pacific cultures the idea of the spirit going on a journey to a land of peace and plenty. In the Maori case, heaven is in Hawaiki far out into the Pacific Ocean.

Different tribal groups might have their own point of departure for the spirits. Te Reinga in the Far North is one commonly referred to in farewell orations. For some of the Mataatua tribes in the Bay of Plenty, Paepae-Aotea (Volkner Rocks) is the departing-place for the spirits. From here they go to Te Reinga and then to Hawaiki-pamamoe.

Contest Between Life and Death

Death is often described as a struggle between life and the forces which conspire to terminate it. These forces include the ill will of adversaries, ritual errors committed innocently or deliberately, sickness, accident, wilful violence and so on. For example, some ceremonial adze handles are decorated with the powerful image of a human figure contending mouth to mouth with a lizard, which is regarded as the symbol of death (Barrow 1972, p.166, Fig. 296). Here the message is easy to read. Life is a continuous struggle to prevent the lizard from entering the stomach of a victim and then slowly eating away its body. The idea of a lizard being the cause of sickness is part of the belief system of the Maori (Best 1941, Vol. I, p.107). Ill health was not caused by a germ caught without design from the atmosphere. Rather, the germ is in the form of a lizard, and someone maliciously directed it to the victim. In other words, one does not 'catch' a sickness such as a cold from another person. A person actually *gives* a sickness. There is usually a reason for this sort of giving.

In other art work, the image might be of a human figure biting the tail of a lizard. In this case, the message is that, rather than accept philosophically that we must all die and so wait for it to come, one should tease the tail of death and lead an adventurous life. In other words, people should follow the example of Maui.

Non-Material Aspects of Life

Each living person has several non-material aspects. Mauri and hau are both regarded as principles of life. Mauri is translated as the life principle (the thymus) and hau is the vitality or vital essence of a person (Williams 1957, p.197). Both are delicate, and an attack on one affects the other. Sorcerers were apt to focus especially upon the hau when they worked their arts of black magic known as makutu or sorcery (Oppenheim 1973, pp.81–6). The expected result of makutu was that the state of being well, hau-ora, would change to a state of near death, or hau-mate. Thus the role of the sorcerer was to negate ora (life) and convince victims that their life principles had been destroyed. If this is not halted, the mauri weakens, the spark of life loses its vitality and warmth, and the victim dies.

Makutu

In traditional times, accusations of makutu were quite frequent and many of the suspected sorcerers were identified and killed (Oppenheim 1973, p.85). The frequency with which sorcerers were killed suggests that the homicides were justified on the grounds that the sorcerers had caused death. In other words, a person, not the gods, had killed out of malice. The family had to establish who exhibited the greatest malice towards them.

Sometimes the reason for a person becoming ill and dying was diagnosed as the victim having committed a ritual transgression. For example, an error in the public performance of a waiata or in the recitation of a genealogy would be regarded as a serious ritual error. Similarly, mistakes in the visual arts, including carving, painting, lattice work and weaving, would result in some expected utu.

Ritual Errors

Another source of trouble was the violation of an important ritual rule such as desecrating a wahi tapu. Any ritual transgression gave cause for reprisal. Sometimes these took the form of a chain of disasters which befell a family. For example, members of the victim family might all die in strange and horrible ways—by murder, by road accidents, by their own hands, and so on. People usually explained such a tragedy as being due entirely to some ritual transgression. No other explanation was acceptable to Maori elders.

In modern terms, the cause is described as a whiu (curse). A whiu is 'caused' by committing ritual errors and is a consequence of them. While some whiu have very serious consequences, others have comparatively mild ones. In some cases a family is described as a whare ngaro because it is believed that a curse was put upon it that resulted in death after death among the children. Only one child may survive the curse, and then only to provide a means by which the family can continue. While Maori elders can cite case after case of whiu operating in modern society, people believe that most such curses can be averted. The solution is karakia. It is necessary for the gods to intervene. Today this intervention often requires people to appeal to both the Christian god and the gods of traditional Maori society.

Role of Tohunga

The more important appeal is to the traditional gods of the Maori using karakia. These must be recited by an acknowledged priest or tohunga. Even physicians in hospital occasionally find it necessary to appeal to tohunga to help save their patients from illnesses which are described as mate Maori. I have also heard of big companies requiring the services of a tohunga to convince factory workers that the proper rituals for their protection in the workplace were indeed carried out and hence their families were not in danger.

Progression Towards Final Death

Death itself is seen to be progressive—that is, a person is transformed from a state of good health to a state of hau-mate (vital essence is dying or dead). When a person becomes very ill, as for example with cancer, the body is described as beginning to whakaheke or descend. There is weight loss and the person's vital essence lacks spark. The metaphors of descending and sinking are used to describe this state of dying and refer to the belief that the dead go into the care of the goddess of death in the underworld.

Transition From Person to Corpse

Just before a person dies, there is a ceremony called tuku wairua which sends the spirit of the dying away while the person is still alive and conscious of what is happening. Death is signalled by the final breath, the expiration of hau. Once the spirit has departed, the person may be medically dead but, in a Maori sense, he or she is not wholly dead yet. An important transformation has occurred: the person is now a tupapaku (standing shallow), a corpse. The ceremonies collectively called the tangihanga commence and the tupapaku is given a space in the meeting-house or house of mourning. The corpse lies in an open coffin so that the face can be plainly seen. It is dressed up and prepared nowadays by professional undertakers, but this task used to be performed by the extended family.

The Fiction of Sleeping

Ornaments, weapons or traditional Maori cloaks may be placed over the corpse, who is now ready to 'participate' in the ceremonies. At this stage, all the orators address the corpse in the first person. Participants act as though the corpse can hear and is merely sleeping. In fact, orators move from statements of 'sleep, sleep, sleep' to 'depart, depart, depart' as though the status of the corpse is ambiguous. What is clear, however, is that all orators address the deceased. To this extent there is a general belief that the deceased is sleeping, still able to hear, and able to convey messages to those gone before.

Three days later, when the tupapaku is buried, a further stage of death is reached. The person's face is now out of sight and the person has gone for good. Mourning is still not complete until a year later, when the memorial stone is erected and the relatives come together once again to confirm that the mourning ceremonies were completed properly. At this stage, the spirit of the deceased is summoned back to the marae to witness the event and one may hear again the words 'sleep, sleep, sleep'. Now the message of farewell is much stronger and so the words 'haere, haere, haere' have a ring of finality about them. After this, death is final. Restrictions upon widows or widowers are lifted and they are free to remarry. The widows and widowers are called pouaru, and women far outnumber men. Women tend to outlive their husbands and many remain as widows.

Obligations of Kin

The assembly of the relatives is an important part of the mourning process. Maori clearly understand that near relatives must attend while more distant relatives should do so. Close relatives are obliged to stay for the whole ceremony because their support is needed. It is a time of social renewal, of ensuring that one's face is seen, of re-emphasising the importance of the social unit, the hapu or whanau, and of getting to know younger members of the unit and the in-laws. This group of relatives is assembled twice, at the beginning of the mourning cycle and at the end. The more important the deceased, however, the more likely it is that the 'kin' group would be required to assemble more often than the two occasions mentioned here. There is another series of ceremonies, the kawe mate already mentioned, which entail taking the death to other kin groups at different places in the country. The obligations upon the kin can be quite demanding in time required, and some people have difficulty obtaining leave from their jobs. The coming together emphasises the importance of the hapu in helping its members through crisis.

The Metaphors of Death

There are many ways of expressing the often devastating effects of death. Occasionally, as in the case of a long illness, death is really a great relief for the whole family. Often, however, death comes unexpectedly or quickly and the family is not ready for it. In Maori society, the effect is variously referred to as the shattering of a canoe, as whales cast upon the shore, as a house destroyed, as a mountain covered by dark clouds, or as a rough cloak which has to be worn. The portents of death are the flashing of lightning, the peals of thunder, the shaking of the earth by earthquakes and the darkening of the sky.

The Flax Bush

For some, warnings of impending death within the family come in the form of dreams, which are then analysed for the message. It is a point of comfort for Maori that the deceased leave behind a pa harakeke or flax bush. This is a family of children to become the living faces of the departed, to become their hands and their feet, and to continue the work they did not finish. There is a strong sense of continuity down a line of descent to children who, in turn, will grow up and do their part in the chain of continuity. There is, as well, a strong belief that the ancestors do live and find expression in their descendants. This might be manifest in voice, in appearance, in mannerisms or in some qualities which remind the members of the group of relatives no longer to be seen. Reflections of them are, however, seen in their descendants.

Thus, while death causes closure on one individual life, in the normal scheme of things there is continuity in the descent line. One lives on in one's children. This is the only way in which death can be overcome.

23. Aspects of Raupatu

I was asked to appear as an expert witness on behalf of Ngati Mutunga and Te Ati Awa in their Waitangi Tribunal case identified as WAI-65. The submission is included in this part of the book as it deals with the definition of raupatu. Raupatu became an issue between the Moriori claimants and Ngati Mutunga. My task was to present traditional knowledge and understanding of the concept of raupatu in order to help the claimants.

The submission was presented at Waiwhetu in July 1994, when my own iwi, Ngati Awa, had began its raupatu case before the Waitangi Tribunal at Whakatane. Our case arose out of raupatu as practised by the Crown. Ngati Awa became victims and we know about the results of raupatu. Since I had studied the concept of raupatu as it applied to us, the opportunity to consider other cases was a useful expansion of knowledge. The paper is in the form of a submission to the Waitangi Tribunal.

1. Introduction

1.0 I am Hirini Moko Mead of Ngati Awa. I am trained as an anthropologist and received by PhD in that field. Maori culture has been of special interest to me for several decades. After training as a primary school teacher, I taught in several Maori communities in the Urewera, East Coast, Hawke's Bay and Waikato. During these years I had first-hand experience of Maori culture at the grass-roots level and was exposed to different histories and customs.

1.1 Following that, I attended university both here and overseas. After graduation I taught at Auckland University, McMaster University in Ontario, UBC in British Columbia and Victoria University of Wellington, where I was head of Maori Studies from 1977 to 1991. I am currently associated with the establishment of Te Whare Wananga o Awanuiarangi at Whakatane.

My family and I were farewelled at Kokohinau, Te Teko before our departure in 1965 for Southern Illinois University at Carbondale. John Waititi of Te Whanau-a-Apanui and Pat Hohepa of Te Mahurehure accompanied us.
From left: Hoani Waititi, Pat Hohepa, Aroha Mead, Hirini Mead, June Mead, Linda Tuhiwai Mead. *(Harry Dansey)*

1.2 I was responsible for introducing into university programmes the study of traditional or customary concepts of our people. This came about as a result of my suggestion in 1979 that we apply a rahui to a Springbok tour. Since then the idea of studying tikanga at universities, polytechnics, teachers' colleges and wananga has become widely accepted. The date can be pinpointed to 1980.

1.3 After Sir Peter Buck blazed the trail as the first Maori to be admitted as a fellow to the Royal Society of New Zealand, there was a long period before another Maori was admitted. In 1991 I had the honour of being accepted as the second Maori scholar to become a fellow and entitled to use the title FRSNZ. Towards the end of last year Professor Hugh Kawharu and Professor Mason Durie were also admitted, so that now mine is no longer a lonely position.

1.4 I have some expertise in the area of Maori customs and am qualified, after many years of studying, teaching and trying, to apply some of these customs to modern situations. The fact of being admitted as a Fellow of the Royal Society of New Zealand recognises that I have some mana in these matters.

2. Brief of Evidence

2.0 I have been asked by fellow descendants of Awanuiarangi to offer some comments on some traditional concepts which have a particular bearing on WAI-65.

2.1 My brief is to speak to and elaborate on specific customs which may be helpful to all parties to this claim.

2.2 I am not an expert on Moriori customs and shall not be commenting on tikanga from that point of view.

2.3 Particular tikanga I shall explore are the following:
    i. Take raupatu   v. Te pana tangata
    ii. Ringa kaha   vi. Te noho kore mana
    iii. Mana whenua   vii. Te whakahoki whenua
    iv. Ahi-ka-roa

3. Take Raupatu

3.0 The report *Te Manawa Moriori (The Heart of the Moriori)* by Mana Cracknell and Maui Pomare suggests that what occurred in the Chatham Islands in 1835 was not a proper raupatu because the attackers had no reason to invade (Cracknell and Pomare 1995, p.14). The allegation is

Aspects of Raupatu 225

that the attack was a take kore on the basis that it was contrary to tikanga Moriori (ibid, p.14) and contrary to 'ancient customs' of the Maori (ibid, p.15).

3.1 Nine points are made to support the proposition that there was no raupatu or conquest according to Maori custom. The first point is that there was a lack of provocation or reason behind the attack and therefore it was deemed a take kore. It is clear from examples in the North Island that there does not need to be any reason for one hapu or iwi to attack another. A contemporaneous example of this is some of the attacks by the Nga Puhi raiding parties on the middle and lower North Island iwi throughout the 1820s and 1830s (Stafford 1991, pp.175, 197–203). There was generally no reason behind many of these attacks—save that perhaps of testing their new muskets! Another example of this is the raids of Te Rauparaha into the South Island.

3.2 The initial lack of a take does not, however, preclude the subsequent occupation of an area once the attack has been successfully carried out. Should the attackers decide that the area is suitable for settlement after defeating their opponents, then they may attempt occupation. The initiative is clearly with the attacker.

3.3 The second point made by the authors is that the attackers were assisted by an English sailing ship and muskets. There does not seem to be much difference here from the example of the use by Nga Puhi of Ngai Te Rangi waka to attack Mokoia (Stafford 1991, p.177). The English ship was a means to an end and should not necessarily negate the defeat of the Moriori.

3.4 An interesting comparison to the use of an English vessel and arms can be found in Ngati Awa's own case. Ngati Awa argue that their defeat by Te Arawa in 1864 at the battle of Te Kaokaoroa was not according to tikanga Maori because the force was paid for and led by Crown officials. Although defeated by a Maori force, Ngati Awa did not relinquish mana whenua (refer Mead and Gardiner, 'Te Kaupapa o te Raupatu: An Ethnography of the Ngati Awa Experience of Raupatu', 1994, pp.54–9. Document A18, WAI-46). Ngati Awa lost the mana over most of its land through raupatu. Because this raupatu was carried out by the Crown and not by another Maori group, however, it was not a valid raupatu in terms of Maori custom.

3.5 The third point is that the Moriori were defenceless and refused to fight, and that the fight was not 'fair' (Cracknell and Pomare, 1995, p.15). There is little evidence of consideration of issues such as fairness and neutrality in combat, in Maori custom. There are numerous examples of groups, pa and individuals being attacked and killed whether they were armed or not, involved in the combat or neutral. The authors also assert that the attack by the Taranaki Maori was contrary to Maori custom because they had been welcomed as manuhiri by the tangata whenua. There are plenty of examples of the hosts attacking manuhiri and vice versa. A case in point is the taking of Maunganui by Ngai Te Rangi (Stafford 1991, pp.129–30). The breaking of this protocol was rarely a hindrance to an attack if the group felt strongly enough.

3.6 The fourth point raised is that not all Moriori were annihilated (ibid, p.15). According to traditional Maori custom, the victors often claimed to have annihilated their enemy and killed them all. This was, in fact, rarely the case. A case in point is that of the Maruiwi, who were partly Ngati Awa. They migrated from the Waimana region in the Bay of Plenty and were supposed to have all perished at Taupo (Best, 1972, p.78). Yet we learn that some eventually made their way to the South Island. In reading some of the documents for this case, I find some of the early members of Ngati Awa went to Wharekauri—they were known as the Maruiwi.

3.7 However, it is not necessary to kill everyone in order to win a fight or attempt to assert mana whenua. As stated above there are usually survivors—nga morehu—usually women, children and old people. Should the victors attempt occupation, some arrangements have to be made to accommodate these morehu.

3.8 The fifth point raised was that the Moriori never left their lands. However, this does not necessarily negate their defeat. There were generally three methods of dealing with vanquished people. The first was to annihilate them completely; the second was to send them into exile somewhere else, while the victors occupied the land; and the third was to allow them to remain, but at the sufferance of the victors, and to be used as labour or to live as 'tenants' at the will of the victors. Iwi forced to live under the third option can hardly be said to retain mana whenua. More important in this case is the exertion of ringa kaha (force of arms) by the victors to ensure the subjugation of the defeated party.

3.9 An iwi living under the ringa kaha of another can escape from the political and economic ties placed upon them. They can either fight their way out of the bond by defeating the victor, and therefore restore their own mana, or they can have their mana restored to them, either by the victors or by an outside party. There are examples of both within the region of Ngati Awa.

3.10 The sixth point argues that there was no inter-marriage between the two groups. Inter-marriage is the usual consequence of conquest. It would be inconsistent with traditional practice for their to be no marriages. Marriage was one way open to a victor to cement mana whenua. However, marriages weren't necessarily required. I discuss this point in more detail later.

3.11 The seventh point is related to the fifth in that the authors claim that the Moriori retained manawa ka and ahi-ka-roa. However, as explained in paragraph 3.8, it cannot be said that an iwi living on land at the sufferance of another is keeping its fires burning. The land is still under the control of the victor through the principle of ringa kaha. The ringa kaha claim is therefore stronger than that of ancestral rights. The basic distinction is that of tino rangatiratanga. Ahi-ka-roa is based on mana and the freedom to practise and enjoy the benefits of tino rangatiratanga over the land and over themselves.

3.12 The eighth point raised in support of the assertion of take kore (negative cause) is that the invaders stayed only thirty years. The question of how long an invader stays in actual occupation is not as important as the completion of the two phases of raupatu: conquest, and undisturbed occupation. Conquest is the actual defeat of an occupying group, but that in itself does not constitute raupatu. It is the second phase—undisturbed occupation—that confirms the raupatu. It is important to note here that occupation did not necessarily entail physical occupation.

3.13 There are at least two examples within Ngati Awa history of an area being conquered but left unoccupied by the victors. The land was taken by ringa kaha—extinguishing the ancestral right of ownership, the ahi-ka-roa—and it was under this principle that the land was held. The original owners could not reclaim the land because the ringa kaha was still in place. An example of this was the invasion of the Maketu area by Te Rangihouhiri. Shortly after that invasion, Te Rangihouhiri's people (who became known as Ngai Te Rangi afterwards) then invaded and captured Maunganui, and left Maketu. Despite this, Ngati Te Rangi retained mana whenua at Maketu through ringa kaha. This involved the occasional show of force at Maketu to ensure the retention of the mana. It was not until the 1830s that this mana was finally extinguished through the defeat and expulsion of Ngai Te Rangi from Maketu.

3.14 The final point raised is that the invasion and occupation took place only four years prior to the signing of the Treaty of Waitangi. It is not clear as to the significance of this point.

4. Ringa Kaha

4.0 As mentioned in paragraphs 3.8 to 3.13, the principle of ringa kaha or occupation by force of arms had the effect of extinguishing ancestral title if employed successfully. This is not to say, however, that the ancestral owners could not regain title through various means, as discussed in paragraph 3.9. The rights gained through the conquest and occupation could be strengthened by marriage with the previous owners, so that the next generation held rights to the land both through ancestral title (ahi-ka-roa) and conquest (ringa kaha).

4.1 It must be emphasised that the defeat in a single battle did not automatically confer the right of ownership; rather, it was the defeat combined with the undisturbed occupation of land. If there was no challenge to the occupation of the victors, then they could be said to hold the land by ringa kaha.

4.2 In Ngati Awa's case the principle of ringa kaha is called 'toa'. It is through the concept of toa that military strength was used to exert or gain influence over land.

5. Ahi-ka-roa

5.0 The principle of ahi-ka-roa entails the occupation of an area of land by a group generally over a long time. This group is able, through the use of whakapapa, to trace back to primary ancestors who lived on the land. This group holds influence over the land and is able to exercise tino rangatiratanga over their land and themselves—thereby keeping their fires burning. The ability to do this is based firmly in the ability to exert ringa kaha over the land.

5.1 As stated earlier, land may be held in the form of absentee ownership, especially where that land has been conquered or did not form an integral part of the tribal estate. This generally required the exertion of ringa kaha to ensure that no one encroached on the land. Therefore, while not actually 'keeping the fires burning' on the land, it was still under the influence and mana of the group.

5.2 Within the principle of ahi-ka-roa is the concept of ancestral title: land that has been within the group for a number of generations and to which there is a whakapapa link. This ancestral title can be removed through the imposition of ringa kaha, as described in paragraph 4.1.

6. Te Pana Tangata

6.0 Banishing people from the district and from their lands was one alternative open to tribal leaders. There are instances of this occurring in Ngati Awa's area.

6.1 Ngati Manawa was banished from Murupara by Tuhoe (Best 1971).

6.2 Two hapu of Ngati Awa—Warahoe and Ngati Hamua—were banished by the Ngati Awa chief Rangikawehea (Best 1972).

6.3 For some, the option of banishment is a better alternative to extermination or having to live as vassals. It should be noted that not all Maori leaders were determined to exterminate their foe and many possessed great diplomacy skills.

7. Te Noho Kore Mana

7.0 The concept of te noho kore mana (occupation without mana) covers the situation where a group is living on land without the mana over that land. This generally occurs where the group has been defeated and bonded to the victor through that defeat, or where the group has been banished from some other place and is living on the land of another. In both cases the group does not have mana over the land and cannot exercise tino rangatiratanga over that land. A group in that situation cannot claim to be keeping their fires burning.

7.1 It is possible for a group to escape from this position either by finding somewhere else to live, by having their mana restored to them, or by restoring their own mana—by defeating the 'oppressor', for example.

8. Te Whakahoki Whenua

8.0 Te whakahoki whenua (the return of the land) can be brought about, as discussed earlier, in a number of ways. The removal of the ringa kaha and restoration of ancestral rights can be achieved either by defeating the group holding the ringa kaha or by arranging to have the land—and therefore the mana over it—restored. An example of this is the retaking of Maketu by the hapu of Te Arawa—thereby restoring the ancestral rights of Te Arawa over that area—some 200 years after Ngai Te Rangi seized the land by conquest.

9. Tangata Whenua Right and Whenua Right

9.0 A traditional right to land may be described as a 'whenua right', which comes from the notion of tangata whenua rights. What is the basis of this right? A reasonable inference to draw from the term 'tangata whenua' is that it refers to persons born of the whenua.

9.1 Whenua should be interpreted in its widest sense to include its more obvious meaning of 'land' as well as the less obvious one of 'placenta'. Thus tangata whenua are people of the placenta and of the land. And, since the placenta is normally buried in the land, it follows that a whenua right is a right by birth that is underpinned by the fact of the individual person's placenta being buried in that land. In other words, a whenua right is based on birthright.

9.2 High value is placed on the tangata whenua status of the person claiming rights to lands. While a whenua right could be obtained by the use of military power, there was a preference for a proper whenua right based on birthright or placenta right. The whenua right basically comes through the female line. It is the mother who produces the placenta and gives it up with the birth of a child. Before birth the placenta nourished the child. After birth it is the land that nourishes and enriches the person.

9.3 There are examples of males being responsible for conquering a territory but the local women holding some of the whenua right. There are examples from our region of fighting leaders marrying into the people they conquered, thus consolidating their whenua right and covering all aspects, as it were, and fully bonding the new people to the land.

10. Conclusions

10.0 In conclusion, it can be seen that in traditional Maori society a group able to take control of an area and hold that area, whether by occupation or by influence, could claim a valid raupatu. There were few generally accepted rules governing raupatu, and issues such as 'fair-play', passiveness and neutrality formed little obstacle to achieving conquest. It was left to the leaders of a conquering group to deal with the conquered in the manner they saw fit.

10.1 Events occurring around the same time as the Chatham Islands invasion, such as the Nga Puhi raids of the 1820s and 1830s and the raids of Te Rauparaha into the South Island, show that the customs of traditional Maori society could be 'bent' or even broken to achieve an end.

10.2 However, it should be noted that this was a feature of Maori society not only in the early 1800s: there are examples in Ngati Awa history from the 1600s of the 'rules' of Maori society being broken in order to beat an opponent. The travels of Te Rangihouhiri provide ample examples of this.

10.3 Therefore, it is difficult to claim on the grounds cited that the raupatu was not a valid raupatu. It may have been without a reason other than the desire to conquer, but that does not invalidate it.

10.4 The raupatu carried out by the Crown in the rohe of Ngati Awa, Taranaki and Waikato were examples of a raupatu that was invalid. These raupatu were invalid because they were carried out by the Crown, not another

Maori group. In Ngati Awa's case, a Maori force was used, but they were not the primary initiator of the raupatu. Even had they claimed land as a result of raupatu, it could not be described as traditional raupatu because the force was Crown-led, Crown-financed and authorised by the Crown.

10.5 The raupatu in the Chatham Islands was carried out by one iwi against another prior to the Treaty of Waitangi within the generally accepted bounds of custom. It did damage the mana of the original inhabitants and, whatever the circumstances, a raupatu is always hurtful. The pain of the Moriori is understood.

24. Whenua Tautohetohe
Contested Land

The following paper was part of a report presented to the Waitangi Tribunal in support of the Ngati Awa WAI-46 case. The basic idea of contested land is outlined in this paper, which was Chapter One of the report, Whenua Tautohetohe: Testing the Tribal Boundaries *(research report No.13, prepared by the author and the Ngati Awa Research Team, 21 November 1994).*

It is argued in this paper that there were zones of contested land lying between iwi groups, that these zones were characteristically rich in resources and were exploited by both sides, and that it was difficult to fix a boundary line within this zone. The reason is the factor of ringa kaha, mentioned in the previous paper. As military strength fluctuated, so did the boundary, so there was always the element of contestability in land zones regarded as whenua tautohetohe.

Introduction

According to Norman Smith (1942, p.8), there were only two categories of native or Maori land. But this was after the establishment of the Native Land Court by the passing of the Native Lands Act 1862 (ibid, p.11). The two categories were:

1. Customary land. This was the land 'owned by the Natives under the customs and usages of the Maori people, the title to which has not been investigated by the Native Land Court' (ibid, p.8). Such land was held under customary title which Smith (1942, p.10) asserted had 'for the most part been extinguished'.

2. Native freehold land. This was 'customary land the title to which has been investigated by the Native Land Court, and become owned by the Natives in fee simple' (ibid, p.8). Such land had been acquired by the Crown through 'voluntary cession' or by order of the Native Land Court, or had been taken by the Crown under various acts.

This was the practical view of a former Maori Land Court Judge, R. Noble Jones, CBE, whose advice Norman Smith obtained. Smith wrote from the point of view of a government official (he was a research officer in the Native Department) and of a solicitor of the Supreme Court of New Zealand.

The indigenous system of land tenure was much more complex than the view given by Smith. Douglas Sinclair (1981a), who was a medical doctor and a keen student of Maori land, provided some useful information about how customary title was acquired. The categories he described are set out below.

Whenua Papa-tipu

Whenua papa-tipu is ancestral land which is regarded as the base upon which the hapu was nurtured. It corresponds to Smith's customary land. According to Sinclair (1981a, p.92), the land 'had to be physically occupied or worked by hunting, fishing or cropping, and all other claimants had to be resisted successfully'. The right to 'own' whenua papa-tipu, he said, depended on keeping the fires burning. He was alluding to the principle of ahi-ka-roa (ibid, pp.190–1), which could be described as possession of the land by actual occupation over a long period of time; the longer the occupation, the stronger the claim. Proof of occupation required the owners to describe and name the places where they had cultivations, buried their dead, gathered food, or hunted birds and rats.

Sinclair (1981a, p.91) was of the opinion that, should a hapu leave their land and stay away for three generations, 'the rights of occupation would be lost'. The return of a grandchild, however, was sufficient in traditional times to rekindle the fires of occupation.

An important point noted by Sinclair (ibid) was the 1840 rule. The Native Land Court decided that 1840, the year The Treaty of Waitangi was signed, was the critical year for evidence of occupation.

Customary land could be acquired by several means:

1. Whenua raupatu (land taken by force). Land taken by means of ringa kaha or by raupatu (the blade of the patu) is whenua raupatu. However, land obtained by military conquest had to be occupied and held in order to extinguish the rights of the former owners. As Sinclair observed (ibid), considerable areas of land were won or lost in battle, indicating that it was a feature of the land tenure system. Occupation had to be defended successfully against challenges. A party who lost land could not appeal to any other authority.

2. Whenua tuku (gifted land). Land could be gifted 'by a chief or a lesser person, but only in the interests, and with the consent and oversight of the tribe or hapu' (ibid). Land could be gifted for military service, or as a marriage gift, or in order to resettle landless hapu. In these instances, it is

not clear whether it is the use of the land that is being gifted or the title to the land. There are examples of land being given to certain hapu 'by a chief', in the case of Ngati Awa. Examples are gifts of land made to Warahoe and Ngati Hamua by Te Rangitukehu at about the time of the treaty (Best 1972, p.185). Land given as a marriage gift had to be occupied by the husband (Smith 1942, pp.121–2). The practice was related to the wish of the wife's hapu to build up their members.

Sinclair observed that claims to land through take tuku were difficult to uphold.

3. Whenua ohaki (deathbed land grant). In this case the land is obtained as a result of a deathbed grant. A dying chief may divide the tribal estate among his sons and apportion districts or blocks of land to each one. By this means sibling rivalry was prevented. In a well-known case affecting Ngati Awa and Tuhoe, the brothers Ue-imua, Tuhoe and Tane-moe-ahi quarrelled over land (Best 1972, p.243). Ue-imua occupied lands at Ruatoki and Owhakatoro and he challenged Tuhoe about a cultivation on his part of the estate. The result was that Tuhoe and Tane-moe-ahi joined forces against their brother and killed him. Tuhoe cut out his heart, which he cooked and ate at a place called Te Ahi-manawa-o-Ue-imua (the fire where the heart of Ue-imua was cooked). This case illustrates the potential for trouble when the sons of a chief are ambitious and one of them wants to take all or most of the land.

Thus the institution of take ohaki was important in the maintenance of stability.

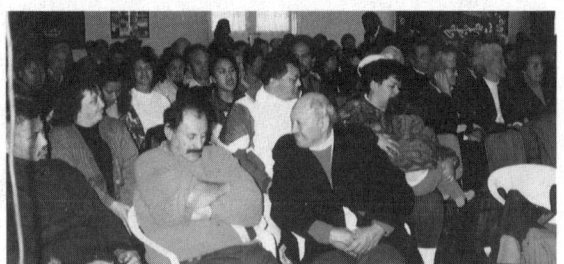

Ngati Awa people attending the hearings at Wairaka, July 1994.
(S. M. Mead)

A group looking at whenua tautohetohe as part of the Waitangi Tribunal hearings, 1995.
(S. M. Mead)

4. Whenua taunaha (named land). Sinclair (1981a, p.89) called this whenua kite hou—that is, land seen for the first time. It is doubtful, however, that the term he used was in common usage in the Bay of Plenty region. A more likely term was 'whenua taunaha', which does occur in Williams' *Dictionary* (1971, p.400). Some land was claimed by right of discovery—for example, by the founders of the waka. Following the same mode of behaviour as European discoverers, they acted as though the land was unoccupied and their leaders claimed land by giving names to various features of the landscape. Sometimes they personalised the names by saying it was a place where the new 'discoverer' carried out some activity—for example, Te Tapapatanga o Taneatua (the place where Taneatua rested) (Best 1972, p.238).

5. Whenua muru (compensation land). Land could be obtained as compensation for breaking some tribal law or tapu (Sinclair 1981a, p.92). A hapu usually lost portable property, such as canoes, food and valuables, but the most severe punishment was the taking of land. Sinclair indicated that land could be given to one party because the negligence of a parent caused the death of a child by drowning or by being burnt.

By whatever means the land was obtained, there were rules to follow and there were threats to occupation. In the case of a gift, the donor might claim back the land before the principle of ahi-ka-roa confirmed occupation. Land ownership required validation by continued occupation. After many generations of occupation, the issue of how the land was obtained tended to be forgotten and the land was regarded as whenua papa-tipu—that is, as ancestral land that was passed down the generations.

The Concept of Whenua Tautohetohe

Standard texts on Maori land tenure, such as Kawharu (1977), do not mention the idea of whenua tautohetohe as land which is frequently contested by two or more iwi at points where their boundaries meet. Instead they write, as did Gudgeon (1885, pp.183–201), about clearly defined boundaries and about sons of chiefs knowing the exact boundaries of their lands. The boundaries marked the extent where rat traps could be set or eel weirs built and generally where food could be gathered. Gudgeon (1885, p.185) went on to say:

> there is not one inch of land in the New Zealand Islands which is not claimed by the Maoris; and I may also state that there is not a hill or valley, stream, river, or forest, which has not a name, the index of some point of the Maori history.

He suggested that the boundary between two tribes was indicated by landmarks, which could be 'a pile of stones or a hole dug in the ground' (ibid, p.184) and that a name would be given to the mark after the 'boundary being agreed to'.

The model he described was an ideal one in which the tribes had agreed on their boundaries and there was no room for political change. It may be described as the 'stability model', which holds when there are long periods of stability. This model, however, does not fit the ethnographic facts for the Bay of Plenty tribes during the early decades of the nineteenth century.

The concept of whenua tautohetohe as applied to the borders between land-owning iwi appears to fit the facts more appropriately. It allows for dynamic political and social relations between neighbouring tribes and reflects the ebb and flow of iwi politics. It also explains why there was so much fighting between certain iwi.

The closest term to whenua tautohetohe was the notion of 'kainga tautohe', which was used by Chief Justice Sir William Martin in 1890 and which he translated as 'debatable lands' (G-1,1890:3). To quote him: 'But between territories of different tribes there are often tracts of land which are called "kainga tautohe" or (literally) debatable lands'. His notion of kainga tautohe is the same as the idea of whenua tautohetohe. The real difference is that Sir William's term appears to be restricted to a particular place or village (kainga), whereas whenua tautohetohe assumes that debatable lands are an essential aspect of tribal boundaries, which are shared with other iwi. However, some parts of the boundary are likely to be more 'debatable' than others.

Basic to all discussions on boundaries is the notion of 'rohe', meaning boundary, set bounds to, or enclose (Williams 1957, p.344). The setting of boundaries appears to be more complicated in the case of Ngati Awa and its neighbours than in other tribal territories. In the stability model, the boundary is a clearly defined line which is marked off by pou (poles) of various sorts. Williams (1957, p.297) gives the following two:

pou aronui	=	opposing boundary post
		opposite post
pou tarawaho	=	outside boundary post

Biggs (1981, p.20) gives 'pou rahui' as another boundary marker. There are other words which could have been used but the three identified here are sufficient for present purposes.

There are also words for setting the boundaries. Williams (1957) mentions the following:

roherohe	=	to mark boundaries (p.344)
kotikoti	=	to divide, lay off boundaries (p.149)

There are many words for the boundary line itself and a sample is given below:

rohe	=	boundary (p.344)
kotinga	=	boundary line (p.149)
ripa	=	boundary (p.341)
kaha	=	boundary line (p.82)

The terminology is generally consistent with the notion of a single boundary line. The two terms identified by Williams as boundary posts, however, could be seen as supporting the idea of whenua tautohetohe as referring to an outer boundary, which implies there is an inside boundary.

The Nature of Whenua Tautohetohe

Typically, the land so classified lies within a zone which is bounded by an inner and outer boundary. This is illustrated in Figure 24.1. The width of the zone varies according to the terrain or to the nature of the resource at the border. The terrain today is not the same as it was originally. Because of the frequent challenges of contesting parties, such a zone is generally unsafe for human settlement.

Some parts of the zone are often totally uninhabited and, if there are settlements within its boundaries, they are frequently abandoned for several years at a time.

The zone is useful from at least two points of view. From a military standpoint, the absence of settlements diminishes the opportunities for further disputes, and thus the iwi which controls the zone is able to achieve a measure of political stability at that section of the tribal estate. Stability comes at a price, however. The iwi has to be strong in a military sense in order to maintain the zone as a buffer between it and aspiring competitors. Thus the contested zone could be viewed as a defensive ring around the borders with each side setting its own 'line in the sand'.

Economically, the whenua tautohetohe zone provided a source of food and building materials for constructing canoes. The resources of the zone become available to the iwi controlling it. An activity which rivals may not allow is cultivation of the land for growing crops. It is not in their interests to allow unfettered use of the land for cropping because this would imply long-term occupation, which is the basis of the principle of ahi-ka-roa. So guerrilla tactics might be used to harass the political masters of the land in order to prevent actual occupation and so maintain the status of whenua tautohetohe. Once an area of land is fully occupied by the attackers, it is regarded then as whenua raupatu (land taken by military action). It is no longer contestable land. In

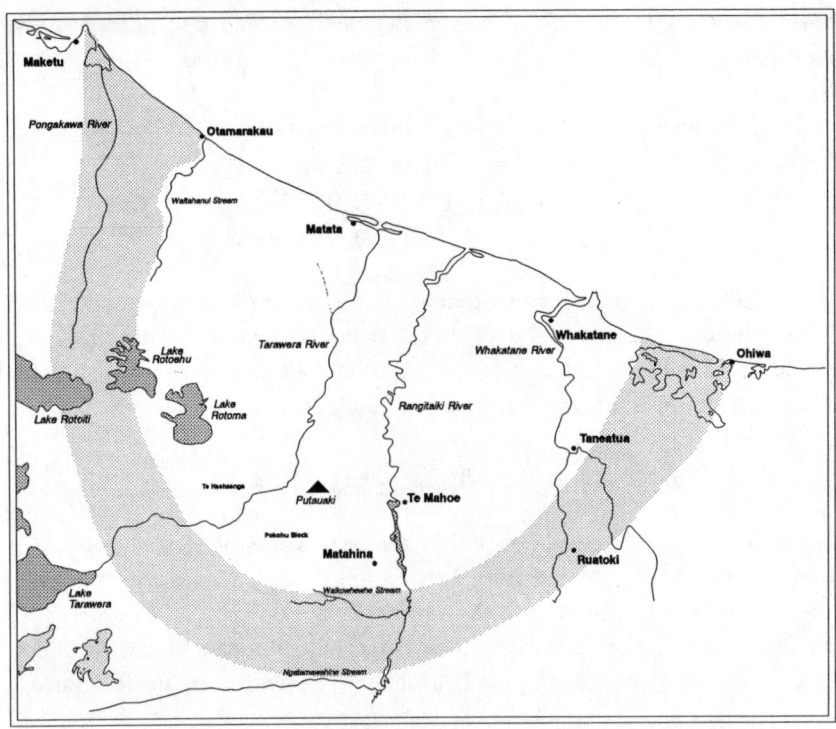

Figure 24.1
The whenua tautohetohe zone around the borders of Ngati Awa. Scale 1:200,000

(Ngati Awa Research)

special circumstances, the land might be reoccupied by the original owners at the invitation of the other party.

The concept of whenua tautohetohe does not rule out the possibility of an agreed boundary line in the middle of the zone. It is possible for such a boundary line to exist, but it is plain that only the foolhardy would set their rat-traps on the edge of the outer border. The trapper runs the risk of being trapped by the enemy.

The concept of whenua tautohetohe embraces the idea that the boundary between tribal territories is not so much like a surveyed line, although a line may exist, but rather is like a band of land which might be likened to a zone of no-man's-land. The zone has an inner boundary which marks the effective defensive ring of the owning iwi (see Figure 24.1). It also marks the line of heightened collective political concern. A challenger who comes as far as the inner boundary triggers an iwi-wide response and a serious territorial battle occurs. A successful challenge could mean that the defending iwi loses some of its land, or signals that stronger alliances need to be made in the near future.

However, there are punitive raids which penetrate the inner defences but which are not seen to threaten the borders. In such cases the raid is allowed by the hapu concerned, and sometimes with the express wish of the hapu, as when it wants to get rid of a troublesome leader. These were usually utu-seeking raids to pay off 'debts'.

Some areas of land are clearly not in the category of whenua tautohetohe as between iwi groups. The township of Whakatane was built on confiscated land.

(S. M. Mead)

Looking over contested land at Rotoehu are some members of the Waitangi Tribunal, representatives of the Crown Law Office and Ngati Awa and legal counsel for Ngati Awa, Stephen Bryers.
Left to right: Sir Hugh Kawharu, Chief Judge E. T. Durie, Gordon Orr (obscured), Hirini Mead (partly obscured), Te Hau Tutua, Ngahuia Rowson, Keith Sorrenson, Stephen Bryers, Andra Moberley (Crown Law Office), and presenters from the Forestry Corporation explaining the lay of the land. *(Onehou Thrupp, Ngati Awa Research)*

Usually, skirmishes occur within the zone and there is a series of challenges until some decisive action is taken by one of the contenders. It is because of the frequent challenges that the term whenua tautohetohe is applied to such land: 'tautohetohe' means to argue from one side to the other.

In respect of the traditional land-tenure system, Smith (1942, pp.32–4) published an essay entitled 'Remarks on Maori Affairs' (*Note on Maori Matters*, 1860). Its early date of 1860 marks it as important because the comments were based on the traditional land-tenure system, which was still in place at that time. The author is not identified, but the text may have been written by Judge Fenton, who was an authority of Maori land law.

> It would appear that, of the attributes of sovereignty, the administration of justice (as far as there was any beyond mere reprisals) and the right of declaring war, as well as the power of temporary alienation of land belonging to the tribes, were all vested in the tribe generally, and although often exercised by chiefs or tohungas, were so exercised with the consent, either express or tacit, of the whole tribe. But the original tenure, by occupation was one which could be maintained by a tribe only so long as they were strong enough to prevent another tribe from depriving them of it; for there was no tribunal, external or common to all the tribes, to which appeal could be made, nor does there seem to have been any compact or understanding, express or implied, that if one tribe should disturb another in its occupation the general body of the tribes should protect the occupier or punish the assailant. Therefore the right of occupation was always liable to be superseded by force, and acquisition of territory by conquest was recognised by all the tribes as rightful possession (other than by sufferance) being the evidence of the right.

This provides a useful background for understanding the concept of whenua tautohetohe. In one sense, all of the land owned at any one time by an iwi or hapu was whenua tautohetohe and subject to being taken by force by a stronger iwi. Here, however, the term is confined to the zone of land that lies on the border between land-owning iwi, as illustrated in Figure 24.1.

It is not wise to describe the zone as 'no-man's-land' as this gives a wrong impression. It is not an area of land that belongs to no one. At any one time, some iwi has political and military control over some or all of the land. And, while the period of dispute might continue for decades, eventually a resolution is worked out, a peace agreement is negotiated and ratified, and stability reigns in that part of the land.

There were two mechanisms in traditional Maori society to stop the fighting. One was outright military conquest, and the other was to negotiate a peace agreement.

Conclusion

In many of the judgements recorded by the Maori Land Court, emphasis was given to the principle of the long-burning fires, ahi-ka-roa. Occupation over a long period of time was held to be crucial and while this was an important principle it was not the only one. There was another principle just as important. This was the principle of ringa kaha or toa (success in war).

Who exercised political control over the land was often the key factor. For example, it was possible for a hapu to keep its fires burning in a particular area of land. However its political status could be that of a vassal group owing its occupation of the land to the protection and agreement of the reigning political tribe. The vassal group occupies through a sort of lease agreement whereby it 'pays' for permission to occupy the land by offering produce and labour to the owning group.

There are many examples in the ethnographic record to illustrate the point made above. In these cases the principle of ahi-ka-roa does not apply and is quite irrelevant. It is possible for the party having the political power or ringa kaha to live miles away from the land occupied by others. The classic example is that of Ngai Te Rangi, living in Tauranga. Their political influence extended to Maketu and, although many groups occupied it over various periods of time, it was not until the battle of Te Tumu, 1836, that Te Arawa could claim it back. Details of the case are described in Mead (1994) and Stafford (1991). What is important here is that Maketu was located within a disputed zone of land: it was whenua tautohetohe.

As long as Ngai Te Rangi was able to exercise the ringa kaha principle by clearing people off the land, it was the dominant political force. Other tribal groups occupied Maketu with its permission. However in 1836, when Ngai Te Rangi attempted once again to clear the land, it failed to do so. Te Arawa then became the dominant political force over Maketu and its occupation was supported by the ringa kaha principle and later legitimated by the 1840 rule. Because Ngai Te Rangi did not reimpose is ringa kaha and political dominance over Maketu before the Treaty of Waitangi was signed, it lost the contested Maketu.

However, this might not necessarily stop verbal arguments over the whenua tautohetohe zone. These arguments will continue into the next century.

Thus, what I have set out to show in this paper is that the principle of ringa kaha is an important consideration in deciding who had real political control over an area of land. Land on the borders between competing iwi often become whenua tautohetohe. Characteristically, contested lands are rich resource regions such as a forested area, a harbour or a large swamp area. The resources are accessed by the border tribes but each has to exercise care in how far into the zone it penetrates. The dividing line is defined by the exercise of ringa kaha by one party or the other.

There was no mechanism in traditional Maori society for arbitrating a dispute over a boundary. The rights of a group had to be defended so that in the end the military power of an iwi was of paramount importance in maintaining territory. A strong iwi was able to defend its borders and sometimes gain ground. Because of this factor the whenua tautohetohe zone was likely to be contested by the parties for decades and never resolved in any conclusive way.

This picture of Maori land tenure differs from the usual one of the idyllic smoke rising from the cooking fires of peaceful hunters and gatherers who are minding their own business. The reality was different.

References

Best, Elsdon, 1972. *Tuhoe: The Children of the Mist*. Wellington, A. H. and A. W. Reed.

Gudgeon, Thomas Wayth, 1885. *The History and Doings of the Maoris, From the Year 1820 to the Signing of the Treaty of Waitangi*. Auckland, H. Brett.

Kawharu, Ian Hugh, 1977. *Maori Land Tenure: Studies in a Changing Institution*. Oxford, Oxford University Press.

Martin, Sir William, 1890. 'Maori Land Tenure', *Opinions of Various Authorities on Native Tenure. Presented to Both Houses of the General Assembly. G-1, 1890*. Wellington, Government Printer, pp.3–4.

Mead, Hirini Moko and Ngati Awa Research Team, 1994. 'Whenua Tautohetohe: Testing the Tribal Boundaries', *Research Report No. 13*. Whakatane, Te Runanga o Ngati Awa.

Sinclair, Douglas, 1981. 'Land: Maori View and European Response', *Te Ao Hurihuri: The World Moves On*. Edited by Michael King. Auckland, Longman Paul, pp. 86–106.

Smith, Norman, 1942. *Native Custom and Law Affecting Native Land*. Wellington, Maori Purposes Fund Board.

Williams, H. W., 1957. *A Dictionary of the Maori Language*. Wellington, Government Printer.

Being Maori Today

25. The Maori World and You

This was the text of an address given at an end-of-year prize-giving ceremony at Turakina School at Marton, 3 December 1977. Turakina is well known as a secondary boarding school for Maori girls, run by the Presbyterian Church.

At prize-giving ceremonies all over the country, probably everything that ought to be said in the department of advice has already been said, and much better, by someone else. This year you chose to invite a professor of Maori as your speaker. It thus seems sensible that I should say something about the Maori world and you. No better justification can be offered for my topic than the undisputed fact that *you* are very important to the Maori world of today and tomorrow.

First, I shall talk very generally about the nature of today's world: about its interdependence, its complexity and its contradictions. Then I shall talk briefly about our own country and some of the problems we face. But the main theme of my address is about imperfection and contradiction, because I want to make a particular point about the nature of Maoritanga. In the last part of this talk, I, the fragile human that I am, succumb to the temptation of giving advice. It might be no better nor worse than advice given before, but I hope it will be useful nevertheless.

One of the lessons which you should have learnt already is that the world of today is enormously complicated and full of contradictions. The ugly and the beautiful live side by side, so too the petty and the great, the dumb and the clever, the starving and the overfed, the rich and the poor, the law-abiding and the criminally minded, the weak and the strong; and, in New Zealand, there are the Polynesians and the Pakeha.

We live in a world that is increasingly interdependent. The recent oil crisis has demonstrated just how interdependent we are, and how an action taken in another part of the world can affect all of us at home here in quite a profound way. For example, going to a tangi by car, bus, train or aeroplane costs a lot more today than it did just two or three years ago. As another example, your parents now pay more for the electricity and gas that they cook with than a year ago. All this and a lot more because the Arabs in the Middle East increased the price of fuel oil.

Yet, given the obvious need for greater international co-operation, we see everywhere evidence of nations fighting against one another, of one country trying to overthrow the government of another, one group of people setting out to exterminate another, and people called terrorists flying planeloads of hostages from one country to another. Everywhere around us we see or hear of rape, violence and murder, and we, the Maori people, are right in there with the rest of the world.

On the other side of the coin are all manner of institutions from the United Nations down in scale to smaller ones which strive to maintain peace, order and harmony among the people of the world. These institutions also strive for justice, for the dignity of man and for equal rights of the individual. We have such institutions in New Zealand, and no less in the Maori world.

Today is the world of the jumbo-jet which crisscrosses the air corridors of the world and eventually links every country within it. There is hardly a country to which you cannot fly as a tourist. The world has opened up and people, young and old, like Marco Polo, visit exotic places, witness the strange customs of other cultures, perhaps stay a while and then return home to tell of their marvellous travels. The Maori is a part of the jumbo-jet age and today you will find them in the strangest of countries—working, just passing through, singing, studying, or married and settled permanently. We are a part of the world out there. But the world we live in is not perfect and may never be, despite our most cherished dreams. And if we leave the world aside a moment and focus upon our own country, one can say the same thing. It is not a perfect country by any means and it, too, has its contradictions. Some of you may well disagree with me about this. There may be even a few very loyal and patriotic New Zealanders who would report me to the SIS for claiming that our country is not perfect and is not God's own country.

My defence is that God never claimed New Zealand as His own. It was the Pakeha who did the claiming, and he used God's name to justify his actions. The country certainly has a lot of good features about it: its varied scenery, its mountains, rivers and lakes, its beautiful beaches and, in some parts, its beautiful summers. We can take pride in the beauty of our native trees and the bird life that once thrived in them.

As descendants of the original inhabitants of New Zealand, we might be excused for saying that, before the coming of the Pakeha, there was this beautiful land called Aotearoa and it was settled by a proud, virile and handsome people who came from tropical Polynesia. They called themselves Maori, the normal ones, the ordinary, and the people of this land. So, when the

Pakeha came, the resources of Aotearoa included the country; with its flora and fauna, the sea, with its bounty of food, and the Maori people, with their culture. What have we done with the natural and cultural resources of New Zealand?

It is when a question of this sort is asked and we ponder the answer to it that we realise we are not perfect. Another question can be asked: are we satisfied with our way of life in New Zealand today? Those who think deeply about this issue will answer in the negative. In my opinion only a fool—albeit our own special brand of fool—will claim that everything is fine the way it is.

The imperfections and the contradictions of our society have a special significance for the Maori people. Because so many of our people are at the lower socio-economic level of New Zealand society, we are lashed by the waves which ripple out from the centres of power and wealth. Many of us are jobless. Others of us earn very low incomes. Many of us are in mental and penal institutions. There are far too many of us failing to make the grade in today's society. We are like the debris washed up on the beach after a storm.

We live in a country which has an international reputation (or did have) for its humanitarian approach to race relations. Ours is supposed to be a paradise for the peaceful co-existence of Polynesian and Pakeha, where there is equality before the law and God. This is but a dream unfulfilled. The Maori is a long way from being equal with the Pakeha, and the rumblings you hear from Maori people, young and old, deny the existence of paradise here.

The signs all around us indicate that we, the Maori people who aspire to maintain our Maoritanga in today's world, are fighting a rearguard action. We are losing the linguistic battle, slowly, but in the end surely. Many of our traditions have disappeared and those which survive today, often in new and adapted forms, are struggling to survive. Our people are confused. Some have given up the idea of doing battle because they think the situation is hopeless. We cannot win against the Pakeha, they say. The best thing to do is to join them. Others keep the faith and hope for a miracle—perhaps a new Ngata to rally the people, or more educated Maori to take up the struggle, or a more sympathetic and understanding government to right the wrongs which we perceive.

But is the situation really that hopeless? I don't think it need be. More than ever before we have a vast army of Pakeha sympathisers and helpers. Hundreds of them are now linked to us by ties of marriage and friendship. Many of them are willing to join the battle on our behalf, if we ask for their help. Others are waiting for some sign that we ourselves are ready and willing to fight for what we believe in. It is true, however, that there is a huge majority of Pakeha who are still to be persuaded that we have a right to be different from them. That formidable majority presents an equally formidable challenge to the leaders of today and tomorrow.

We also need to look at ourselves and try to mend some of our broken fences. Too many Maori people have opted out, and have deserted the ship at a time when their help is urgently needed. Some of these people speak too loudly against us, perhaps, in an effort to justify what they have done. What we need are more Maori people supporting, with their money, labour and dedication, the local marae and the various committees which struggle to keep the Maori world together.

There are far too many young Maori men and women who are playing fox, hiding in their dens and displaying far more loyalty to the local pub than to the Maori world. There are literally thousands of them all over the country who are purposely being 'lost' in the cities. We cannot sustain this massive loss of talent. Something must be done to bring the youth into the Maori fold. This is another challenge of our time.

There also needs to be a drastic change of attitude among our own people. If it is to survive well into the twenty-first century, Maoritanga must have the majority of Maori supporting it. Urbanites must seek out its covens, as it were, and go to those places of their own accord. If they don't know its ways, they had better find a learner's coven. But the important thing is that an effort has to be made to find the nearest convenient centre of Maoritanga and support it. If we sincerely believe in the worth of being Maori, we must be prepared to reach out towards Maoritanga.

Now, what can you girls do to help with the survival of our culture? First, while at this school you should become as expert as possible in the ways of Maoritanga. This includes learning the language. By the time you leave this school you should be speaking Maori, especially if you could not speak a word of it when you enrolled. You have a unique opportunity here and, if you have not made use of it, you disappoint me, because a dedication to the task is not evident.

Second, try to become an excellent all-rounder who is just as capable in a Maori setting as in a predominantly Pakeha one. This is something we have talked about for years but have not pursued with sufficient vigour. All too often, the students become one-sided and are educated *out* of the Maori world instead of *into* it. Education then becomes an agent of alienation and hence an enemy of Maoritanga. Good education is not supposed to be that.

Another piece of advice is to think positively about your identity and heritage as a Maori. 'Maori is beautiful' is a slogan you might keep with you always. Nobody likes an apologetic Maori who, like Judas, tries to deny the truth. This sort of person is just as embarrassing as the other who militantly screams her lack of Maoritanga to the whole world.

Later, when you become mothers, give your children Maori names, but not just any name. Rather, choose names which belong to your subtribe, to your ancestors, and so keep their memory alive. Your ancestors are part of your identity and the children have a right to be familiar with them.

Keep in touch with your families and your relatives. One useful thing to do now is to begin compiling your own personal whakapapa book while your elders are still alive. Too many of us, including myself, left this task too late. The result is that I am frequently embarrassed by not knowing the kin relationship of my own relatives. Usually every family has at least one person who either holds or has compiled books of whakapapa. You should find that person.

Just as the world is full of contradictions and imperfections, so is the Maori world. You are a romantic dreamer if you expect everything in Maoritanga to be beautiful, peaceful and strewn with pohutukawa flowers. Nor should you expect it to be logical and orderly: it is your task to find an order and logic with which you can be comfortable. There are bound to be contradictions and we learn to live with them. Perhaps, the greatest contradiction—to many Pakeha, at least—is that, by being a capable Maori, you become a good citizen of New Zealand.

26. The Significance of Being Ngati Awa

Paper given to Hui Whakapakari at Ohope, 15 June 1990. Organised by the New Zealand Planning Council and Te Runanga o Ngati Awa.

Introduction

Tēnā tātou Ngāti Awa, ngā uri a Awanui-ā-rangi, a te whānau a Toi-kai-rākau. Me mihi ki ō tātou kuia, koroua, ō tātou tīpuna kua ngaro ki te pō. Nā rātou tātou i kiia ai he Ngāti Awa. Ka mihi ki ō tātou mate. Haere rā koutou, haere, haere, oti atu ki te pō. Ka huri ki a tātou te hunga ora, tēnā koutou, tēnā tātou.

In this talk I will trace some of the history of Ngati Awa in order to show that as a people we have a rich and complex history that is exciting and challenging. I want to emphasise the point that we are heirs to a valuable heritage or taonga tuku iho that we can be proud of. I also want to deal with the problem of the raupatu and its consequences for us. This is seen as a very negative part of our history, but that depends on how you look at these events in the light of what we now know.

From here, I go on to list some actions we can take to give some significance to being Ngati Awa; for belonging is a two-way process. There is a process of taking from the group to give strength to the individual, and there is a process of the individual giving strength to the group. We all want Ngati Awa to continue into the next century and we have a common purpose in making sure there is something to hand on to the next generation.

The Toi Family

Ngati Awa as a tribal name is known widely but especially in the Bay of Plenty region, Te Taitokerau (the north) and Te Taihauauru (west coast). In the first two regions the name is Ngati Awa, while on the west coast and in Wellington the name is Ngati Awa in the early literature, or more commonly today it is Te Ati Awa. Ngati Awa covers three of the four tides.

There is a way of including the fourth tide in the south, but to do so requires establishing links with Ngati Kahungunu, whose region extends down the eastern coast to the South Island.

The ancestor of all divisions of Ngati Awa is Awanuiarangi, brother of Rauru. The names Rauru and Awanuiarangi go together; thus in Taranaki there is a tribe called Nga Rauru and another called Te Ati Awa. According to Mataatua whakapapa, the brothers are sons of Toi. To the Taranaki branch they are grandsons.

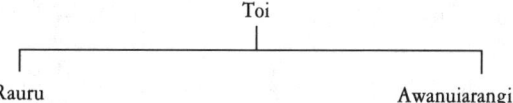

Most whakapapa lines from Toi comedown through the tuakana Rauru, not through Awanuiarangi, and in fact it is difficult to find a published whakapapa showing a clear descent from the younger brother. The following composite whakapapa makes the point. It can be seen immediately that the Awa line is short on generations and tends to focus on different Awa names.

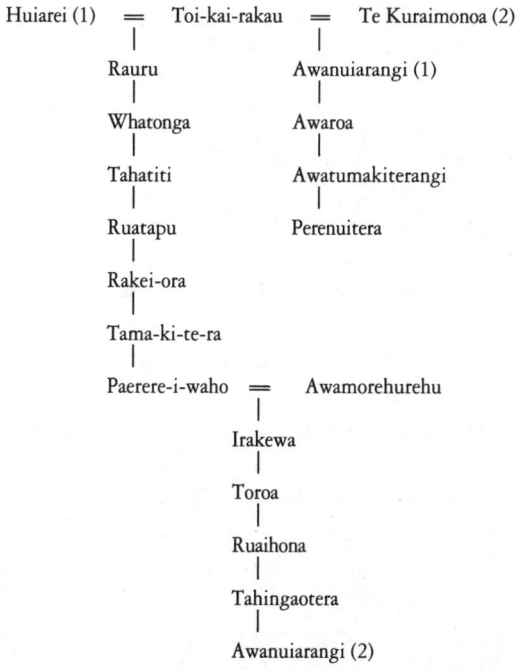

Sources: Toi line, Smith 1910, p.368, and Steedman 1996:327. Awa line, Steedman.

This whakapa comes down to Awanuiarangi (2), with whom the Bay of Plenty branch of Ngati Awa is clearly associated.

From Awanuiarangi comes all branches of Ngati Awa, including some Toi-associated groups such as the Maruiwi. (Best 1972, p.64)

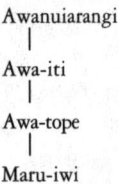

The Maruiwi lived in Hawke's Bay and migrated from there to the Bay of Plenty. Their migration route took them to Turanga, to Te Kaha and eventually to Waimana (Best 1972, p.66). In time they were forced out of the area and migrated back to Heretaunga by way of Rangitaiki and Kaingaroa. While at Kaingaroa they were engaged by the sons of Tuwharetoa, and in a battle called Owhakatihi the Maruiwi were successful. But the Kawerau people retaliated with a ritual weapon called 'kete pounamu'. This was a special ritual in which a sacred fire was lit at a place since called Te Ahi-a-nga-tane and the power of the atua Irakewa was invoked. The Maruiwi were pursued to Mohaka and then a terrible thing happened to them: in darkness they rushed over a cliff at Te Pohue and perished. Only seven survivors reached Heretaunga, or so it is claimed.

Toi himself lived at his hilltop pa at Kaputerangi, from where he could see the coastline from Nga Kuri-a-Wharei at Tauranga to Tikirau. It was a beautiful site for a village. His immediate people, Te Tini o Toi, lived at Ohiwa and some were at Owhakatoro. Te Whanau a Tairongo was a branch of Te Tini o Toi and this hapu too lived at Ohiwa. It is tempting to refer to the stories of how Repanga, son of Maruiwi, was killed and how utu was sought by Repanga's son Tuamutu. His form of utu was novel. He succeeded in catching them in his fish net, hence the name Karihi-potae (the cover of net-sinkers). Some of the survivors of this slaughter, descendants of Awaheiroa, migrated to Taranaki under their chiefs Kahurua and Ngatata-nui. One of the hapu that migrated was Ngati Tama (Best 1972, p.97).

Local evidence suggests that Ngati Awa began in the Whakatane region as part of the Toi people. Various related divisions of Ngati Awa, such as the Maruiwi, Te Tini o Awa, Waitaha, Te Kawerau, the Hapuoneone, occupied various parts of the land and gradually spread out. Ngati Awa traditions mention a large migration to the north when Tihore moved from Rangitaiki and finally settled in the north.

In his book *Peopling of the North*, Percy Smith (1898, pp.38–47) provides an interesting record of the occupation of the North Auckland region by Ngati Awa. At one time our ancestors controlled an expanse of land that ranged from Pukepoto to Aurere (Taipa) and included places such as Hokianga, Awanui, Kaitaia, Victoria Valley, Rangaunu, Whangaroa Harbour and Whangarei.

Smith (ibid, p.45) says that Ngati Awa was in the north for many generations and that the migrations southward may have begun at about 1450 (p.47). Several causes are given for the migrations. One was a series of conflicts with Ngapuhi and Ngati Whatua which exacerbated as the populations grew and food-growing areas became very valuable. Disease is given as another cause. The group which left from Kaitaia at Rangaunu Bay was led by Kauri, chief of Ngati Te Awa. An informant called Timoti Puhipi told Smith that Tamatea was the son of Kauri and Tamatea was Kahungunu's father.

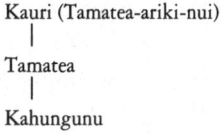

In the north they remembered an ancestor called Kahu-unuunu, who might have been a different person from Kahungunu, founder of Ngati Kahungunu.

Smith (1898, p.47) thought the last exodus of Ngati Awa from the north occurred about 1600. Their leader at the time was Titahi, a descendant of Rahiri. His group moved slowly southward, spending considerable time at Kaipara. They eventually went to Taranaki and occupied that region as a homeland.

The migration led by the Tamatea line of chiefs went to Tauranga and there founded the Ngati Ranginui tribe, which today acknowledges a Takitimu connection and sees itself as part of the history of Ngati Kahungunu.

The early history of Ngati Awa shows that the Tamatea family was part of the chiefly lines of Ngati Awa and that there are connections between Ngati Kahungunu and Ngati Awa which continue down through history.

Tamatea was the father of Whaene and Kahungunu.

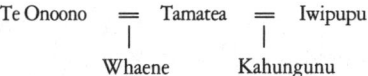

There are traditions about the two sons, such as the well-known disagreement about tamure (snapper) which resulted in one brother throwing fish at the other's face. The incident is remembered in the name of a famous Whakatohea warrior called Tutamure, and there is a meeting-house with that name.

The line from Whaene comes down to Taka, to Hourangi, and then to Uiraroa, who married Awanuiarangi (2) of the Toroa line. This marriage brought the two groups together and established a strong Mataatua connection. Kahungunu went on to found the large tribe which takes his name. In the course of time, their Ngati Awa origins have been forgotten. There seems to be no doubt, however, that Ngati Kahungunu came out of the north as did Ngati

Awa, and that both derive from the same stock. This explains why Kahungunu ancestors are in the meeting-house of Ngati Awa.

Another line from Tamatea comes down to Ranginui.

$$\begin{array}{c} \text{Tamatea} = \text{Te Moana-i-kauia} \\ | \\ \text{Iranui} \\ | \\ \text{Ranginui} \end{array}$$

The chief Ranginui also founded a large tribe but, unlike Kahungunu, his group stayed at Tauranga, where they remain today.

More research is needed to provide information about the beginnings of Ngati Awa. Percy Smith (1898, p.39) thought that the name Ngati Awa came from Rarotonga, where the original tribe was called Ngati Ava, and that our ancestors came from there. This needs to be checked out.

Te Aratawhao Waka

I turn now to the coming of Mataatua waka. This event is linked to the coming to Whakatane of Taukata and Hoaki in search of their sister Kanioro. The two brothers landed at Whakatane and were discovered by Te Kurawhakaata, daughter of Tama-ki-Hikurangi, and taken to Kaputerangi, the pa of Toi. There they were entertained and given the food of the forests, hence Toi's name Toi-kai-rakau. The visitors brought dried kumara and introduced the people to this important food.

Later they built a canoe called Te Aratawhao and went to Parinuitera to fetch kumara to bring to Toi's people. Best (1972, p.693) says they went to Polynesia to fetch it. There is a body of opinion that says Parinuitera was in North Auckland and that Taukata and Hoaki thus never left Aotearoa. However, the popular story is that they sailed far away to Hawaiki. There was built a new canoe named Mataatua. This new canoe brought the kumara to Whakatane and it was planted in the garden called Matirerau. Also a small portion of soil was brought from Hawaiki, and this gives rise to the saying: 'He iti oneone i kapua mai i Hawaiki.' Mataatua became associated with the other well-known canoes: Te Arawa, Tainui, Takitimu, Kurahaupo and Aotea.

Mataatua

The captain was Toroa and his navigator was Tama-ki-Hikurangi. On board was the family of Toroa, which consisted of his sister Muriwai, his brother Puhi-kai-ariki, his half brother, Taneatua, his son Ruaihonga, his daughter Wairaka, his grandson Tahinga-o-te-ra and his nephew Rahiri, son of Puhi.

The family whakapapa is very important and is illustrated here.

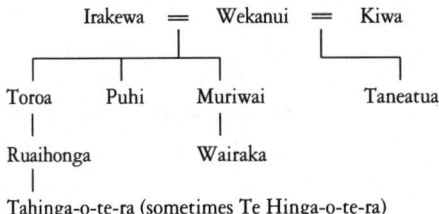

Tahinga-o-te-ra (sometimes Te Hinga-o-te-ra)

The adzes used to make Mataatua were Te Apa-a-rangi and Te Kore-kai-tangata. Rongomai was the spiritual caretaker of the waka. The canoe brought three kawa or sacred chants:

1. Hangaroa-i-te-kaaunauna
2. Hangaroa-i-turiroa
3. Tiki.

Mataatua landed at Whangaparaoa, and some say it moved on to Uawa and Turanga, where passengers of Kurahaupo were dropped off. Then the waka went to Katikati at Tauranga, which marks one boundary of the waka area named Nga Kuri a Whaare (Whaarei). Whaare is said to have come on Mataatua and his name is remembered for all time at the rocks named after his dogs.

From there the canoe came along the coast to Te Awa-a-te-atua. This place, now called Matata, was named by Wairaka because of a comment she made: 'Ha! He atua ki uta ra!' (Best 1972, p.721). There are other versions of what happened but all of Mataatua agree that Wairaka was the principal player.

Mataatua then went on to Whakatane, where the well-known canoe incident took place and Wairaka's famous words are remembered in the name of Ngati Awa's city, Whakatane. You should be aware that Whakatohea gives the credit for this deed to Muriwai. She, of course, is remembered in the name of the cave Te Ana o Muriwai, which is now a famous spot for tourists to see. Wairaka was also responsible for the name given to Koohi Point. Evidently, Wairaka, daughter of Toroa, was quite an adventurous woman and her travels and deeds are remembered in placenames from Whakatane to Owairaka in Auckland.

According to Best (1972, p.720) when Mataatua arrived the lands were already occupied and settled as follows:

Tribe	Locality
Hapuoneone	Opotiki to Whakatane
Ngai Turanga	Ruatoki, Opouriao
Nga Potiki	Ruatahuna
Te Marangaranga	Rangitaiki
Wai-o-hua, Kotore o hua	Whakatane to Matata
Te Tini o Kawerau	Upper Tarawera River
Te Tuoi	Matahina

The principal leaders of Mataatua waka were Toroa, Muriwai and Taneatua, and they became the focal points of whakapapa reckoning. For example, Muriwai is the founding ancestor for Whakatohea. Toroa is the ancestor for Tuhoe and Ngati Awa. Taneatua was an explorer and a seer. Many places were named by him, such as: Te Kuri a Taneatua, Te Tapapatanga o Taneatua, Nga Tamahine a Taneatua, Te Whakaumu a Taneatua, and so on. He was reputed to have taken the ahua of Mataatua waka—that is, the puhi—and hidden it. While Puhi took the canoe to Te Taitokerau, Taneatua kept its spiritual essence within the district, which is clearly identified as being Mataatua.

The Northern Connection

Toroa and Puhi quarrelled over their gardens at Whakatane, and this is given as the reason Puhi and Rahiri took Mataatua to the north and anchored it at Takou Bay, where its stone remains can be seen in the riverbed. Many Mataatua people travel to the north to see the resting-place of our canoe.

Because Puhi and Rahiri belong to the Toroa family, this establishes important links between Ngati Awa and Ngapuhi. And, while the name Ngati Awa is no longer seen as a tribal group, there are many hapu who acknowledge whakapapa connections with us. Ngati Kahu and Ngati Wai are clearly related iwi, but the connections go back a long way. Similarly, there is a link to all of Ngapuhi through the relationship of Toroa and Puhi. Iwi such as Ngai Takoto acknowledge a relationship, as do the people at Te Tii.

Ngati Awa Interrelationships

Whakatane is sometimes referred to as Te Puku-o-te-wheke (the stomach of the octopus). If we use the metaphor of the octopus, we can site its head at Whakatane and trace its longest tentacles to the far north, to Taranaki, to Whanganui (Ngati Apa), to Waiwhetu in Wellington, to Heretaunga. This is the large octopus with long tentacles. A smaller octopus can be used to stretch out to Te Whanau-a-Apanui, to Tuhoe, Tuwharetoa and Ngai Te Rangi, who have all developed out of Ngati Awa. I do not have time to trace out all of these linkages for you at this time.

Enough has been said to indicate a very rich and complex history for Ngati Awa. Thus the first point I wish to make is that being Ngati Awa is to link with a rich and fascinating history and to become a part of it. This can be done by helping to do the research to unlock some of the mysteries of the past. Or you could help by becoming history shapers and shakers. You can make things happen for your people and know that you played a part in influencing the course of history.

Through a very rich past we all become inheritors and trustees of a tribal legacy—of what we know of it at the present time, and what we can claim back from the recorded literature, from museums, from private collectors and from families who are holding manuscript material that we are unaware of. The legacy includes information, knowledge, history, songs, karakia, haka, artifacts, art objects and ritual objects. It includes placenames and the stories about them. It includes whakapapa lines and stories about our various ancestors. These are all esteem-enhancing aspects of our heritage.

Raupatu

You should also be aware that Ngati Awa was one of the tribes involved in raupatu. In fact, we were at the end of a chain of confiscations that began at Taranaki then moved to Waikato. From there the battles shifted to Tauranga, and after Tauranga the guns were turned onto Whakatohea and Ngati Awa. We lost over 200,000 acres of land, which were confiscated because we were accused of being in rebellion against the Queen.

If you are aware of our history, our hara was in killing one of our relatives, James Te Mautaranui Fulloon, who at the time was working for the government. This happened at a time when the Hauhau missionaries were active in converting Ngati Awa to a new religion which asserted a right to be strongly pro-Maori. Coming at the end of a chain of government confiscations, our ancestors were quite right to fear for their lands, and they were right to try to protect them by well-known traditional means, such as the placing of a rahui to keep out the Pakeha and our neighbours, Te Arawa.

We might have held out against the forces of the government of New

The Waitangi Tribunal sitting at Wairaka to hear the Ngati Awa case, July 1994. The Ngati Awa team: Stephen Bryers giving evidence, Hirini Mead, Tom Woods, Jeremy Gardiner, Andrew Macdonald, Joe Mason, Te Hau Tutua, Himiona Hunia. *(Mead collection)*

Zealand if Te Arawa had not joined in to take advantage of a chance for utu. They were still smarting over Te Rangihouhiri driving them out of Maketu and Tauranga and settling a region rich in sea resources. To cut a long story short, we were defeated on the battlefield at Te Kupenga, Te Teko, our men were court-martialled at Opotiki and jailed at Auckland. Some paid the supreme sacrifice of being hung; others died miserably in jail and their bones were only recently brought back; others suffered various periods of hard labour and, after being thoroughly humiliated as a lesson to other tribes, they were finally released to find their usual land-base had been removed from them. Some pockets of land were given back, but Ngati Awa was still short by some 120,000 acres.

Ngati Awa was classed as rebels, and it mattered little whether or not hapu were involved in the battles or in the killing of James Fulloon. The purpose of the exercise was to confiscate land for Pakeha settlement. This was part of Sir George Grey's assimilation policy and euphemistically called a Plan for Peace.

The confiscation or raupatu brought about a dark period for Ngati Awa, which meant a loss of land, loss of rangatiratanga, loss of treaty rights, and the imposition of Pakeha military settlements at Whakatane, Ohiwa and Te Teko. It was a time not unlike the situation in Israel today, when Arab land has been taken for settlement. There was nothing Ngati Awa could do but watch the process of a complete takeover of its territory by the victors in the battle: the military, and Te Arawa at Matata and at Otamarakau. In addition, other iwi were settled in our district to ensure that Ngati Awa would never rise again. That is, we were systematically crushed and our resources taken away for Pakeha use.

Thus, the second point I want to make is that being Ngati Awa means coming to terms with the bitterness of the raupatu and its aftermath, knowing what happened and why it happened and then arriving at a sensible personal position about it all. My personal position is this: nothing is to be gained by trying to deny what happened. We have to support our ancestors. They did what they thought was best for us at that time. That they failed should not be held against them. In fact, we should be proud of the fact that they actually tried to (a) protect the rangatiratanga of Ngati Awa; (b) protect our treaty rights; and (c) maintain tikanga Maori in our territory. We can actually feel quite good today about being one of the iwi who has a raupatu claim before the government and the Waitangi Tribunal.

The Beginnings of Justice

This year the Ngati Awa Station, which was part of the raupatu lands, was returned to Ngati Awa. The date of the return was Tuesday, 24 April 1990, and it occurred at the Maori Land Court at Whakatane, later finished at the marae at Wairaka. On 14 December 1988 a general pardon was granted to Ngati Awa to lift the stigma of being labelled as rebels. That same day our runanga was established. These have all been positive moves which have raised our self-esteem as Ngati Awa considerably.

I am able to tell you that our runanga has established an investment company and that we are now entering a phase of acquiring real estate in Whakatane. We have quietly acquired a building to which our runanga will move soon.

Developments Today

We are about to begin a tribal radio station this week, and do a trial run for three days (14–16 June). In addition, we are negotiating to establish a whare wananga. These initiatives are listed not in a spirit of showing off, but rather to show that there is a new mood taking over our iwi.

We were a pretty sullen, disorganised and very oppressed people who carried a heavy sense of being unfairly treated by the government and people of New Zealand. There is the case of Mataatua, for example, our carved house which went to Australia and England and is now at Dunedin, in the Otago Museum. We did a lot of complaining and did not make any headway. Now that has changed and Mataatua is coming back.

Shaking Off the Shackles

Thus, my third point is that being Ngati Awa today means shaking off the shackles of feeling oppressed and put down and rising up to meet the challenges of today's world. But I realise that this is easy for me to say because I have been through the educative process of helping to change the course of our history from negative to positive. Those of you who do not know what to do might like to consider a number of options. These include offering your services to the Runanga, to the Youth Council (Te Huinga Rangatahi o Ngati Awa), to the Elders Council (Te Kahui Kaumatua), to a Ngati Awa kapa haka, to a marae, doing time back home, or joining our research units, or offering to give your help to our Ngati Awa wananga.

Ambassadors and Trustees

The next point I wish to make is that you can be Ngati Awa wherever you are. There are two aspects of identifying as Ngati Awa and generally letting everyone around you know about it. This identity can be carried into meetings, into the workplace, on to the sportsfield, in the classroom, and so on. In other words, one should not be afraid to be clearly identified as Ngati Awa.

The other aspect is the role of ambassador and trustee. Each of us can be an ambassador and a trustee wherever we are, at home, in the city, or abroad. As an ambassador you carry the Ngati Awa flag around and as a trustee you do your part to see that our heritage is protected or returned to our own control. As a trustee you help to maintain our traditions and do your part to pass on the heritage to the next generation. Sometimes the actions that are needed appear small but are nonetheless very important in the long term.

The author's whanau, or extended family, taken during a reunion. These are the descendants of Moko Haerewa, my grandfather. The whanau is part of Te Whanau a Maata and of Ngati Pahipoto, a hapu of Ngati Awa. Taken in front of Ruataupare. *(Maata Taiawatea Reunion photo)*

A Naming Policy

Take, for example, the relatively common event of naming our children. We can adopt a name-giving policy that is simple but effective. Instead of receiving names like mine, Sidney Moko, it is easy to say that the first name we give to any Ngati Awa child is a tribal name, which might be a tipuna name or the name of an event. Thus my first name should be Moko Haerewa, which is my grandfather's name. If an English name is given, it should be the third name or dropped altogether. What is wrong with a name like Moko Haerewa, which is a tipuna name? What is wrong with Te Whare-wera, which is the name of an event as well as a tipuna name? The point is that a name-giving policy such as this can become a way of ensuring that a connection is established with the tribe and its heritage. Everyone should have a tribal name, and we can make it happen.

Te Reo o Ngati Awa

To be an effective trustee and ambassador of Ngati Awa obviously requires some preparation and self-education. Being able to speak the lingo of Ngati Awa is certainly a high priority, because this unlocks the doors into general conversation, into information, into the sharing of laughter and of grief in a more satisfying manner, and into the traditions. The point is so obvious that I do not need to push it.

He Tangata Mohio: the Knowledgeable Person

It is a very frustrating experience to lack certain key pieces of information about ourselves, our marae, our tribe. Being Ngati Awa does require us to become knowledgeable about our traditions, our waiata, our proverbs and so on. Without this knowledge we cannot play the role of trustee very well.

Developing our Pumanawa

Being Ngati Awa does not mean cramping your style. In fact, it is an expanding experience. Your iwi could want you to develop your pumanawa (talents) to the highest levels you are able to manage. You need skills for your own sake and sustenance, and also for your iwi. Ngati Awa of the modern era needs expertise in all sorts of fields, from managing a marae to electronics, physics, geology, education, performing waiata and so on. The person who has developed their talents is more likely to be happy in themselves and will have more to contribute than someone who has nothing to offer. Besides, as an iwi we need fresh ideas and we need talented people to carry us into the next 100 years.

Integrity and Commitment to Iwi

One's attitude to tribal affiliation is very important. Particular qualities in our people that are urgently required by Ngati Awa are integrity and commitment. If we are able to recruit a group of dedicated and committed people to our marae and to our three councils, Ngati Awa will not be left behind by other iwi. We need to be constantly reminded today that there are many iwi and that several of them are well organised; others have had runanga or trust boards for a

Mrs Linda Tuhiwai Smith, the first woman of Ngati Awa to gain a PhD. She is pictured with her parents, Hirini Mead and June Te Rina Walker Mead, and her aunties of Ngati Porou, Mrs Keita Te Hauauru Walker-Haig and Mrs Heneriata Walker Kawhia, on the occasion of her graduation at Auckland, 3 May 1996. (S. M. Mead)

much longer period than ours; some are larger than we are, richer in resources, and have more political power. We are trailing behind but will catch up if we can recruit the dedicated people of integrity that I mentioned earlier.

Iwi Service

Ask not what your iwi can do for you, but consider what you can do for your people. Our kuia Matarena Reneti, who died this year, was a keen advocate of our runanga. She was disdainful of people who asked what the runanga could do for them. What she demanded of our rangatahi was service to Ngati Awa, to the survival of the iwi, to its future development, to the maintenance of its mana and the fierce protection of its mauri. She is not here now, but her message is one we can adopt as a policy. Every Ngati Awa person should do iwi service, and the service rendered can take many forms and ought to be recorded in a book entitled 'Service to Ngati Awa'.

Conclusions

I traced parts of our history, which took us into the Pacific and then to many parts of our country. Events of history showed that we were once a powerful people that ruled most of the north. I looked at the coming of Mataatua and dealt very briefly with the interrelationships of Ngati Awa with other regions and with other iwi.

All of this was done to demonstrate that there are powerful reasons for identifying as Ngati Awa, and much to be proud of. I emphasise that you can be Ngati Awa wherever you are and that each Ngati Awa person can and should become both an ambassador for Ngati Awa and a trustee. A necessary part of the trustee role is becoming knowledgeable. While the trustee role emphasises protection and cultural maintenance, there is also the role of sharing information so that our culture can be shared with the next generation and maintained by this means. We have to find a place for everyone who is Ngati Awa in the affairs, and especially in the future, of our iwi. We cannot afford to alienate our own people: it is the Pakeha who does that. Our job is to link our people together, to focus them on our iwi, and then to work together to guarantee the survival and development of our heritage and of our people.

The common link is our Ngati Awatanga by whakapapa and by inheritance. My view is that we must find ways of enjoying our membership and our participation in the affairs of our iwi. I also believe that to be strong we must overcome the dislocation of our population and turn this fact to our advantage. I don't know how we do this, but I think we must address this problem. The fact is that more Ngati Awa people live outside our tribal territory than in it.

Our little octopus must stretch its tentacles outwards to draw in our people towards the centre.

In drawing our people towards the tribal centre, we must also find ways of removing any feelings of threat that the people at home might experience. They kept the home fires going, they protected our ahi-ka while we enjoyed careers, full employment and opportunities in the outside world. How do we include everyone, without threatening the iwi kainga? In the end it is not our feelings or our egos that are of paramount importance to our development as a tribal people. What is important is the iwi, that it survives and develops. We are all part of the development and we are all part of what makes Ngati Awa what it is today and tomorrow. No reira kia kaha koutou ki te whai i to koutou Ngati Awatanga.

Glossary

ahi-ka-roa	long-burning fire of occupation
aitua	disaster
aroha	love
aukati	boundary marking a declared trespass, line in the sand
haka	ritual war dance
hapu	subtribe
hara	transgression, sin
hau	vital essence of life
hau-mate	ill health, near death
hau-ora	well-being
hohonutanga	depth of (eg knowledge)
hui	discussion meeting
huringa	turning
ihi	power
iwi	tribe, social unit bound by common genealogical links and, formerly, common residence
iwitanga	being iwi
kaha	strong
kaiarahi	guide
kai moana	seafood
kainga	village
kairamua	offence against a rāhui
kakano	seeds
karakia	prayers, chants
karanga	ceremonial call
kaumatua	elder
kawanatanga	government
kimihanga	the searching
kiri mate	literally, skin of death; metaphor for the immediate kin of the deceased
kohanga reo	Maori language nest
korero	talk
koroua	male elder
kuia	female elder
kura kaupapa Maori	Maori language school

māhunga	head
maia	brave
makutu	witchcraft
mana	status, prestige
mana motuhake	autonomy
manawanui	stout-hearted
manu hou	new bird
manuhiri	visitor
Maoritanga	Maori culture
marae	communal centre
māramatanga	light and understanding
mātāmua	first born
matauranga Maori	Maori knowledge, philosophy
mate Maori	Maori sickness
maunga	mountain
mauri	life principle
mauriora	well-being, survival
moenga	bed
mokopuna	grandchildren
muru	ritual plunder
pa harakeke	literally, flax bush; metaphor for living descendants
pānui	publication
Papatuanuku	Earth Mother
patu	club
pou	post
pouaru	widow, widower
poupou	wall post, usually carved
pōwhiri	welcome ceremony
puawaitanga	flowering
rahui	prohibition
rangatahi	youth
rangatira	chief
Ranginui	Sky Father
rarangi	line, row
raupatu	confiscation
ringa kaha	strong arm, military power
rongonui	famous
rourou	basket
runanga	council, meeting to discuss issues
take	cause
tamaiti whāngai	adopted child
tangata	man, mankind
tangata whenua	people of the land
tangi, tangihanga	mourning ceremony
tangohanga	acquisition of wealth
taniwha	monster
taonga	prized possession
tapu	sacred
tautohetohe	contested

te reo Maori	the Maori language
tikanga	customs
tino rangatiratanga	self-determination, home rule
tipunga	growth
tohunga	priest
toi	knowledge, art
toki-pou-tangata	adze to despatch men
tukutuku	latticework
tupuna	ancestor
turangawaewae	place for feet to stand
tu tangata	stand tall
utu	payment, reciprocity
wahine pukupa	barren woman
wāhi ngaro	the lost portion
wahi tapu	sacred area
waiata	song, chant
waihanga	to build, construct
wairua	spirit
waka	canoe
wa kainga	home base
waka pakaru	broken canoe
waka taua	war canoe
wana	authority
wananga	a tertiary institution that caters to Maori learning needs, established under the Education Act 1990
wehi	awesomeness
whaikorero	oration
whakairo	carving, art
whakaiti	to be humble
whakapapa	genealogy
whakaruruhau	sheltering
whakatahe	abortion
whakatauki	proverb
whanau	family
whanaungatanga	relationship
whāngai	to adopt, literally 'to feed'
whanuitanga	breadth of (eg knowledge)
whare hou	new house
whare ngaro	lost house; metaphor for an endangered descent line
wharenui	meeting-house, big house
whare wananga	house of learning
whatu	sacred stone associated with a rāhui
whenua	land; placenta
whenua muru	compensation land
whenua ohaki	deathbed land grant
whenua raupatu	confiscated land
whenua taunaha	named land
whenua tuku	gifted land